DATE DUE

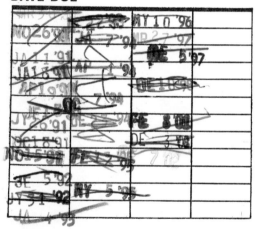

JUSTIFIABLE HOMICIDE

JUSTIFIABLE HOMICIDE

Battered Women,
Self-Defense,
and
the Law

Cynthia K. Gillespie

Ohio State University Press
Columbus

Library of Congress Cataloging-in-Publication Data

Gillespie, Cynthia K., 1941-
 Justifiable homicide.

 Bibliography: p.
 Includes index.
 1. Self-defense (Law)—United States. 2. Abused women—legal status, laws, etc.—United
States. 3. Homicide—United States. I. Title.
KF9246.G55 1989   345.73'04   88-18014
ISBN 0-8142-0466-X   347.3054

The paper in this book meets the guidelines for permanence and durability of the Committee on
Production Guidelines for Book Longevity of the Council on Library Resources.

Printed in the U.S.A.

Contents

Preface

Several years ago, when I was the director of the Northwest Women's Law Center in Seattle, Washington, a woman named Janice Painter came to us asking for help with her case. She had killed her stepson, Ted Painter, a violent young man who resented her marriage to his father. Ted's behavior had become so aggressive and threatening that Janice, at her husband's insistence, had begun carrying a gun to protect herself from him. She killed him when he assaulted her during a family argument. She had tried to get to the phone to call the police, but Ted knocked her to the floor and then came at her with his hands outstretched towards her throat as she lay there, literally paralyzed, on the floor. Although Janice believed that she was acting in self-defense and had no other way to save herself from being severely beaten up or killed, she was arrested and charged with first-degree murder. During her trial, everything she and her husband had done to try to deal with Ted's violent and abusive behavior was twisted around by the prosecutor and used against her to persuade the jury that she had planned to lure Ted into a situation where she could murder him and make it look like self-defense because she couldn't get rid of him any other way. They had, for example, tried to have the young man committed to a mental institution and had tried to get him a job in a distant state; when everything else failed, Janice got a permit to carry a gun and asked the sheriff's department to tell her under what circumstances she could use it to defend herself. The jury, convinced that she was plotting to kill him, found her guilty of premeditated murder. She was sentenced to life in prison. The Law Center was asked to write a brief in support of her appeal, and I took on the job.

My research was unexpectedly brief. Although there had been a few highly publicized cases before 1980 that involved women's right to self-defense and feminists were beginning to recognize that there were some serious problems with the way these cases fared in the courts, there had been almost nothing written on the subject other than a handful of scattered articles in law journals. The prevalence of violence against women in this country had begun to be extensively studied and written about in the late seventies, but books about rape and wife-beating tended to skirt nervously around the subject of women victims fighting back and killing their attackers. No one, understandably, wanted to appear to advocate murder as a solution to personal problems. It was not until 1980 that Ann Jones, in a fine and angry concluding chapter to her book, *Women Who Kill*, brought the subject to light for a general audience.

Janice Painter's appeal was successful, I am happy to say, and she has gone on to become an active and effective advocate of women's right to self-defense. The Northwest Women's Law Center, too, has gone on to represent many other women in self-defense cases. After the brief was written, I continued, out of curiosity, to gather stories about women who had killed men in self-defense, both official case-reports and stories of trials published in newspapers, expecting to turn up a dozen or so. I was amazed at what I found.

With very little effort, I was able to find over two-hundred stories, and this was clearly only the tip of the iceberg. The only cases that appear in official case-reports are those that have gone to trial, resulted in convictions, and been appealed. Incidents in which a woman has not been charged, has pleaded guilty in a plea-bargain agreement, has been tried and acquitted, or (the most common outcome, I suspect) has been tried, convicted, and not appealed— are not collected anywhere. Although a few of these cases have generated a lot of publicity, most are given a few paragraphs on a back page of a local paper, if that; they are very hard to find. Thus, I have no doubt that the cases I turned up represented only a fraction of the total.

The numbers were not the only surprise, however. Another was the recurring pattern in what happened during these lethal confrontations. Almost all the cases involved women who killed men to whom they were married or with whom they lived in an intimate relationship. The men they killed were men who had beaten and abused them in the past and were assaulting or threatening to assault them again. In case after case the scenario was the same: the man, threatening to "whip her ass" or kill her, lunging toward her, holding her and beating or strangling her; the woman grabbing a knife from a kitchen drawer or counter and jabbing it at him trying to break his hold or grabbing a gun—usually his gun—and pointing it at him, telling him to back off and leave her alone; the knife suddenly hitting a vital spot or the man grabbing for the gun and the woman pulling the trigger; the woman calling the police or the ambulance and sitting on the floor cradling her husband's head in her lap begging him not to die. This story was played out, with minor variations, so many times that I sometimes had the feeling that I was reading the same case over and over again.

The other scenario (not quite as common) involved women who, after years of brutality, despairing of any way of stopping the beatings or escaping their mates, took advantage of an opportunity to catch them off-guard when their backs were turned or they were asleep or passed-out drunk, and killed them to defend themselves against the beatings that they believed were inevitably to come. There were also a number of cases in which a woman killed a man who was raping her or threatening to rape her.

The outcome of all these cases was depressingly similar. The woman was arrested immediately and charged with murder. She subsequently pleaded guilty to murder or manslaughter, hoping that the circumstances of her case would move the judge to be lenient; or she went to trial, was duly convicted, and went to prison. Either way, she was clearly considered to be guilty of a terrible crime.

In every case, the woman freely admitted that she took the man's life and claimed she was acting in the sincere belief that she had to do so to save herself from death or serious injury. However, self-defense cases present particularly difficult problems for someone trying to tell the story of "what really happened and why." Usually the only person who is able to testify about what took place is the person who did the killing, and he or she arguably has every reason to give a self-serving version of the facts. Unless there was an eyewitness, the only person who could tell a different story is dead. Because women who kill in self-defense are most apt to kill violent husbands or lovers in response to domestic assaults, their acts most often take place at home where there are likely to be no witnesses other than an occasional terrified child.

When such women are charged with murder, the prosecution's case is usually, of necessity, an indirect and circumstantial one. Lacking eyewitnesses or other direct evidence to contradict the woman's story, the prosecutor's two main weapons are most often to cast doubt on her credibility and veracity as a witness and to convince the jury that, even if her story is true, her perception that she was in such serious danger was unreasonable. Generally, the case against her consists not of hard evidence but of speculation and innuendo about what really happened and what her true motive might have been.

How, then, can the readers of this book have any confidence that they are being told the "true" story or even the "whole" story in any of these cases? I have concluded that the best approach is to rely whenever possible on the version of the facts accepted and reported by an appellate court.

There are a number of advantages to using appellate court reports, and some disadvantages. The whole purpose of a criminal trial, of course, is to determine what happened. A jury is a fact-finding body. When a higher state court considers an appeal of a criminal conviction, it has before it the entire transcript of the trial as well as briefs from the attorneys on both sides, each of which will present a version of the facts that it urges the reviewing court to accept. That court, at least in theory, draws on the transcript and the lawyers' arguments to determine the facts of the case as they were proved by the evidence at the trial. It then sets out those facts in its opinion and bases its decision on them. All of the testimony at the trial, which is reproduced in the transcript, will have been given under oath and subject to cross-examination. This is, I believe, as close as we can come to a "true" version of what happened in any given case.

One drawback, of course, is that an appeals court opinion will only exist in cases where the woman was charged with a crime, put on trial, convicted, and her conviction appealed. In those rare cases where a woman kills in self-defense and is not charged or is tried and acquitted, or where (as more commonly happens) she does not appeal her conviction, or accepts an offer to plead guilty to a reduced charge, we must look to the press and other sources for the facts.

Another drawback is that appellate court opinions usually only recite those facts of the case that are necessary to explain its decision. This frequently leaves tantalizing questions unanswered. When I have been able to go to other sources, I have tried to use court records or newspaper reports of trial testimony. The reader is thus at least assured of receiving the same version of the story that the jury heard, told under courtroom conditions designed to ensure its veracity. Beyond this, I have assumed throughout that, in every case, to the extent that her story is uncontradicted by direct evidence, the woman is telling the truth.

It is my hope that the reader will come to share my view that there are far better reasons to believe than to doubt these women's tragic stories because what emerges from them with stunning clarity is this: we as a society are unwilling to grant women the same right of self-defense that we grant to men. Under the law, a person, regardless of gender, is entitled to kill another if that person reasonably believes that he or she is in imminent danger of death or serious bodily injury at the hands of the other. But when a woman kills a man, especially a man with whom she lives intimately, we are loath to acknowledge that she was acting in self-defense.

This book explores the historical, legal, and societal reasons why women are rarely granted the right to act in self-defense. The problem appears to result from a combination of two things: first, the law itself, which over many centuries has come to embody masculine assumptions about the circumstances that entitle a person to act in self-defense; and second, our society's ambivalent and biased attitudes about women and its acceptance of violence against them. These two components of the problem interact to create a no-win situation for women charged with homicide in these cases. Even where they were clearly acting in self-defense, the law of justifiable homicide often cannot be made to fit the kinds of situations that female victims of male violence find themselves in and the ways that they often must act to defend themselves. Moreover, even where the law does apply to the facts, juries are so beholden to our society's prevailing misconceptions about rape and domestic violence and the myths, stereotypes, and fears about women which are so widely shared by our culture, that they almost always manage to find the women guilty anyway. It is not my intention to argue that women are entitled to special treatment or that we should apply different legal rules to men and women in self-defense cases. Quite the opposite, I am arguing that we must find ways to fairly extend the right of self-defense, which men already enjoy, to women who must kill to save themselves from serious injury or death.

Not every woman who kills her husband or lover is acting in self-defense, of course, but what little data there are indicate that self-defense *is* the reason far more frequently than most people assume. Women, in fact, seldom kill anyone for any reason. Men commit 85 percent of the 20,000 or so homicides that occur in the United States every year, a percentage that has held steady for several decades. Of the homicides that occur between spouses or lovers, men are also far more apt to do the killing. In 1986, for example, men killed wives and girlfriends at nearly twice the rate of women who killed husbands and boyfriends (7.4 percent of all U.S. homicides vs. 4.2 percent for women).

Men and women do not only kill their spouses and lovers at different rates; they appear to kill them under different circumstances as well. There are no hard statistics but there are clear indications that in a large percentage of instances in which women kill their mates, they are acting to defend themselves against violent assaults. In his study of spousal homicides, sociologist Marvin Wolfgang found that 53 percent of the victims were wives killed by their husbands and 47 percent were husbands killed by their wives. However, over half (60 percent) of the husbands who were killed had precipitated their own deaths by assaulting their wives, who responded by killing them. In 1969, a report by the National Commission on the Causes and Prevention of Violence concluded that women who commit homicides are seven times more likely to have been acting in self-defense than are men. An unpublished study of women inmates of the Cook County Women's Correctional Institute in Chicago (conducted in 1975 and 1976) found that, of the 132 women awaiting trial for murder or manslaughter, 53 (40 percent) said they were defending themselves against violent husbands or boyfriends when they killed.

Other studies of spousal homicides have also found that when women kill their husbands, they are apt to be responding to the man's violence. A study of spouse killings in Florida between 1970 and 1980, for example, found that 73 percent of the wives who killed their husbands had been beaten by them in the past and were reacting to yet another assault by their mates. Every woman in Peter Chimbos' study of spousal homicides in Canada had been beaten by her husband and three-quarters of them were being beaten or had just been beaten when they struck back. Sixty-seven percent of the women incarcerated for killing their spouses, who were interviewed by Jane Totman, reported that they had acted to defend themselves or their children; 93 percent reported that they had been abused during their marriages. Whatever the actual figure, these data suggest that when a woman kills a man she is married to or lives intimately with, there is better than an even chance that she was acting in self-defense. If this is so, then there may be as many as 500 such killings every year.

As the stories in the following chapters will make clear, when a woman kills her husband or boyfriend in self-defense, that fact is usually perfectly obvious from the moment the police arrive and ask her what happened. Such a woman should not even be charged with a crime, much less tried and convicted. That so many are is a miscarriage of justice that has too long gone unrecognized in our society.

On its face, the law of self-defense is the same for men and women. It ought to treat them exactly alike. As we shall see, however, it operates very differently for women than for men because of the assumptions built into it and the sex bias that all of the actors in the criminal justice system—but especially jurors (including women jurors)—bring into it. In recent years women's rights advocates and feminist thinkers have been turning their attention more and more to these intractable situations where there are equal legal rights but, for women, disproportionately unfavorable legal results. Most of this attention has been focused on employment rules, such as minimum height and weight or load-lifting requirements, that apply to everybody but effectively bar mostly women from certain jobs. More recently, concern has been raised about divorce and custody laws that, in operation, leave women far worse off than men and disability-leave policies that are inadequate to cover even a normal pregnancy and, in effect, allow pregnant workers to be fired. *Treating people the same, on paper, is no guarantee that justice or fairness will result.* I believe that self-defense law provides a chilling example of how this can happen in the arena of the criminal law.

JUSTIFIABLE HOMICIDE

1
OVERVIEW:
When Women Fight Back

In the early morning hours of November 12, 1979, Caroline Mae Scott, a twenty-nine-year-old mother of five from Kankakee, Illinois, picked up a .357 magnum pistol from where it lay on her bed and fired six shots at Arthur Lee, her housemate of eight years and the father of three of her children. He was sitting down when she shot him, about four feet from where she stood. She called the police immediately and waited for them to arrive and arrest her.

Caroline Scott was charged with murder. At her trial, the prosecutor argued that she killed Arthur Lee in a jealous rage when he threatened to leave her for another woman. The judge refused the defense attorney's request to allow the jury to consider a verdict of manslaughter or a finding that she had acted in self-defense. Lee had been seated a safe distance away and had made no move toward her. She picked up the gun and deliberately shot him dead. Murder, pure and simple. The jury found her guilty, and she was sentenced to serve twenty years in prison. Hell hath no fury like a woman scorned, as everybody knows, and she never denied that she pulled the trigger. It would appear that Caroline Scott got exactly what she deserved.

But the killing of Arthur Lee was not the vengeful act of a jealous woman. It was, instead, the last desperate attempt of a woman who had suffered eight years of unspeakable brutality to save herself from another round of torture and—this time, she feared—quite probably death.

Caroline Scott had every reason to fear Arthur Lee and to believe that he was capable of killing her. She and her two children had moved in with him in 1971 after her first marriage had ended. She was a high school dropout, only twenty years old. It was just a few months later that he beat her up for the first time when he came home to find her dressed up and, without giving her a chance to explain, accused her of getting ready to go out with another man. From that time on, Caroline was the target of an unfounded jealousy that rapidly grew to insane proportions. He made her a virtual prisoner in her own home, cutting her off from contact with friends, neighbors and her own family. She was not allowed to go out or to allow anyone in. Even so, he imagined that she was constantly engaged in sexual relationships with other men. He would accuse her of having an affair and then beat her unmercifully until she "confessed." He beat her with his fists, his gun, a blackjack, belts, broomhandles, coat hangers, and extension cords. He kicked her and threw things at her and several times tried to smother her with pillows. Once he threw her out of the house stark naked. When she was eight months pregnant, he accused her of having an affair with the landlord and threw her down a flight of stairs. Another time, he held one of the children's teddy bears next to her head and, telling her she might be next, pulled out his gun and shot a hole in it. By 1973 (she testified at her trial) these beatings were coming as often as two or three times a week.

Lee was always armed because he worked as a correctional officer at the Kankakee jail, and he always carried handcuffs. He frequently tied Caroline up or handcuffed her before he beat her. The handcuffs, in fact, became such an integral part of his torture routine that he had only to give a signal—tapping his left wrist with his right hand and pointing to where they were kept—to tell her to get the cuffs and bring them to him so he could shackle her and begin the beating.

Several times she left him, going to stay with her mother, but that was never more than a temporary refuge. Lee always found ways to get her to come back. He would come and tell her how sorry he was and how much he loved her; he would promise never to do it again. And she wanted to believe him because she loved him; because she wanted so badly to keep her family together for the sake of the children; and, no doubt, because—as a black woman who had dropped out of high school to marry and who had five children to care for—she didn't perceive herself to have very many other options. When she wavered and it appeared his pleas and promises might not work, he would threaten to kill her if she refused to come home, threats which his past behavior gave her every reason to take seriously.

Through it all she loved him, amazing as that might seem to those not familiar with this very common aspect of the battered woman's experience. She did not want to leave him; she wanted him to stop beating her, and she just kept hoping, desperately, that someday he would stop treating her the way he did.

The night her hope ran out, Lee came home extremely drunk and pounded on the door. Caroline went to the door with the .357 magnum in her hand because Arthur had ordered her never to answer the door unarmed. When he came in, he shoved her around and began accusing her of having an affair for the past eight years with a man named Slim, once a friend of Lee's. When she denied it, he took his 9 mm. pistol from the clip on his pants and began smashing her in the face with it. She was still holding the .357 magnum, but he took it away from her and threw it on the bed. Then he hit her some more with his own gun and with his fists. He let her go then and made a phone call to a woman named Bonnie, telling her that Caroline would be "gone" in forty-five minutes.

Afraid that this time he was intending to kill her—and knowing that, at the least, she was in for another of the severe beatings that always followed his accusations of infidelity—Caroline wandered around the house trying to figure out a way to take her youngest child and get away without his catching them. Finally, hopeless, she sat down on the bed where at least she could keep an eye on Lee, who was still on the telephone and still holding his gun. The .357 magnum remained on the bed where Lee had thrown it earlier. At length, he hung up the phone; and she saw him give the dreaded signal, tapping his wrist and pointing to the handcuffs. She got up and walked toward where they were kept but suddenly turned back toward the bed, picked up the pistol, pointed it toward him, closed her eyes and pulled the trigger. She intended to fire only one shot, to frighten him, but the gun kept firing until it was empty. Arthur Lee died instantly.

Under the law of Illinois, as in every other state, Caroline Scott would not have been guilty of murder, or any crime at all, if she was acting in self-defense because she reasonably believed that it was necessary to kill Arthur Lee to avoid an immediate danger of being killed or seriously injured by him. Surely Caroline Scott believed that she was about to be seriously hurt or killed. Surely she believed that firing the gun was the only way she could stop him from doing what he was about to do. Surely her belief was reasonable. He had seriously hurt her and threatened to kill her many times before. The situation was the same as the ones in which he had beaten her most severely in the past. That night he had told her that he would make her confess everything "or else." His remark to Bonnie on the telephone that she would be "gone" in forty-five minutes sounded like this time he intended to kill her. He was armed with a gun. He was about to render her absolutely helpless. She could not get away.

How could what Caroline did have been anything but self-defense? How could she conceivably have been convicted of murder and sentenced to twenty years in prison for her desperate act? How could everyone along the line—the police who arrested her, the prosecutor who decided to seek a murder charge and argued that she was a cold-blooded killer, the judge who believed her action was so clearly not self-defense that he wouldn't allow the jury even to consider that possibility, the jury that convicted her—have been so determined to assume the worst about her and so unwilling or unable to understand what had happened in that house that night?

The answer lies partly in the law itself and partly in attitudes about violence toward women that are shared by many people in our society and are reflected in the workings of the criminal justice system—especially in the deliberations of juries. These two factors operate together to create a situation that is extremely unfair to women defendants in self-defense cases. Caroline Scott's case was by no means a fluke. Hundreds of women like Caroline are found guilty of manslaughter or murder and sent to prison for defending themselves against the life-threatening assaults of violent men. Our society is simply unwilling to grant to women the same right of self-defense that it grants to men.

The law of self-defense is a law for men. It developed over many centuries in response to two basic kinds of situations that men found themselves in. The first was the sudden assault by a murderous stranger, such as when someone, perhaps bent on robbery, comes out of a dark alley with a gun and threatens to kill a person walking innocently down the street. The second is the fist fight or brawl that gets out of hand and suddenly turns deadly. Usually this is the sort of bar-fight situation where both participants willingly enter into a punching match; and one of them, believing he is losing, suddenly pulls out a weapon and threatens to kill the other.

These were the only situations in which a self-defense killing was traditionally excused by the law, and the rules surrounding each one were different so that it was important that such a killing fit into one category or the other. However, the assumption in both situations was that the antagonists were men of relatively equal size, strength, and fighting ability. A further assumption was that the antagonists were strangers, or perhaps acquaintances, whose confrontation was an isolated incident occurring in a public place from which one or both could withdraw or escape and so end the conflict without bloodshed, unless the attack was so sudden as to make retreat impossible.

The self-defense situation that a woman is most likely to find herself in, however, is very different. Women rarely kill to defend themselves against violent assaults by strangers although there are some cases in which women have killed rapists, and we will look at a number of them. Nor do women often get involved in punchouts in which one antagonist finally kills the other. Like Caroline Scott, the overwhelming majority of women who kill men in self-defense, kill their husbands or lovers—violent men who have beaten them and threatened them many times before. Such a woman's situation does not fit within either of the traditional, masculine, self-defense categories. Her assailant is neither a stranger nor someone with whom she has voluntarily engaged in a fist fight. The result is that when she does strike back, in the sincere belief that she is acting to save herself, the law of self-defense often cannot be made to apply to her action.

As we shall see, a whole series of rules and requirements grew up in the criminal law that were intended to restrict self-defense pleas to only those situations that men recognized as legitimate. Moreover, the law was concerned to make certain that, even within these situations, no one could use the plea of self-defense to excuse a killing that was not absolutely necessary. Such a killing would only be considered necessary if the person acting in self-defense had conformed to the standard of behavior that was expected of a *man* facing dangerous circumstances.

A man was expected to meet his adversary face to face and knuckles to knuckles. He was expected to use no more force than was needed to repel the attack, which meant that he was not to use a weapon unless one was being used against him. If forced to resort to a weapon, he was expected to handle it with sufficient expertise to disable, rather than kill, his opponent if possible. He could not use deadly force to defend himself against a mere threat or an anticipated attack that had not yet begun. He was not permitted to indulge in cowardly behavior like ambushing his opponent from behind or catching him off guard or making any kind of pre-emptive strike. If he could avoid killing by escaping or backing down from the fight, he was expected (at least in some states) to do so.

All of this translated into a law of self-defense that held a killing was only justified if it was in response to an armed assault that was already underway, if one had tried to escape or retreat, and if one wielded a defensive weapon no more violently than necessary to repel the attack. The touchstone was whether one had acted, under the circumstances, the way a reasonable man would act.

It was a law that made perfectly good sense in the sorts of situations that it was developed to apply to, and still does. It is clearly in society's interest to discourage unnecessary violence—especially the use of deadly weapons—in people's everyday interactions with one another. If a man is walking down a dark street and is suddenly confronted by a stranger whose appearance is menacing but who has done nothing overtly threatening, he has no right to pull out a gun and kill the stranger, no matter how genuine his fear might be that the stranger means to do him harm. If two men are drinking in a bar and get into an argument that they can't or won't settle without coming to blows, it is reasonable to expect them not to fight with anything more lethal than fists. No matter how badly he is losing, a man who has willingly entered into a fist fight has no right to resort to a weapon if all he faces is a humiliating thrashing at the hands of his opponent. Even if he is minding his own business and is unilaterally attacked, he ought not to defend himself against another man's fists with a deadly weapon. He must rely on his own fists as well. If, during the course of their argument, one man threatens to kill the other or tear him apart or cut off his balls, it would hardly be reasonable for the target of the threats to react by killing the man who makes them. The harm threatened is serious, certainly, but there is no reason to assume that the threats will ever be carried out. One is, in short, never justified in making a lethal confrontation out of a nonlethal one. The assumption is, always, that a man can avoid letting this happen by fighting fair, by taking his medicine if he comes out the loser, or by backing off and simply walking away before things reach the point of turning deadly.

But these options were not available to Caroline Scott, and they are not available to most women who are assaulted in their homes by violent men. The situations that such women face are light years away from the kind of pugilistic combats between gentlemen that the law contemplates. Men and women are not of equal size, strength, and fighting ability. Arthur Lee was able to brutalize and terrorize Caroline Scott over those many years precisely because she could not defend herself against him. He was bigger, stronger, and infinitely meaner. She was entirely at his mercy physically; she knew it, and he knew it. Once he made up his mind to start beating her, nothing she did, or could possibly do, would stop him. This had nothing whatsoever to do with putting up her dukes and fighting fair. She could not back off, cry "uncle," offer to shake hands and buy him a beer. Nor was this a one-time-only episode between strangers, with no past history and no future. She knew, with painful certainty, that his threats were not idle barroom bluffs; he was able and more than willing to inflict horrible injuries on her. She knew that if she submitted to him and "took her punishment," that would not be the end of it: he would not just walk out of her life like a stranger after a bar fight. Their life together would go on as it had before; he would be free to shackle her and beat her at will, and she would be powerless to prevent it.

Caroline Scott's situation that night, however, did not fit the masculine pattern that the law of self-defense anticipates, and so her actions did not seem to meet the law's requirements. The law says that in order to justify using deadly force in self-defense, a person must be in danger of death or serious bodily injury. Even though Lee had a gun in his hand, he wasn't threatening to shoot Caroline with it as long as she obeyed his orders. Although he had threatened to kill her in the past, on the present occasion he did not clearly do so. He didn't, arguably, intend to kill her that night. He was "only" going to beat her up, and he had done that plenty of times before without killing her or permanently maiming her. Since the damage he was proposing to inflict on her would only be inflicted with his fists or some other handy nonlethal object, under the law, strictly applied, she was only entitled to use her own fists or a similar object to defend herself.

Moreover, the law requires that the death or serious injury faced by a person acting in self-defense be absolutely imminent. The assault must be already under way or, at the least, clearly about to begin. But Arthur was sitting on the sofa by the telephone when Caroline shot him. He had not made any move toward her; he had merely made a gesture that signalled her to go and get the handcuffs. Under the law, strictly applied, she was not entitled to fight back with a weapon until he was actually beating her severely enough to make it clear that he was going to beat her to death or nearly so. By that time, of course, she would have been rendered helpless to resist at all, but the law does not make room for such considerations. It was simply never designed for situations like Caroline Scott's. That is not the sort of situation, short of war, that most men would ever be likely to find themselves in.

The law of self-defense is inflexible and embodies male standards of behavior. It is not the law alone, however, that is responsible for Caroline, and so many other women victims of violence, being found guilty of criminal homicide when they fight back against their attackers. Our society's attitudes about women, their nature and their proper roles, also play a significant part.

Violence against women is so ingrained in our society and so widely tolerated that it has been only in the last few years that its real scope and seriousness have begun to come to light. This acceptance of violence against women has served to obscure the reality of the truly desperate choices its victims are often forced to make—between staying to protect one's children, who may also be targets of abuse, and abandoning them to protect oneself; between staying and being beaten and leaving to face the very real risk of being pursued and murdered; and, too often, between killing and being killed. Society's unwillingness to see what happens to such women has allowed the criminal justice system to operate under stereotyped and mistaken assumptions about why women in these circumstances make the choices that they do. When a woman who is trapped in a situation of ongoing violence finally fights back and kills her tormentor, her action is seen not as self-defense but as murder or at best manslaughter. When she is arrested, tried, and convicted, that outcome appears to most people to be the proper one. When, in fact, such a woman is acquitted by a jury, society's reaction is apt to be one of outrage.

Nothing could make this more clear than the uproar in the press when women defendants, in the 1970s, began to assert their right to defend themselves against assaultive spouses and argue vigorously in the courts that their actions were justified. The first few cases to come to nationwide attention did not involve domestic violence, and the defendants were treated rather as tragic heroines by at least some segments of the media. In 1974 Joanne Little, a young black woman confined to a North Carolina jail, stabbed a white jailor to death with his own knife as he was raping her. Her cause was taken up by both women's rights and civil rights groups, and her acquittal was generally regarded as a victory over a particularly vicious form of southern racism. The same year, Inez Garcia shot and killed a man who had participated in raping her shortly before and then telephoned her to threaten to do it again. Although Inez Garcia was convicted by her jury of second-degree murder, her conviction was overturned on appeal; and, in 1977, a second jury acquitted her, finding that she had acted not to avenge herself for the first rape but to defend herself against the threatened second one.

The third case from the early seventies that received national attention was that of Yvonne Wanrow, a Colville Indian woman from Washington state, who shot and killed a known child-molester who had broken into her house in the middle of the night and made suggestive gestures toward a child who was sleeping there. Wanrow, too, was convicted at her trial, but her conviction was overturned on appeal. Although she chose to plead guilty to a reduced charge rather than face a second trial, the Washington Supreme Court opinion was the first anywhere to acknowledge that the traditional approach of self-defense law might not work fairly for women defendants.

From the press's point of view, these were three extraordinary women who faced extraordinary circumstances. All three of them were defending themselves against virtual or total strangers who had behaved in ways our society agrees are outrageous. All of them were members of minority groups, and there were *bona fide* questions of how large a part racism played in their being brought to trial at all. Nothing in their situations came close enough to home to be particularly threatening to the public at large.

But around the same time a handful of quite different self-defense cases involving women began to come to public attention around the country. These cases involved battered women, ordinary housewives mostly, who struck back in defense against their husbands' violence and then claimed (usually to a chorus of support from feminist groups) that their actions were completely justified. That women killed their husbands was not new; that they argued they had a right to do so definitely was.

The public and the press were horrified. In November of 1977, *Time* magazine, in an article entitled "A Killing Excuse," complained that women were managing to "walk away unpunished after killing their husbands or even their former husbands." The article referred to the upcoming trial of Jennifer Patri, a Waupaca, Wisconsin, housewife who shot her brutal estranged husband when he threatened to kill her with a butcher knife. Curiously, the magazine didn't find the fact that Mr. Patri was wielding a weapon during his final confrontation with his ex-wife significant enough even to mention, leaving its readers with the impression that the shooting was unprovoked. The article closed with a quote from the local sheriff about the support Patri had gained from women's rights organizations: "I wonder if these people know what they're doing. If they get their way, there's going to be a lot of killings."

Around the same time the *Chicago Daily News* published an article entitled "Are Women Getting Away With Murder?" that discussed the trial of Francine Hughes. As everyone who saw *The Burning Bed* on television knows, she was acquitted, on grounds of temporary insanity, of murdering her ex-husband after years of abuse. A spectator at her trial was quoted as announcing that the verdict would result in "an open season on men." A short time later, *Newsweek* took up the subject and after reviewing several cases, including Patri's and Hughes', concluded that the feminist effort to broaden self-defense law to take the man's previous violence into account had "worrisome" legal implications. "If it is left to run its course," cried *Newsweek*, "such a trend smacks uncomfortably of frontier justice."

In Ohio, an article headlined "Self-Defense Decision Causing Double Standard: Women Get More Than Equal Rights After Killing Spouse," a writer for the *Columbus Dispatch* lamented that "it's a simple matter for the defense to present witnesses who say the husband beat the wife. If a jury or judge believes them they find for the woman." The article reported the observation of a local prosecuting attorney that, "Hey, it's open season on husbands."

Why should the public and press be so shocked by a handful of acquittals? These women had broken two unwritten rules. First, they had fought back to the death against their husbands' violence.

And second, they had claimed that they were entirely justified in doing so. Their actions suddenly shed some stark light on a number of confused, contradictory, and mostly unarticulated beliefs about women and violence that are widely shared in our society.

We, as a nation, suffer from a painful ambivalence about violence against women. We simultaneously deplore it and excuse it. Far too often, instead of blaming the perpetrator of the violence, we go to great lengths to find ways to blame the victim.

Rape, for example, is generally regarded as one of the most serious of crimes. Indeed, it is the only crime besides premeditated murder that many states have, until recently, made a hanging offense. And yet, it is extremely difficult to get a jury to convict a man of rape. Our society has developed a whole mythology devoted to excusing rape or blaming the victim for it: that no woman can really be raped against her will, that all women secretly want to be raped, that when women say "no" they really mean "yes," that when a woman is raped it is her own fault because she dressed seductively or behaved carelessly, that women consent to sex and then cry rape when they subsequently regret it.

Even when sexual violence is directed at very young girls we are ambivalent. We regard child-molesters with revulsion, and yet sexual abuse of children is widely practiced and tolerated in our society. Some experts say that as many as one young girl in four will be sexually molested by the age of thirteen. Our legal system is just as reluctant to arrest, try, convict, and sentence men who are accused of raping children as they are of those who rape adult women. As a society, we prefer to believe that children lie about such things or—taking a page from Freud—that their stories are just fantasies, or even that grown men are helpless to resist the seductive blandishments of little girls. The Lancaster, Pennsylvania, judge, who recently characterized a five-year-old victim of sexual abuse as "an unusually promiscuous young lady" who had led her mother's innocent twenty-four-year-old boyfriend astray, was not just displaying his own peculiar view. He was expressing what a lot of people in our society prefer to believe.

Our attitudes about domestic violence against women are no less contradictory. Once again, we simultaneously deplore it and excuse it, tolerating it by pretending it doesn't exist. Nearly two million women are severely beaten by their husbands every year in this country, according to one authoritative study. Although the authors of the study were taken aback by the size of that figure, they acknowledged that their research probably seriously undercounted the actual incidence of such violence. Other experts believe the true number is many times that. According to the F.B.I., a woman is beaten in the United States every eighteen seconds. It goes on all around us, but we don't want to know about it. When we are forced to acknowledge it, once again we call up a whole mythology devoted to justifying it and blaming the victim for it: she nags, she asks for it, provokes it, deserves it, or masochistically desires it. Men don't hit women without good reason; nice women don't get hit by men at all; women who don't like being beaten are always free to leave; if they stay, they probably want and deserve exactly what they get.

Significantly, while we register great disapproval of male violence against women, we do not teach women to defend themselves against it. Our culture's expectation is, always, that a woman is not supposed to defend herself; she is supposed to rely on a man to defend her—her husband, her boyfriend, her father or brothers, or the police. We still prefer to believe that the greatest threat of violence that women face comes from strangers in dark alleys, although that is manifestly not true. Women are far more at risk at home and from men whom they know. If the man that she most needs protection from is the very man who is supposed to protect her, a woman is just out of luck.

A woman who wields a deadly weapon, even to defend herself, presents a deeply disturbing image. Our prevailing ideal of women's true nature is that they are nurturers and life-givers, not life-takers. There is something that strikes us as obscene, against nature, or unholy about a woman who kills, that goes way beyond the illegality or even the immorality of her act. It shakes some of our most deeply held cultural stereotypes to their roots.

Society is outraged when a woman challenges all of these assumptions, refuses to take the blame, refuses to be a helpless victim but instead picks up a weapon and defends herself. It is doubly outraged when she then brazenly claims that she was reasonable and justified in doing so and should pay no penalty at all. If a woman, driven absolutely to the wall by a violent assailant, does have to kill him in order to save herself from being killed or grievously injured, she has traditionally been expected to do one of two things: plead that she was temporarily insane or plead guilty to manslaughter and throw herself on the mercy of the court. A woman who defends herself against a man's violence is either a criminal or crazy; our society is very reluctant to say that she is ever justified.

Everywhere she turns in the criminal justice system, a woman who must defend herself against male violence is confronted by people who share these attitudes. If she has called the police for protection in the past, she has already learned that the police seldom view the battered wife's situation with much sympathy. Domestic violence calls have a low priority in many police departments. The police respond slowly, if they respond at all. When they do arrive, it is usually with the attitude that they are there to cool down an argument, not to investigate a crime. The man is seldom arrested, even when an assault has obviously taken place. The woman is frequently told that being beaten by her husband or boyfriend is not a criminal but a civil matter. She should call a lawyer, get a restraining order, or file for divorce; but she should not look to the police for protection. Their job is to prevent and solve crimes, not to act as social workers.

Many women who have ultimately killed violent mates tell of their inability to get police protection. When Roxanne Gay, the wife of Philadelphia Eagles defensive lineman Blenda Gay, would call the police for help when he beat her, they would end up sitting around talking football with her husband. Eventually, believing that he was going to kill her, she stabbed him to death. Clara Miles stabbed her boyfriend with a kitchen knife as he was twisting the belt that he had been beating her with, around her neck to strangle her. Half an hour before, she had called the police for help in getting him out of her apartment because he was drunk and violent. When they came, not only did they refuse to arrest him; but they asked him if he wanted them to arrest *her* since he had sustained an injury to his hand in the melee and was bleeding. He declined to press charges and, according to her later testimony, the police laughed at her and left.

Caroline Scott, of course, could not call the police because the man who beat her so savagely for eight years *was* the police; and Ms. Scott is not unique in having to defend herself against the violence of a peace officer. Rose Lucas, for example, was married to a highway patrolman for twenty-three years, but during the last five years of their marriage, Mr. Lucas began drinking heavily and had become increasingly violent toward her. She testified that during that period he had made violent assaults on her, trying to strangle her at least two or three times a month. She felt a little safer when her grown sons were in the house, but they were not able to protect her all the time.

Two evenings before their final confrontation, there had been a violent scene; and she had called the police for help. The following night she had avoided him by staying with a neighbor until midnight, waiting to return home until he was asleep. When she went into the bedroom, she found that he had left his loaded revolver on the dresser. She removed the bullets from it and put it in a drawer. The next night there was another violent argument during which Lucas told her to get out and repeatedly threatened to kill her. She called the police again, and they came and talked to her husband but did not arrest him. After they left, Lucas' death threats resumed. She went into the kitchen to start dinner while he sat in the living room shouting at her that he was going to kill her. She went into the bedroom and got the revolver out of the drawer, reloading it with the bullets she had removed the night before. She walked into the hallway leading to the living room, telling him that she did not want him to kill her and pleading with him to talk to her about their problems. He started to get up from the chair, at which point she may have fired her first shot at him, although exactly when that first shot was fired was never established. At any rate, he came at her with his arms reaching for her. Convinced he was going to kill her, she emptied the gun at him. Rose Lucas was charged with murder, and the jury convicted her of manslaughter.

Delores Churchill, in a story that was eerily similar to Caroline Scott's, testified at her trial for attempted murder that her marriage to a police officer had been a seven-year nightmare of beatings, rape, torture, forced prostitution, and armed assaults. She said her husband had beaten her with his fists and with a belt. He had raped her and sexually assaulted her with such objects as a wine bottle, a broom handle, and his gun. Twice she was beaten so badly that she required medical care. He often threatened her with his gun and once had shot two holes in a pillow that she was clutching to her chest for protection. He held a gun to her head and ordered her to go out into the street and solicit passing men for sex, telling her he would be watching from nearby and would shoot her if she refused or tried to call for help. The Churchills separated four times; but every time, he stalked her and haunted her every move. Not once, but a number of times during these separations, he abducted her at gunpoint, drove her to their former apartment, and forcibly raped her.

She told the jury that the day she shot him, they were once again living apart. He had taken her to his house where he had punched her in the head, raped her, and then held a .38 caliber pistol on her and forced her to sign a property deed. He then drove her to a liquor store and put the gun in the glove compartment while he went in to buy some wine. In his absence, Delores removed the gun and put it in her purse, fearing that he was going to kill her with it. When he returned to the car, he drove her to the place where she worked in San Francisco. When they got there, there were some harsh words exchanged about the property deed, and she got out of the car and started walking toward her office building. He came rushing after her and, fearing another assault or abduction, she pulled the gun from her purse, turned, and fired, wounding him. She was charged with attempted murder and assault with a deadly weapon but, mercifully, was acquitted by a jury.

If the police don't regard wife-beating as a "real" crime, if they tolerate it in themselves and their buddies, if many of them share society's belief that women who get hit like it or deserve it, it is hardly surprising that—when the police are called to the scene of a domestic homicide, where a woman has killed her husband or boyfriend—they are going to be far more inclined to look for evidence of murder than of self-defense. There is seldom any question about who did the killing: in the typical case, it is the woman herself who calls the police and freely acknowledges that she wielded the knife or pulled the trigger. The police investigation, then, focuses on the circumstances of the killing. Although the purpose of a police investigation is merely to gather all the facts (those that would explain or excuse as well as those that incriminate) so that the prosecutor can decide whether criminal charges should be filed, the police (in these cases) often give the impression that they see their job as building a murder case. What the woman usually describes to them is a beating, a physical assault on her by the man she killed, often accompanied by a clearly expressed intention to kill her. What the police put into their official reports is that the parties were engaged in a "quarrel" or a "domestic altercation" that led to the killing. By characterizing the situation thus, the woman's actions are made far more likely to appear to have been motivated by aggressive anger than by fear and self-preservation. The ensuing investigation then becomes focused on digging up facts that would appear to give her a stereotypical motive for murder, such as jealousy or revenge.

Sometimes the police can become so complacent in assuming that their view of the facts is the only possible one, they are downright careless in preserving evidence that might support a different interpretation. In one Washington state case, the victim's body was released for cremation prematurely, which meant that the defense was unable to effectively challenge the autopsy report's conclusions about crucial matters involving the angle of the shots and thus the relative position of the parties when those shots were fired. In a North Carolina case, the house where the killing took place was permitted to be torn down although it contained the only evidence that could corroborate the defendant's version of how the fire started that killed her husband.

Sometimes, in their zeal to obtain a conviction, the police can clearly overstep the bounds of legality in pushing a confused and distraught woman to make a damaging confession. Joyce Hawthorne, for example, was arrested at four o'clock in the morning of a sleepless night of threats and violence which ended in the shooting death of her husband. She was read her *Miranda* rights—the right to remain silent and to have an attorney—and taken to jail. Her five children— the youngest only six years old and two of them ill—were also hauled off to the jail for questioning. She obtained a lawyer who advised her, quite correctly, to make no statement to the police. A bail hearing was held at eleven that morning, at which she appeared so shaken and upset that there was some consideration of sending her to a hospital rather than back to jail. However, this was decided against, bail was denied, and she was driven back to the jail by Officer Dunn of the county sheriff's office.

Although he knew that she had been advised not to make a statement, during the drive Officer Dunn began to pressure her to do so. He told her that her children were still being "interrogated" and that it was extremely upsetting for them to have to answer questions about the problems between their mother and father. He told her that she could spare them further anguish by making a statement; the police had to know what happened, she was the best source of information about it, and her refusal to talk was forcing the police to get the story from the next best source—the children. Ms. Hawthorne insisted that she was going to follow her attorney's advice. She was too upset to eat any lunch when they got back to the jail. At two that afternoon, she was taken to Dunn's office where he resumed his efforts to extract a confession. He told her that the children were still at the jail and were still being questioned. He told her that she did not have to follow her lawyer's advice; that she could fire him and get a public defender to represent her; that advising a client to remain silent was just a meaningless, routine piece of advice that all lawyers gave, even when it wasn't in their client's best interest. In response to her repeatedly expressed concern about the children and who would care for them, he told her that if she made a statement, he would see to it that she got out on bond that night. She could go home to her kids and wouldn't have to spend the night in the jail cell "with the lesbians." But it was getting late; he couldn't arrange with the state's attorney for a bond after five o'clock, so she would have to make up her mind soon.

Joyce Hawthorne had not slept for thirty-six hours nor eaten in twenty-four. She was ill, exhausted, and distraught about her children. Finally, after two-and-a-half hours of Dunn's browbeating, she agreed to waive her rights and make a statement without her lawyer present. Tape recorders were turned on and for another two-and-a-half hours, interrupted only by periods when she was too upset or exhausted to continue, she was grilled by the police. Finally, at seven o'clock in the evening, she was returned to her cell, handed a pad and pen and told to keep on confessing. Officer Dunn did not obtain a bond for her release that night.

Joyce was tried and convicted of first-degree murder. Her statements to the police were allowed into evidence by the trial judge despite defense objections that she had been improperly coerced into making them. The Florida Court of Appeal ultimately agreed that Ms. Hawthorne's constitutional rights had been grossly violated by the sheriff's department's treatment of her. It threw out the conviction and granted her a new trial in which her statements to the police, and any evidence deriving from them, would not be admissible.

The vindictiveness of some police officers toward women who defend themselves against violent men is illustrated by a pair of letters that were attached to the presentence report to the judge who presided over the Idaho murder trial of Thelma Griffiths. Ms. Griffiths shot her husband when—during an argument in which he had shoved her violently—he lunged at her with the same expression on his face that he had had when he had attempted to strangle her and succeeded in choking her almost into unconsciousness. She was charged with second-degree murder; however, the jury returned a verdict of involuntary manslaughter, which indicates they believed she had not intended to kill her husband but had acted with criminal recklessness by firing a gun under those circumstances.

In their letters to the judge, the two police officers who had investigated the case were clearly outraged at the jury's failure to find her guilty of murder and tried to convince the judge to give her a murder sentence anyway. In the words of a dissenting justice on the Idaho Supreme Court, which upheld Ms. Griffith's conviction, "A cursory glance shows that these letters were highly prejudicial and constituted an attempt to in effect retry the case by influencing the sentence." The dissent goes on to quote portions of the two letters. From the Chief of Police:

> We could find no reason for anyone to shoot him...Why didn't she leave the house, she had plenty of opportunity to do so...[she] followed him [into the bedroom]. She claimed that he had been hitting her. Was she asking for more?...When the gun was pointed at Joe he had no other way out of the room except through Thelma...We all hope that we aren't called out to investigate another homicide at the Griffith's residence.

From Officer Tony Young:

> Throughout the entire investigation of the death of Joe GRIFFITHS, I came to the conclusion that a great injustice had occurred. From the moment that I was contacted on the night of the shooting, to the last day of the trial I felt that Mrs. GRIFFITHS was guilty of first degree murder...
>
> . . . .
>
> I believe that Mrs. GRIFFITHS is guilty of first degree murder and that she should have been found guilty of that charge. I believe that her actions on the night of the shooting were premeditated and occurred with malice aforethought. I believe that Mrs. GRIFFITHS placed the gun in the storage cabinet in the bedroom for the purpose of using the firearm later in the evening when Joe arrived home. As she apparently did. Furthermore, I believe that Mrs. GRIFFITHS is a dangerous person, and that she should be strictly dealt with when her sentence is passed. I might also add that I don't believe that I would be surprised if I were called to that same house tonight to investigate another shooting.

As Justice Bistline so aptly observed in his dissent, "...it is indeed a sad day when a defendant is virtually attacked and pursued so viciously by the very officers entrusted with the public safety, to the extent that they would attempt to influence the court to disregard a jury verdict—long considered as one of our greatest protections—and continue to seek that punishment which *they* feel is warranted.'' Although he argued for a reversal, the majority of the court felt otherwise; and her conviction, and three-year prison sentence, stood.

After a woman's arrest, the next person whose stereotyped and sex-biased ideas can affect the working of the criminal justice system is the prosecutor. It is the prosecutor, in most states, who decides whether criminal charges will be filed and what those charges will be. If the woman suspect is charged with a crime and put on trial, it is the prosecutor's job to try to convince the jury that she should be convicted. In both of these aspects of his or her role, a prosecutor who has benighted notions about women—or is willing to pander to the worst possible prejudices of the jurors—can cause great injustice to be done to women defendants in self-defense cases.

Whether a state requires a prosecutor to convince a grand jury to issue an indictment or permits filing the charges with the court directly, a prosecutor has an enormous amount of discretion in deciding whether to charge a person at all and what charges to bring. There is virtually no way to compel a prosecutor to bring charges, even when a crime clearly has been committed and a suspect identified, as any number of rape victims have learned to their sorrow. Nor is there any way to prevent a prosecutor from filing charges and bringing someone to trial, even where it appears that the accused person acted justifiably under the law. Any number of factors can influence the charging decision, some of them legal (the admissibility of key evidence or the credibility of witnesses) and some of them extra-legal (politics, community pressure, or racial or sexual prejudice). Prosecutors are elected officials. Every few years they must face the public and seek reelection, usually on the basis of how tough they are on crime and criminals. The easy convictions that prosecutors can win against women who kill men can be a tempting way to add a few notches to their guns when the decision about whether or not to file charges in such cases must be made.

It is not surprising, then, that many people I have talked to who have dealt with the problem of women who defend themselves against male violence—including experienced defense attorneys—claim that women are more frequently charged with such crimes or are charged with more serious crimes than men would be. It is a claim that is difficult to verify, in part because prosecutors do not have to account to anyone publicly for their charging decisions but, equally important, because the sorts of things that happen to women that they must defend themselves against so seldom happen to men. It is hard to imagine, for example, a man being in Caroline Scott's situation—brutalized, terrorized, and tortured over a period of years, either at the hands of a woman or of another man. On the other hand, it is hard to imagine that if such a thing did occur—a man held prisoner by terrorists, perhaps, or a lunatic—such a man would *ever* be charged with murder for shooting his way out when an opportunity presented itself.

Occasionally a case does come along that presents circumstances in which one can imagine a man finding himself. Alene Collier's, for example, was such a case. Alene Collier shot Leon Mitchell at the end of a night that must have seemed to her like a waking nightmare. Alene lived with her mother and her two small children in her mother's house in Morgan County, Alabama. Although Leon Mitchell was the father of her children, they were never married. Mitchell did not live with Alene and did not help to support the children.

Leon was a heavy drinker and a violent man. He carried a knife and, on more than one occasion, he had attacked Alene and cut her up with it. She may have loved him, but she had every reason to fear him.

The night of his death, he came to her house very drunk and with his opened knife in his hand. He told her that he had lost thirty dollars gambling that night. He wanted her to give him some money and, brandishing the knife, he said that he would kill her if she didn't. Alene gave him five dollars and told him that she could not come up with any more. Enraged, Mitchell began slashing at her with the knife and chased her out of her house. Then, while she stood in the yard and he remained inside the house—which was not his and in which he had no more right to remain than any stranger would have—he shouted at her that if she came back inside, he would kill her.

In the meantime, of course, Alene's two little children and her mother were still in the house with this apparent madman. She waited in the yard for a little while; and when she thought it might be safe she went back inside, but Leon went after her again with the knife and chased her outside once more.

While she was in the house, before this second armed assault, she managed to take a single rifle bullet from a drawer. Outside again, she went across the street to her grandfather's house and picked up a .22 rifle that she brought back and hid under her mother's house.

Leon Mitchell, still in the house and still in a rage, began beating one of the children, and Alene went back inside once more. Although Mitchell was still armed with the knife, Alene left the gun where she had hidden it. This time, knife still flailing, Mitchell chased both Alene and her mother out of the house. Still terrified for her children but still unarmed, Alene returned to the house one final time. When she got inside, she found that Mitchell had used his knife to slash up her purse that had been lying on a table. When she asked him why he had done that, he swore at her and threatened once again to kill her. When he charged at her with the knife, she fled her house for the last time.

Picking up the rifle from where it lay hidden, Alene carried it around the back of the house to the window of the room where Mitchell was standing. She tried to talk to him through the open window, but he brandished the knife at her and said, "If you come in the house I'll kill you." At that point, Alene fired one shot at Mitchell through the screen. He closed the knife and sat down on the bed, saying, "You got me now." Afraid that he was play-acting, Alene waited outside the window for a few minutes before she ventured back into the house once again. When she saw that he was bleeding, she called an ambulance and administered what aid she could until it arrived. She rode with him to the hospital where he died of a single bullet wound.

Alene Collier was arrested and charged with second-degree murder; the jury found her guilty of first-degree manslaughter, her conviction was upheld on appeal, and she was sent to prison for her crime.

Suppose, now, that Alene Collier had been Al Collier, divorced or widowed perhaps, living with his old mother and his two little children. And suppose that the drunken man who came to the door had been a total stranger or a casual acquaintance, someone with a local reputation for violent behavior. If that man had burst in brandishing a knife, demanding money—which is armed robbery and an assault with a deadly weapon—had taken over the house and had driven the rightful occupants out, had repeatedly threatened to murder the father and had physically attacked one of the children, would Al Collier have been charged with murder for finally getting off a shot at the intruder through a window? No. Of course not. It's highly unlikely that any charges at all would have been filed, much less that a jury would have found him guilty of anything. He would have been hailed as a hero, defending his home and his children and his women against a violent criminal, exactly the way a man is supposed to do.

Similarly, it is difficult to believe that a man in Bernadette Powell's situation would have been charged with murder or any other crime. Bernadette (along with her six-year-old son) was kidnapped at gunpoint by her ex-husband, Herman Smith, driven around aimlessly for most of the night—all the while being threatened with death if she tried to escape—and finally was taken to a room in a motel. When it appeared that Smith had fallen asleep, Bernadette tried to slip the gun out of the waistband of his pants so that she and the boy could escape unharmed; but Smith jerked awake, and the gun went off, killing him. If Bernadette Powell had been a man, kidnapped with his young son by an armed desperado or even if (as a woman) she and the child had been kidnapped by a total stranger, her actions would probably have been perceived by everyone—including the prosecutor—as entirely justified under the circumstances and in fact courageous and praiseworthy. Why, then, should those actions be any less justified because they were performed by a woman, or because the man whose criminal violence she was trying to escape was someone with whom she was once intimate? There is a double standard operating here.

If prosecutors charge women in circumstances in which they would not charge men, it is in part because they know that they can get juries to convict women in these circumstances. The trial courtroom provides a forum for a biased or cynical prosecutor to trot out every myth and stereotype and misconception about women that could conceivably inflame a jury against the defendant and that could encourage the jurors to ascribe the worst possible motive to her actions.

Testimony about the deceased's past violence toward the defendant should always be admissible in a self-defense case because it is relevant to the crucial determination of whether the defendant's perception of the danger she was in was reasonable. If the man had inflicted serious injuries on her before, the woman's assumption that he was about to do it again might well appear more reasonable than if he had never before laid a hand on her. However, a zealous prosecutor has a whole panoply of arguments with which to counter this assumption. One of the favorites is that the woman (like all women perhaps) is a masochist who invited and enjoyed the violence and, therefore, couldn't have been motivated to kill by fearing more of it.

The prosecutor in Bernadette Powell's case—who it later turned out was at the same time being divorced by his own wife on the grounds of his violence toward her—hammered away relentlessly at this theme. Although there was not a shred of evidence to support his innuendoes, the picture of Bernadette that he painted for the jury was that of a woman who (during the course of her marriage to the man she eventually killed) had gotten her sexual kicks from being tied up and beaten, scalded with hot water, burned with cigarettes, kicked down flights of stairs, and imprisoned for hours in the trunk of a car.

Similarly, when Linda Anaya was put on trial for murder in the stabbing death of her lover Frank Williams, the prosecutor argued to the jury that her injuries—sustained during a horrendous five-month-long live-in relationship with him—were all part of a "loving game," and that, consequently, she had no reason to fear him. She had been beaten, kicked, stabbed, mutilated with a chisel, and struck hard enough on the head to cause a concussion. Five times he had injured her seriously enough to require medical treatment. Williams had held a knife at her throat and threatened to kill her if she left him. Linda's roommate, who had gone on living in the apartment with them after Williams moved in, testified that life at the apartment was "like a madhouse." Linda was afraid to leave Williams because of his threats. A few days before the final, fatal episode she had tried to kill herself—her second suicide attempt in five short months.

According to the Supreme Court of Maine, "The State's closing argument focused on the 'bizarre' behavior of the victim and the defendant, implying that the defendant could not have been fearful of Williams since she never attempted to leave him, and suggesting that the injuries received by defendant over the course of several months were part of a loving game, not attempts to commit suicide or the result of physical abuse." The jury apparently bought this "loving game" theory and found her guilty of manslaughter.

There are any number of other ways that a prosecutor can belittle the seriousness of injuries the defendant suffered and can imply that she is exaggerating them or flat-out lying about them. Ignoring the past decade of research about the way battered women typically behave and the problems they face, the prosecutor can argue to the jury that if there had indeed been the violence that she claims, she would surely have left him long ago. She would have called the police, who would have records of her calls and would, by implication, have arrested the man and solved her problem. She would have told her neighbors, her friends, her minister, her mother. All of the ways in which so many beaten women manage to hide what they perceive as their humiliating and shameful situation is turned against them. If the man's violence was usually accompanied by heavy drinking, and the woman drank with him prior to the final incident, she is portrayed as having knowingly contributed to the assault and therefore is not entitled to defend herself against it. One woman, Ivy Kelly, was accused by the prosecutor of having faked her injuries with makeup.

Bernadette Powell's prosecutor argued that the violence she experienced during her marriage was "only" sexual, since most of her husband's attacks on her culminated in his forcibly raping her. As he put it in his appellate brief, "The point that is relevant and material out of all this is that these acts were sexually motivated on his part, regardless of her acquiescence or lack of it, and that they are not any proof of his violence toward her or of any reasonable fear on her part of serious physical injury at his hands."

If the woman's story about past abuse inflicted on her by the man she killed is too ghastly or too well-documented to be denied, the prosecutor can turn it against her with another set of sexual stereotypes. He or she can argue to the jury that the defendant must have been motivated by revenge, on the assumption that any woman who had suffered such treatment would undoubtedly be hungering for vengeance; that she murdered him because it was the easiest way she could get out of a hopeless and horrible situation; that, since he had beaten her so many times before without killing her, it was unreasonable of her to think he was going to kill her this time. If she was hysterical when she called the police or when they arrived, it can be argued that the killing was the unreasonable act of an out-of-control person; if she was not hysterical, she is a cold-blooded, calculating murderess; if her husband was unfaithful to her then, as

Caroline Scott's prosecutor argued to the jury, she must have murdered him in a jealous rage. Indeed, this constant speculation about motive, arising from an unspoken assumption—that a woman who kills a man with whom she has been intimate *must* have had some base and ugly motive for her act, which she is subsequently lying about—is at the center of virtually every prosecution of a woman's self-defense case.

The prosecutor, of course, is not the only lawyer a woman defendant has to deal with whose perception of her actions may be distorted by stereotypes about lying, vengeful, jealous, masochistic women. Her own lawyer may be just as much a victim of these cultural myths and just as unable to perceive her act as self-defense. This can result in a defense strategy that sees a manslaughter conviction as a victory and fails to raise self-defense issues at all. It can also lead to a decision to raise an insanity defense, which not only inappropriately labels the woman as crazy for fighting back but is also apt to result in her being committed to a mental institution for a far longer time and under far worse conditions than if she had been convicted of a crime and sent to prison.

Much more often, however, she is advised to plead guilty to a reduced charge of manslaughter or even second-degree murder, not because that is the best among a range of bad options (as of course it sometimes is), but because her own lawyer believes that is what she is indeed guilty of. It is impossible to determine how many women—who were in fact acting in legitimate self-defense—have followed such advice and quietly gone off to prison. However, it is interesting that, since a woman's right to self-defense has begun to be acknowledged by the courts, we are beginning to see suits brought by such women seeking to have their guilty pleas set aside on the grounds that they were improperly advised by their lawyers or that they pled guilty without even being informed that they might have raised a self-defense plea.

In Washington state, for example, Alice Keyes pled guilty to second-degree murder, on her attorney's advice, in the shooting death of a man she claimed was trying to rape her. Alice, who had recently arrived in Washington from Philadelphia, had taken a job in a cafe, cooking, cleaning, and washing up in exchange for $50.00 a week and room and board. Her boss put her up in a room next to the cafe. Late one evening, he burst into her room with sex obviously on his mind. She says that he fought with her and slapped her around, calling her a black bitch and asking why she didn't act like a woman. He took off his pants and put them on the dresser. She knew that there was a gun in one of his pants pockets. There was a struggle on the bed as he was trying to force his head between her legs. She fell off the bed; and as she did so, she knocked the pants off the dresser onto the floor. Remembering the gun, she got her hands on it and fired two bullets into the back of her assailant's head.

As luck would have it, the man Alice shot was the father-in-law of a candidate for county sheriff; and the county prosecutor threw the book at Alice, charging her with first-degree murder and asking for the death penalty. On her attorney's advice and assurances that she would probably only draw a sentence of five years, she pled guilty to second-degree murder. Her sentence was fifty years in prison. After serving five years of it, she was able, with a new attorney, to convince the same judge that he had improperly accepted her guilty plea because there was not an adequate factual basis for it at the time. The judge allowed her to withdraw her plea and granted her the right to a trial. When the prosecutor then threatened to charge her all over again with first-degree murder, she decided to plead guilty to a reduced charge of manslaughter. The length of her new sentence matched the time she had already served, so Alice Keyes was finally released.

Another Washington woman, however, was not so fortunate, if that is the appropriate word for the outcome of Ms. Keyes' legal ordeal. Elizabeth Knott was a young black woman who had married Bernard Knott at twenty-one and lived with him in Kentucky. He began to beat her early in the marriage, and eventually she pressed assault charges against him. He lost his job and joined the Navy, which assigned him to a base on Whidbey Island, Washington. Fearing his violence, Elizabeth told him she was not going to accompany him; but he begged and pleaded with her, and ultimately she gave in and went, taking her two daughters from her previous marriage with her. A short time later, she gave birth to a third child, fathered by Bernard. The violence continued and escalated after the move. Once, she went into the hospital for surgery; and when she returned home, Bernard raped her, injuring her so badly that she had to return to the hospital. Bernard began to abuse the stepchildren as well, beating one of them so badly that the child had to be hospitalized. Elizabeth pressed charges against him, and he was convicted of assault. He was put on probation for one year and confined to the base where he could not have contact with Elizabeth or the children. She sent the two older girls back to relatives in Kentucky.

The day that Bernard was released from probation, he came home and beat her up. Many other beatings followed, and finally Elizabeth fled back to Kentucky. Reluctantly, she left her youngest daughter behind with Bernard, believing that under the circumstances, she had no other choice. Within two months, however, Elizabeth's concern for the youngster was so great that she went back to Washington. She found her daughter badly injured and confronted Bernard, telling him she wanted a divorce. Bernard charged at her in a rage, and she shot him.

Elizabeth Knott was charged with first-degree murder and convicted of manslaughter. She claims that she was advised by her attorney not to appeal her conviction because she would feel better if she served her sentence and paid her debt to society. Her sentence was ten years in prison, five years of which was mandatory because she had used a firearm. Her attempts to get the appellate courts to permit her to file an appeal after the deadline for filing had run out were unsuccessful.

Although it is the jury which ultimately decides a defendant's guilt or innocence, a trial judge who has a mind to can do a great deal to influence the outcome of a trial. There is nothing necessarily wise or enlightened about judges. They share the same prejudices and stereotyped beliefs as the rest of the population; and to the extent that state court judges tend to be white males past middle age, their attitudes about women may be more traditional than most. Furthermore, a judge who has been on the criminal bench for a long time, or who is a former prosecutor, is apt to share the criminal justice system's traditional assumption that a woman who kills her husband or lover has always at the least committed manslaughter; he or she may well be resistant to a defense attorney's attempt to put on a vigorous justifiable homicide defense, as recent battles to get expert testimony admitted in women's self-defense trials demonstrates. Some judges may even believe that it is in the woman's best interest to be found guilty. I recall a chilling conversation with a former judge—and avowed feminist—who argued that battered women were in need of counseling; thus, finding the defendant guilty and putting her on probation was an effective way of ensuring that she would get it. An acquittal, on the other hand, would put her beyond the reach of the court's benevolence.

We have seen that the judge who tried Caroline Scott's case refused to allow the jury the option of finding that she had acted in self-defense. It is the judge's responsibility to instruct the jury about the law. The jury is then supposed to apply that law to the facts as they are developed in trial testimony in order to reach a verdict. By refusing to instruct the jury about either self-defense or manslaughter, the judge left the jury with only the choice of finding Scott guilty or not guilty of murder. It could not consider any justifying or mitigating circumstances. Since there was no question that she had pulled the trigger, the guilty verdict was virtually assured.

Where a judge does give the jury self-defense instructions—and most quite properly do if there is any possibility at all that the defendant might have been acting in self-defense—he or she can define self-defense so narrowly that the jury cannot fit the facts of the case at hand within it, although the jurors may honestly believe that the woman was in fact defending herself. A judge can also influence the outcome of a trial by controlling what testimony the jury is allowed to hear. Although it is established law that past violence against the defendant by the man she killed is relevant and admissible in a self-defense case, some judges still refuse to permit it; or attempt to limit it by ruling that it happened too long before the final episode; or, if there is more than one witness able to testify to it, that it is cumulative and therefore unnecessary. In Joyce Hawthorne's first trial, for example, the judge only permitted the jury to hear testimony about her husband's violent acts during the two weeks previous to the shooting, although she had endured endless abuse throughout the seventeen years of her marriage.

A judge can also refuse to allow testimony by expert witnesses, often psychologists or psychiatrists, who are brought in by the defense to explain to the jury about the phenomenon of wife-beating and how battered women typically cope with their violent situations. As we shall see, the presentation of expert testimony often makes the crucial difference between a conviction and an acquittal in these cases. Two such experts were standing by at Caroline Scott's trial, but the trial judge refused to allow either one to testify.

Judges can be wrong, of course, and these sorts of discriminatory courtroom decisions are more and more often being overruled by the appellate courts. Caroline Scott's conviction, for example, was overturned on appeal because of the judge's refusal to allow the jury to even consider a finding that she had acted in self-defense or that her act was not murder but manslaughter.

It is important to remember, however, that all that a woman wins in a successful appeal is the right to be tried all over again and quite possibly convicted again. Joyce Hawthorne's first-degree murder conviction was overturned on appeal on the grounds that her statement to the police was improperly coerced, and she was granted a new trial. At that trial, she was convicted, again, of second-degree murder. That conviction was also appealed and overturned, in part because the second trial court had refused to permit an expert witness to testify about battered women. She was tried a third time; and at that trial she was found guilty only of manslaughter, but the sentence of fifteen years was the same as the one she had been given for the second-degree murder conviction. She appealed yet again; and the third conviction, too, was overturned by the appellate court. At this writing, Joyce Hawthorne is facing her fourth trial for an act that took place in 1977.

Joyce Hawthorne's incredible tenacity is unusual. Many such women, unable to face the expense and emotional ordeal of a second trial with such a high risk of another disastrous outcome, choose to plead guilty to reduced charges just to have it finally ended. Winning an appeal is surely better than losing an appeal, but justice for women who kill in self-defense will not be obtained until they can win these cases at the trial level or, far better yet, never be charged and put on trial at all.

The fate of a defendant in a criminal trial is ultimately, of course, in the hands of the jury. It is the jury's role, after listening to all the testimony and viewing all of the evidence, to determine the facts of the case—what really happened and why—and then to do its best to apply the law to those facts and reach a just verdict. It is in the jury box and the jury room that the rigid, archaic, male-oriented law of self-defense, interacting with the social attitudes that jurors quite naturally bring with them to the courtroom, creates a no-win situation for women defendants. A juror who believes the myths and stereotypes about battered women—and also believes that any woman who kills her mate *must* be guilty of some crime and deserves to be punished—can find ample justification in the twists and turns of self-defense law to convict her, no matter how compelling her claim that she was acting to defend herself. And a sympathetic juror who has been convinced by the evidence that the woman's act was completely justified can still feel obliged by those same twists and turns to convict her anyway. The first juror can say that although the defendant met all of the technicalities of the law, her actions were simply not reasonable. The second juror may have to find that, although her actions were eminently reasonable, she did not meet the technical requirements of the law. In the following chapters we will examine just how this lamentable interaction of law and bias works to deprive most women of any effective right to self-defense at all. First, however, it is useful to take a brief look at how the law developed historically, since the dead hand of history, still lying heavily on the law of today, is one of the major sources of the problem.

2

A Law for Men

The notion that killing in self-defense is excusable is an extremely ancient one in English law. It was a European view, brought to England by the Normans after 1066, and was one of the first exceptions to the Anglo-Saxon idea that the taking of life is culpable regardless of the circumstances. The earliest reported cases date from the early 1200s. Although the law of self-defense has evolved over some nine centuries, its basic parameters were established very early and have changed remarkably little.

Prior to the Norman conquest and the subsequent imposition of French and Italian notions of justice on Anglo-Saxon customs, English law imposed absolute liability on everyone whose actions, or even whose possessions, caused injury or death to another. It did not matter whether the injury came about as the result of accident, negligence, or malicious intent. If a man hung up his sword on the wall and it fell on someone sitting beneath it and killed him, the sword's owner was every bit as blameworthy as if he had taken the sword in his hand and intentionally run the other fellow through. In the case of a deliberate killing, no account was taken of motive, intent, or mitigating circumstances. The only inquiry that the system of justice, such as it was, made into the facts was whether or not the accused caused the death or injury; and this inquiry was addressed not to any human agency but directly to God. Trial was by ordeal, usually fire or water, or by compurgation, wherein the accused had to present a prescribed number of witnesses who would swear to his or her veracity. If, in the course of the ordeal, the accused drowned, or the wounds caused by the hot irons or the boiling water festered and failed to heal, it was a direct heavenly indication of guilt. In a trial by compurgation, if the requisite number of oath-helpers could

31

not be produced or if any one of them tripped over his words when reciting the formula, the accused's denial of guilt was divinely repudiated. The defendant's motives or the circumstances of his act were sublimely irrelevant to the whole proceeding.

Originally, English law did not distinguish between civil and criminal matters. The local government, or the king, did not bring charges against an alleged wrongdoer. All wrongs were avenged by the injured party or, in the case of a killing, by the next of kin either directly and bloodily or by appeal to the local court for monetary compensation. Once the accused's responsibility was ascertained through an ordeal or oath-swearing, the injury was compensated through the payment of a sum of money, called *bot* or *wergild*, by the wrongdoer to the victim or the victim's survivors. Although there were almost no crimes (short of treason) that were not compensable by monetary damages, vengeance killings that sometimes resulted in long-lasting blood-feuds were common.

The Norman invasion brought social and political changes that were accompanied by lasting changes in English law. William the Conqueror and his successors imposed a strong central government on England, and one of the prerequisites for accomplishing this was the elimination of the custom of taking the law into one's own hands. Personal vengeance and *bots* and *wergilds* had to go. One of the wrongful acts that had historically never been compensable by a *bot* was a breach of the king's peace. Gradually, one after another of the acts that are now regarded as crimes were included in this category, and a system of royal courts and circuit-riding judges grew up to enforce the king's peace. Trial by battle replaced the oath and the ordeal, eventually to be replaced in turn by the forerunner of modern juries. Private compensation for criminal acts was replaced by public punishment, which in most cases was mutilation or execution, accompanied by a forfeiture of one's lands and property to the Crown.

This process, of course, took place over many years. Reforms took root slowly and for long periods of time old and new ways of doing things existed side by side. It was during this period of legal—not to mention political, social, and religious—turmoil that the notion began to emerge that the circumstances surrounding an act that injured or killed another ought to be taken into account in deciding how to deal with the killer. The earliest recorded English cases, which date from the beginning of the thirteenth century, reflect this. Although there was growing acknowledgement that killings that were the result of accident or self-defense were somehow different from intentional murders, there was considerable uncertainty about how such killings should be treated by the courts.

A very early pair of cases, from the same local jurisdiction and the same year, reflects this confusion. Interestingly enough, they are the first recorded English cases involving women defendants in self-defense circumstances. In the Assize of Northumberland in the year 1256, a woman named Alice drew a knife and killed a man who attempted to rape her. She fled and became a fugitive, but subsequently her father went to the local court and offered to pay a fine of forty shillings if she were allowed to return. The offer was accepted but, on her return, she was taken into custody and held until she was able to obtain a royal pardon. A short time later, another woman, Matilda, who killed a man in identical circumstances was acquitted outright by the same court. In both cases the court apparently felt that the circumstances excused the homicide. The confusion arose out of what the court's power was to respond to the facts.

The English courts and judges had no power to pardon or even mitigate. Once responsibility for a wrong was established, the court could only impose the compensation or the punishment. Consequently, the rule evolved, and was formalized in the Statute of Gloucester in 1278, that in all cases of homicide in which accident or self-defense was an issue, the accused still had to be tried and, if found responsible for the death, convicted of murder. The defendant then could apply to the king for a pardon. This remained the law until the end of the sixteenth century, although more and more the granting of a pardon became a routine matter in which the king was not personally involved.

In 1532, Henry VIII enacted a statute that abolished forfeitures in such cases, and in the ensuing decades the necessity of obtaining a pardon fell into disuse. By the seventeenth century, when Sir Edward Coke and Sir Matthew Hale were writing their discourses on English common law, it was firmly established that a necessary killing in self-defense was no crime at all. A person who committed such an act was entitled to a complete acquittal, if indeed he or she was made to stand trial in the first place. This has continued to be the law to the present day.

When a pardon for a homicide committed in self-defense ceased to be purely a matter of the king's grace and began to be a legal right asserted before a judge and jury, a body of law began to develop that would provide guidance about when an acquittal for self-defense was appropriate and when one was not.

The common law of England was, and is, unique among the world's legal systems. Rather than being exclusively handed down from above in the form of statutes adopted by king or Parliament, the law was perceived simply to exist in the common usages and conscience of the English people. It was the task of the judges of the Crown Courts to "discover" this law and apply it to the facts of each case. In earliest times, the law that the judge discovered was likely to reflect nothing more than his private sense of justice, such as it was. However, over time, and especially as written records of cases began to be kept, the judges developed the habit of looking to previous decisions in similar cases to find the law. This precedent system, which is still in use today in England and America, provided a continuity and uniformity of decisions that to some extent tempered the individual prejudices of judges. More important, it provided litigants and the criminally accused with some guidance about how their cases would fare and what arguments to make to the court.

The common law system had its most extraordinary flowering in the area of criminal law. Since statutes were few, a citizen could not look to the criminal code to discover what actions were prohibited and what were not. Simply by virtue of participating in English society, he or she was expected to know right from wrong and behave accordingly. Murder, rape, robbery, burglary, and arson were crimes by common agreement, not because they were outlawed by statute. And it was the common law judges who defined and refined them and gradually developed a body of case law that was sufficiently sensitive to the varieties of human behavior to distinguish, for example, between homicides committed with premeditated malice, those committed in the heat of a momentary passion, and those that were the result of a reckless desregard for another's safety.

The common law judges were also quite free to identify new crimes when changing times or plain criminal ingenuity presented them with behavior that appeared to them obviously improper even though it had never been encountered before. Similarly, the judges could recognize as a defense to criminal charges any justification or excuse put forward by a defendant if justice seemed to demand it. Most of the defenses recognized by modern criminal law, such as alibi, insanity, and self-defense, came into being in just this way.

It cannot be emphasized too strongly that all of these judges were male, as were the jurors and most of the criminal defendants brought before them. Their cases involved the sorts of situations men were apt to get themselves into; and the excuses or defenses they offered were those that made sense—to themselves, their judges, and all-male juries—in terms of acceptable or understandable masculine behavior. The body of case law that began very early to grow up about self-defense in the centuries following the Conquest inevitably reflected the male-centered point of view of a rigorously male-centered society.

Medieval England was a fertile ground for the development of a legal right to self-defense. The times were disorderly and, despite the determination of monarch after monarch to establish "the king's peace," violent crime was common, especially in the countryside where 90 percent of the population lived. The rate of homicide was many times what it is today, and robbery-murder was so frequent as to be characterized by one historian as a "major social phenomenon." Another has observed that, "So common was violent death from homicide in Medieval London or Oxford the man in the street ran more of a risk from dying at the hands of a fellow citizen than from an accident."

There was no standing army, and there were no police to enforce domestic law and order. The Normans retained the Anglo-Saxon system of "hue and cry" which made all adult males collectively responsible for law enforcement by pursuing wrongdoers when an alarm was raised, but it was not a very effective system. A man generally must have assumed that he must provide his own protection for himself and his family.

It was a responsibility that most would have had no trouble meeting. Feudal England was a masculine world, organized for warfare. Since every man's primary obligation was to render military service to his lord, he was a soldier and a fighter, in addition to whatever his other occupation might be. Besides the regular military service he owed, every adult male was subject to general mobilization in times of danger; and from 1181 onward, royal decrees specified what weapons men from sixteen to sixty, of every social status, were obliged to keep ready to hand in case they were called out. In any confrontation a man in those days might have had with other men, there would have been no question about his ability to give as good as he got. Court records reflect that the earliest situations in which a recognition of justifiable homicide began to appear were those in which the defendant, in a sort of law-enforcement capacity, killed someone who was committing a violent felony against him. Fighting and brawling were so commonplace, however, and so frequently resulted in someone's being killed that the concept of self-defense was gradually applied to those situations as well.

A man had to be able to protect himself because there was precious little the state would do to protect him. Women, on the other hand, were not expected to protect themselves but to look to males to protect them. They were passed, often at an early age with no say in the matter at all, from the protection of their fathers to the protection of their husbands and later, if widowed, to the protection of their brothers or the church. Women who did not marry were expected to seek the protection of the convent. Although medieval women, especially of the lower classes, were remarkably tough and took an active part in work and social life, they were involved in far less violence than men were. Indeed, historian Barbara Hanawalt has noted that, "Medieval women were less physically aggressive than medieval men and somewhat less prone to personal violent attacks than modern women." Whether because they tended to spend their lives closer to home or because when they went out in public they were seldom alone or unprotected, women seem to have been much less apt to find themselves in circumstances where they had to defend themselves. Hanawalt observes that "women were less apt to be found in situations conducive to becoming victims. They were not actively engaged in the heavy work in field and on ships and therefore were less likely to become the victims of homicidal arguments related to these activities. Women infrequently traveled with valuable chattel and animals, so that they were rare victims of robberies." James B. Givens, in his study of homicides in thirteenth-century England, found that while men met their fates in a variety of public places—"in fields, on ships, in stables, in meadows, on bridges, or at markets, parties, and fairs," as well as in taverns— women were not killed at all in these sorts of places. Indeed, the great majority were killed in their own homes.

Although women committed far fewer homicides than men did (8.6 percent in Givens' study, 7 percent in Hanawalt's), when they did kill, they were apt to kill their husbands. Considering that wife-beating was common and the home was such a lethal place for women, many of these homicides must certainly have been in self-defense; but two aspects of medieval family law kept them from ever being considered as such. The first was that a woman lived her entire life "under the rod" of men. Her husband, just like her father, had the right to beat her all he wished, as long as he was doing it for her own good—as punishment for wrongdoing or to keep her from "falling into error." Even though he was not supposed to beat her seriously enough to maim or kill her, his right of chastisement was so taken for granted that little was probably done about it if he did. One commentator tells the story of an early fifteenth-century Hampshire man who beat and kicked his wife to death. He was put on trial, but the jury acquitted him and had it entered in the official records that the poor woman had died of plague.

The second aspect of medieval family law was that a woman's relation to her husband was that of a subject to his lord. He was her "baron," and she owed him absolute fealty and obedience. If he killed her in cold blood, it might be murder; but if she killed him, she was guilty of treason. The punishment for that was the same as if she had killed the king. She was burned alive at the stake, a horror that persisted at least until 1763 when à woman named Ann Beddington was executed in this manner at Ipswitch. The crime of petty treason was not actually abolished in England by statute until 1828. Barbara Hanawalt reports in her study that not a single woman who killed her husband claimed she acted in self-defense and suggests that such a plea would have been legally impossible for a woman charged with treason.

The medieval Englishwoman seldom found herself in a situation where she had to defend herself against a stranger. The very idea that she might be justified in defending herself against her husband was unthinkable. The law of self-defense was very early set in its course of ignoring the one situation in which a woman's life was most apt to be put at risk: a lethal assault by her own husband.

By the seventeenth century, when the American colonies were founded, self-defense law was firmly established in the common law of England and had by that time developed into a fairly complex legal doctrine. It was still entirely case law, and the cases on which it was based stretched back over the previous six centuries. Long after the Middle Ages were over, the law continued to reflect the medieval society in which it had developed.

The law of the time had come to distinguish between two different types of situations in which the question of self-defense might arise. The first was the sudden murderous assault, in which a perfectly innocent person is set upon by someone bent upon violent crime, whether murder, mayhem, robbery, rape, or assault. Since most of this development of the law took place before firearms were in widespread use, or even existed, it must be remembered that robbing and murdering someone must frequently have amounted to the same thing. The victim would have had to be physically overpowered—likely as not bashed over the head or beaten into unconsciousness—with death no doubt frequently the outcome. In these circumstances, the victim's right to self-defense was unquestioned. Such a victim could stand his ground and kill the assailant on the spot. He was also justified in pursuing his attacker and killing him, if that was the only way he could put himself out of harm's way. Likewise, a woman's right to kill a stranger who tried to rape her was clear, as was the right of her husband or father to protect her from a rapist by killing him.

The second self-defense situation that came to be clearly recognized by seventeenth-century common law was called the "chance medley," or ordinary fist fight or brawl. The rules of self-defense in this situation were much more complicated. In a society where survival depended on physical strength, civil police were nonexistent, and everyone went about armed with some type of weapon, a simple argument (entered into with no intention of doing more than throwing a few punches) could easily escalate into a deadly combat. Sometimes, where the two parties to such a melee were both willing participants, one suddenly found that the other had pulled a dagger or other weapon and meant to use it. Sometimes, both antagonists drew their swords or knives, and one began to get the best of the other. In either case, the fighter who suddenly found himself in deadly danger from the other was not privileged to kill his adversary in self-defense unless he first retreated "to the wall." Originally, this meant that he literally had to back away from the fight until his back was against the castle wall or city wall or some other impassible barrier and he could retreat no farther. At that point he was permitted to stand and fight back. Later the term came to be used more symbolically, and required retreat to a position of safety if one were available, and permitted killing an opponent in such a situation only if no safe avenue of retreat presented itself.

The only exception to the retreat requirement in the chance medley or mutual combat situation was when the person subject to it was in his own "castle" at the time. The safest place a person could expect to find in those dangerous days was his own home, and he could not be required to abandon it to an adversary to seek theoretical safety elsewhere. This became known as the "castle doctrine" and it is still a part of the law of self-defense today.

It was this medieval world of castles and swordplay, highwaymen and rough and ready peasants with daggers in their belts that was reflected in the common law of self-defense that the English colonists brought with them to America. It was a way of looking at self-defense that easily took root in the new world. Although the new society growing here could not have been less like feudal England in its social and economic arrangements, many of the conditions that contributed to the English common law of self-defense prevailed here as well, particularly on the frontier as it edged westward.

America was a wild and dangerous place. The native tribes were often distinctly unfriendly to the new intruders, and with reason. Law enforcement outside the towns was nonexistent. Survival depended upon brute strength and a hunter's skill with a rifle. From the earliest colonial days, it was commonplace for men to go about armed; and once again they found themselves in the same two situations that seemed legitimately, to them, to raise a claim of self-defense: sudden murderous attacks by strangers and fist fights, mutually entered into, that escalated into deadly combats.

The women who came to the colonies, and their daughters who moved westward as settlers, had a courage and toughness that is truly awe-inspiring to their modern descendants. Yet, for all they endured and accomplished, they were still "ladies." They had no legal rights or identities separate from their fathers and husbands. They still lived very much "under the rod." It was not until the 1860s that American courts began to put some limits on a husband's hitherto unbounded right to beat his wife for her own good. As the property of men, women were expected to rely on men's protection, not to protect themselves. The idea that a woman might justifiably defend herself from her own husband was still unthinkable.

The original colonies adopted simple codes of laws for themselves that met their own needs. As the colonies burgeoned into busy commercial centers in the eighteenth century and life became more settled and complex, there was an obvious need for a more elaborate system of law. Although there were enthusiastic advocates of other solutions, the colonists turned back to the common law of England and adopted it as their own.

Fortuitously or not, this movement coincided with a rich period of legal scholarship in England. Not only were cases meticulously collected and judges' opinions published, but commentators—usually judges—began systematically searching those opinions for common threads and distilling from them the legal principles that underlay the common law. By far the most influential of these was Sir William Blackstone, whose great four-volume *Commentaries on the Laws of England* was published between 1765 and 1769. Blackstone's *Commentaries* provided the first really readable and accessible treatise on virtually the whole of common law. Instead of laboriously searching through reported cases or trusting to the hunches of judges, litigants and lawyers, and judges too, could simply look up the law in Blackstone and quote it like holy writ. Although they were published in England and for an English audience, the *Commentaries* provided exactly the shortcut route back to English law that the newly formed states needed in the second half of the eighteenth century, and the work sold here in phenomenal numbers. In many courts, especially on the frontier, it was the only law book anyone—lawyers and judges alike—ever laid eyes on.

By Blackstone's day, the difference between the law's treatment of the two kinds of self-defense situation was clearly recognized and had become more marked. Although a person's right to stand and fight back against a sudden deadly attack by a stranger was unchanged, an extremely elaborate set of rules had evolved to govern the applicability of self-defense law to the seemingly endless variety of contingencies that can arise when two men get into a fist fight.

When two people voluntarily enter into a fight, according to Blackstone, and one kills the other in the heat of combat, it is manslaughter if not murder. But in some circumstances, one man's killing of another in the course of a fight might be excusable. If one man tried to start a fight and the other refused to fight back and the original aggressor then escalated his attack into life-threatening violence, his victim (being totally innocent) was permitted to defend himself, then and there, by killing his attacker. Similarly, if the original nonaggressor in a fight did fight back but subsequently clearly signalled his unwillingness to continue the combat, and his adversary refused to stop but continued the attack, the nonaggressor could kill his adversary if that was the only way to save his own skin. There was disagreement among Blackstone's sources about whether or not the original aggressor in a fight could also plead self-defense if he made it clear that he wanted to stop fighting but was still being set upon by his original victim who had taken up the challenge. It was clear, however, that where both parties had voluntarily entered into a mutual combat (as in a duel), neither one could subsequently plead self-defense if he tried but failed to end the fight and was thereupon obliged to kill his adversary to save himself. No matter what the circumstances, the victim of the original assault in a mutual combat situation was required to retreat as far as he could, until he was stopped either by reaching some impassible barrier or until the fierceness of the attack prevented further movement. Only then was a man who was not the original aggressor in a fist fight or brawl privileged to stand his ground and kill his attacker.

It should begin to be clear why, when the courts two hundred years later began to try to apply self-defense law to situations in which battered women killed their husbands, it was so hard to make the law fit. In some ways, a battered wife's situation is rather more like that of the assaulted stranger, in that a husband's beatings are more apt to be unilateral assaults than fist fights mutually entered into by equals. On the other hand, since the parties are not strangers and the beatings usually arise out of a context of argument or anger, they are rather more like fist fights than assaults by strangers. In fact, of course, they are neither, but the law was far too settled in its masculine assumptions to acknowledge that.

The law of self-defense in the mutual combat situation had, by Blackstone's time, clearly taken on the character of a code of acceptable manly behavior for a person who was facing a dangerous adversary in a fight. It was all very masculine, two-fisted stuff; and it suited the needs of the Eastern colonies-turned-states, or at least their male population, very nicely. It was not quite two-fisted enough, however, for the Western frontier, where the notion that a man should be required to run away from a fight did not sit well at all.

In classic common law fashion, the law developed in the Western territories in response to the peculiar needs that were imposed by harsh geographical and political realities. Most parts of the West were being explored and settled, however sparsely, long before the organization of governments that could make and enforce laws.

Although some of the people went west specifically to escape the reach of the law, most went to settle; and they took their eastern, and basically English, sense of law and order with them. Everywhere that people stopped and settled, institutions arose to maintain order and to protect people's rights as they saw them. In the midwest there were claim clubs, on the western ranges, cattlemen's associations, and in the far-western mining camps, miner's courts. Citizens organized into "regulators" or vigilantes as the need arose; and later, as towns grew, they often hired the toughest gunslingers they could find as sheriffs and marshals. Where courts existed, they were presided over by judges who, lacking laws, lawbooks, and sometimes any legal training at all, improvised according to their own highly subjective sense of right and wrong just as the English common law judges had done before them.

All of this amounted to very rough justice indeed; but it was all the justice there was, and the concept of self-defense played a crucial role in it. The introduction of the Colt revolver (the "great equalizer") in the 1840s meant that, for the first time in history, killing other people became an equal-opportunity undertaking. It required neither size nor strength nor even any considerable marksmanship to hit somebody in six tries. Where law enforcement was nonexistent—and danger from others, similarly armed, was all too real—the availability of such an easy and accurate weapon made the temptation to shoot first and ask questions (or offer explanations) later almost irresistible. But the prohibition against cold-blooded murder was equally strong. The key to reconciling these conflicting pressures was the concept of self-defense, drawn in part from what English common law sources, such as Blackstone, were available, but primarily from frontier notions of the way a man was supposed to behave in dangerous circumstances.

In the first place, it was neither manly nor justifiable to shoot another man in the back or from ambush. That was cowardice, morally, and therefore murder, legally, no matter how much of a threat the dead man might have been to his killer or to the community at large. "Real" men, brave men, faced each other, eyeball to eyeball, and had it out in a fair fight.

This notion is reflected very clearly, for example, in the famous story of the killing of Jesse James. In the fifteen years following 1867, Jesse James and his gang had terrorized Missouri and its neighboring states, robbing banks and trains with no regard for the lives of company employees or innocent citizens who got in their way. In April 1882, probably in response to an offer of a reward of $10,000, dead or alive, Robert Ford, a member of the gang, shot James in the back and killed him while James was standing on a chair dusting off a picture on the wall. The populace's sense of fair play was so outraged that instead of being proclaimed a hero, Ford was condemned as a man who, in the words of a contemporary, had "put a blacker stain on the fair name of Missouri than years of outlawry had ever done." Ford fled the state and spent his remaining years being hounded from place to place. Jesse James, in death, became a sort of folk hero; Robert Ford is remembered only as "that dirty little coward" who put Jesse James in his grave.

Similarly, it was neither manly nor justifiable to shoot an unarmed man. If a man was attacked by fists, he was expected to defend himself with his fists. He could only draw his own gun if his adversary was wearing, and presumably about to draw, his own. Conversely, at least in the wilder days of the mining camps and cattle towns, virtually any killing could, and would, be justified as self-defense if the dead man was wearing a gun.

Another aspect of manly behavior in dangerous circumstances that the self-defense law of the frontier reflected was the deeply held belief that a man should never, ever, be expected to turn tail and run away from a fight. The requirement of retreat to the wall, imported with the English common law, never took hold in the west. Even today, the eastern states generally require retreat where possible before one is entitled to resort to deadly force in self-defense and the western states do not.

The stories of the notorious gunslingers and lawmen of the old west present many examples of the free-wheeling way self-defense law worked in those days. Before he became a U.S. Marshall, Wild Bill Hickock was twice tried for murder and twice acquitted on grounds of self-defense. One incident involved a gunfight of the classic sort we all remember from western movies, where the two men faced each other in the street, and Hickock managed to draw his gun and fire a split second faster than his opponent. In the other, however, he shot down a man who had come to his home, with his young son, to collect some money Hickock owed him. Hickock, hiding behind a window curtain, shot him down from inside the house as the man stood, without having drawn his gun, on the front porch. Even so, a jury found this to be self-defense and acquitted him. Later in his life, Hickock boasted that he had killed nearly a hundred men, every one of them in self-defense or in the performance of his duty as a lawman.

Bat Masterson, the famous sheriff of Dodge City, described an incident in which a friend of his, a notorious gunslinger named Levi Richardson who prided himself on his new-learned ability to fan shots from a Colt .45, picked a fight with a gambler named Cockeyed Frank Loving. Both men went for their guns and Richardson quickly fanned off five shots across the poker table. When the smoke cleared, Richardson learned that all of his shots had gone wild and he stood there with his empty gun in his hand while Loving coolly took aim and shot him dead. Even though Cockeyed Frank clearly fired after any danger to himself was over, the killing was ruled self-defense at the inquest that followed. Ironically, Loving himself was killed in a gunfight three years later, and the man who killed him also pled self-defense and was acquitted.

In another incident witnessed by Masterson, a long-simmering dispute between two peace officers in Dodge City erupted into violence when an undersheriff named McGraw provoked a gunfight with a city policeman named Goodell. Goodell managed to get his gun out and fire first, and his shot hit McGraw in the arm, sending his gun flying. Goodell then shot the unarmed McGraw again and, as he fell, shot him twice more. Although by then a deputy sheriff had grabbed him from behind, Goodell picked up McGraw's fallen gun and shot McGraw twice more before he was finally subdued. Two days later, Goodell was released by an inquest jury which held that the shooting was self-defense.

One of the most bizarre self-defense acquittals on the old frontier involved the killing of New Mexico lawman Pat Garrett, best known as the man who killed Billy the Kid. Garrett had had a long-running feud with a man named Wayne Brazel, who had leased some of Garrett's land. On the first of March 1908, as Garrett and another man were riding in a buggy down a deserted country road they met up with Brazel riding a horse. Garrett got down from the buggy to urinate, cradling his shotgun, which was loaded with nonlethal birdshot, under his right arm. He turned his back on Brazel, removed his left-hand driving glove, unbuttoned his fly and had begun to urinate when he was shot in the back of the head. Brazel immediately turned himself in and confessed to the shooting. At his trial he pled self-defense, citing the threat of the shotgun in

Garrett's gloved right hand. The jury was only out for fifteen minutes. Brazel was acquitted.

The law of self-defense was stretched about as far as it possibly could be on the American frontier but only, it appears, when the actors were male. Stories about women killing men in those days are extremely rare, although it must certainly have happened. One story that has come down to us indicates that a woman's prospects for justice if she killed a man were no better on the frontier than they are in the courtrooms of today.

In the California gold mining camp of Downieville, in 1851, there had been a particularly raucous Fourth of July celebration. The whole town was very drunk. Late that night a miner named Joe Cannon and a group of rowdy friends kicked in the door of the shack in which a Mexican woman named Juanita, one of only a handful of women in the camp, lived with a man who dealt cards in a local saloon. Cannon staggered drunkenly through the door but was pulled back by his friends and went on his way. The next morning, however, he went back to Juanita's house, quite possibly still drunk, and tried once again to force his way in. There was an angry confrontation in the doorway. In the course of it, Juanita stabbed Cannon to death with a Bowie knife.

An angry mob of miners began to gather. Juanita and the card dealer were seized and taken to the town square where a "court" was convened. Juanita's companion was hastily acquitted, but the mob was so set on lynching Juanita that rope barricades had to be strung up to keep them back. Only one man had the courage to speak out in her defense, and he was beaten up and run out of town. A doctor who argued against hanging her because she was three months pregnant was also beaten up by what one eye-witness called "the hungriest, craziest, wildest mob that ever I saw any-where." Amid cries of "hang her" and "give her a fair trial and then hang her," Juanita was found guilty of murder and sentenced to die immediately. A gallows was constructed on the town bridge and later the same day she was taken there. With enormous dignity, she climbed a ladder to a platform suspended by ropes from the superstructure of the bridge, lifted her heavy black braids and placed the noose around her own neck. Far from repentant, she told the crowd that she would do the same thing again in the same circum-stances. Then she cried, "Adios, amigos," the ropes holding up the platform were chopped through and she fell to her death.

The lynching of Juanita shocked many people when news of it spread. Although there seems to have been agreement, after the fact, that she should not have been executed without a proper trial, opinion was divided over whether her killing of Cannon was self-defense or murder. There was no such divided opinion in Downieville that day, however; nor was the lynching just the work of a mob of whiskey-crazed miners. Among the respectable folk who apparently stood by and did nothing were John B. Weller, a rising young politician who later became a United States Senator and the Governor of California, and Stephen J. Field who subsequently served as a Justice of the United States Supreme Court. It is clear that, in 1851, the people of Downieville were not about to apply the wide-open rules of self-defense that prevailed on the frontier to a woman, especially a Mexican woman who killed a white man and, worse yet, a woman who acted to protect herself when she had a man whom she could, perhaps, have prevailed upon to protect her in an appropriately manly way.

By the turn of the century, America's frontier era was essentially over and it was time for even the wildest western states to settle down to the business of becoming civilized. The kind of frontier justice that permitted virtually any killing of one man by another to be justified in the name of self-defense clearly would no longer do. A reaction set in that saw the law gradually become more and more narrow and rigid in its application. It was a reaction that was no doubt triggered by a rejection of the romanticism and sentimentality with which the eastern press and the dime novel industry had come to treat the west and the westerner, as well as a growing revulsion at the extremes to which self-defense law had been stretched by the gunfighters of the frontier. The figure of the lone hero—be he cowboy, sheriff or outlaw—had reached truly mythic proportions in the popular mind in the last decades of the nineteenth century. He was a "man's man," a two-fisted fighter, never a coward or a bully, never entangled by the cloying Victorian society that his idolizers were tied to, beholden to no one but himself. As Teddy Roosevelt described him in his paean to the rangerider, "A cowboy will not submit tamely to an insult, and is ever ready to avenge his own wrongs, nor has he an overwrought fear of shedding blood. He possesses, in fact, few of the emasculated, milk-and-water moralities admired by the pseudo-philanthropists; but he does possess, to a very high degree, the stern, manly qualities that are invaluable to the nation."

The mythic westerner never existed, nor did the "code of the west" that supposedly governed his behavior, but it was important that so many people at the time, and since, believed that he did. The frontier hero represented an ideal of manliness that left an indelible mark on the law of self-defense, not just in the western states where he supposedly lived, but in the east, where the legends really grew, as well. By the end of the nineteenth century the law of self-defense was, more than ever, a law for men.

In an influential article published in the Harvard Law Review in 1903, Professor Joseph H. Beale, a prominent criminal law scholar, analyzed the law of retreat in self-defense situations, as it existed at that time, and made an impassioned plea for the adoption of a retreat requirement in all jurisdictions—not just in the mutual combat situation but in that of a sudden assault by a murderous stranger as well. Beale called the right to stand one's ground and fight back when assaulted a "brutal doctrine" which was "found in the ethics of the duelist, the German officer and the buccaneer." He recognized that the widespread use of handguns made the possibility of retreat problematical: "It is of course true that to retreat from an assailant with a revolver in his hand is dangerous, and one whose revolver is in his pocket is not to be despised; the hip-pocket ethics of the Southwest are doubtless based upon a deep-felt need." Nevertheless, argued Beale, the "advance of civilization and culture" enabled, and required, men to control their instincts toward vengeance and lynch law and could ultimately enable them to give up the notion that retreat amounted to dishonor as well. "A really honorable man, a man of truly refined and elevated feeling," said Professor Beale, "would perhaps always regret the apparent cowardice of a retreat, but he would regret ten times more, after the excitement of the contest was past, the thought that he had the blood of a fellow being on his hands." It is interesting to note that, although Beale was arguing for a change in the law, he saw clearly that, even in the early twentieth century, the function of self-defense law was to define "manly" behavior in threatening circumstances. The definition of what was manly had begun to change, at least at Harvard, but the resolute masculinity of the whole business clearly had not.

As the frontier era gradually came to a close and the western territories gained statehood, one of the first things that most new state legislatures did was adopt a criminal code. These were, of course, not made up out of whole cloth but were based to some extent on territorial law and frequently were borrowed from the legally more developed eastern states. Those eastern law codes, in turn, were based upon English common law and, in particular, on Blackstone. Although a few of these state criminal codes contained specific provisions about self-defense, in most states self-defense was not statutory but was recognized as a common-law defense that could be raised in appropriate circumstances to counter a murder or assault charge. The law was to be found in the reported opinions of the appellate courts rather than in the statute books. Every time a case was appealed on the issue of self-defense, the appeals court judges— drawing on previously published opinions, upon published authorities such as Blackstone, and upon their own inner sense of justice which grew out of their own experience—would elaborate a point here or clarify an issue there. Read together, all of the published opinions of a particular state would—and will still today—embody that state's law of self-defense.

By the early years of this century, virtually all of the continental United States had achieved statehood, and the state courts had all begun this process of developing case law. In some, of course, it had already been going on for over a century. Although each state's law was bound to be different in some particulars from that of other states, self-defense law everywhere turned out to be basically the medieval English common law recorded by Blackstone with a frontier, "code of the west" overlay, but with the law ever more strictly and narrowly interpreted as the frontier era was left behind. Men were no longer permitted to behave in the freewheeling homicidal way the gunslingers got away with. The courts began to insist that a man could use no more force than was absolutely necessary to counter the threat he faced. Even if his adversary was armed, he could not use his weapon in response to a mere verbal threat or before his adversary had begun an actual assault on him. He had to disarm or disable his opponent if he could; and once he had done so, he had to halt his defense and could not go on firing shots until the other was dead. As we have seen, he was increasingly obliged to back away from a fight or escape from a dangerous confrontation if he could rather than stand his ground and take a life.

What was strikingly absent from this development of the American law was the experience of women. During the period from the founding of the American colonies to the beginning of this century, hundreds of self-defense cases were decided by the appellate courts. Among them I have been able to find only three that involved female defendants, all from the 1890s. None of these were cases in which a woman killed her husband or partner. The earliest American appellate opinion I have been able to find involving a woman killing a violent mate and claiming self-defense was decided in 1902.

As a consequence, as the American law developed, the only two situations in which a self-defense plea was felt to be appropriate (by male judges and male legislators) were still the ancient ones in which men most frequently found themselves: the sudden attack by a stranger and the fight between equals that gets out of hand. The law of self-defense may have been becoming increasingly stricter and more "civilized," but it was not in any way becoming more responsive to the circumstances faced by women who needed to defend themselves against violent husbands or lovers. Indeed, as we shall see, the growing rigidity and ossification of the law merely created more legal obstacles for a woman claiming self-defense to surmount.

The law of self-defense has changed remarkably little since the turn of the century, or indeed since the middle ages, although the society which it serves has changed dramatically. It is still, in the 1980s, entangled in such fourteenth-century concepts as the "castle doctrine" and "retreat to the wall." This has no doubt been because the law has appeared to observers, mostly male, to work quite well in most circumstances. Those for whom it has not worked have not had a voice, from behind the walls of prisons or asylums, with which to complain. It has only been in the last few years that women have finally begun to protest the way the law works for them in cases where they must defend themselves against violent men and look for ways to make the law respond to changed social values and needs.

3
The Law in Action

I

The law of self-defense, of course, is meant to apply equally to men and women. Whatever one's sex, one has the right to take another's life if one reasonably believes that it is necessary to do so to avoid imminent death or serious bodily injury at the hands of an assailant. On the surface, the law does not discriminate. In its application, however, the law treats men and women very differently. The historical function of self-defense law (to spell out manly behavior in the kinds of dangerous circumstances in which men traditionally have found themselves), together with the virtual ossification of the law since its narrowing in reaction to the closing of the frontier era, have left it woefully unresponsive to the needs of women defendants. Too often it simply cannot be made to apply to a woman's actions although there is no question that she sincerely believed she was defending herself against death or serious injury. The result is that women are effectively deprived of the same right to self-defense that men have always had under the law.

Three aspects of the modern law of self-defense in particular cause problems for women defendants: the requirement that the threatened harm be sufficiently serious, the requirement that the threatened harm be imminent and, in many states, the obligation to retreat or seek to escape from an attack before one can defend oneself against it.

The law of self-defense has never been limited to a kill-or-be-killed situation. A victim of an assault need not be in danger of certain death before being justified in killing an attacker. In every state, the law permits a person to use a deadly weapon in self-defense in the face of an assault that is likely to cause serious bodily

50

harm or grievous bodily injury. The question is, just what sort of harm is sufficiently serious to justify killing in self-defense?

The assumption underlying the law as it developed was always that the antagonists in these situations were men of roughly equal size, strength, and fighting ability. Furthermore, as we have seen, the code of manly behavior that justifiable homicide law has historically embodied held that it was never acceptable to kill an unarmed adversary. What this added up to was that a punch in the nose or a right to the jaw were properly met by the victim's putting up his own dukes and fighting back "like a man." He was never justified in pulling out a weapon and blowing his opponent away.

This notion of a fair fight among equals became embedded in the law in case after case involving men where the courts have held that a "simple assault" or an "ordinary battery" or, in other words, an assault by an unarmed person, could not justify a killing in self-defense. This is sometimes stated as an equal force rule: a person can use no more force in self-defense than is being used by the attacker he is defending himself against. One can find, sprinkled among these cases, occasional ones that recognized an exception where there was some great disparity between the antagonists in size, age, or strength. However, the general rule has always been that the attacker must be armed with a deadly weapon or, at the very least, some kind of object that can be wielded like a weapon. An assault with the hands, fists, or feet does not ordinarily constitute a serious enough threat of bodily harm to justify a defensive killing.

Whether or not such a rule was likely to produce a just outcome in cases involving male adversaries, there can be no question that it has operated to the detriment of women defendants in self-defense cases, particularly those involving victims of domestic violence. Virtually every study of battered women has revealed that in the overwhelming majority of cases, wife-beaters use their hands, fists, and feet in their assaults. The 120 women in a study by Doctor Lenore Walker were slapped in the face, punched with fists on their faces, heads, and bodies and stomped and kicked after they were knocked to the floor. Their arms were twisted and broken, they were thrown across rooms and down stairs, and choked until they passed out. They were hurled against objects and had objects hurled against them. When they raised their arms to defend themselves, their arms and ribs were broken. Although some of the assaults involved knives and guns and dangerous objects, the overwhelming majority of the women's injuries were inflicted by the man's hands, fists, and feet.

Maria Roy's survey of 150 battered women found that every one of them had suffered from physical abuse (blackened eyes, broken ribs, choking, and biting) that did not involve the use of an object or weapon. Gayford's study of 100 British women revealed that every one of them had been hit with a clenched fist; and all had, at the minimum, suffered bruising. Other researchers, such as Straus, Dobash and Dobash, and Stacey and Shupe, have also found that battering episodes typically involve slaps and punches, kicking, stomping, and choking; and that a wife-beater's primary weapons are his hands, fists, and feet.

Nor is there any doubt that a man can inflict serious harm, or even death, on a woman with these weapons. In addition to black eyes, broken bones, and knocked-out teeth, Walker's subjects reported broken necks and backs, concussions, severe internal injuries, and bleeding. Walker and others have frequently noted the propensity of battering husbands to punch and kick their pregnant wives in the stomach, with resulting miscarriages and injuries to reproductive organs. Fully 42 percent of the women in Stacey and Shupe's study reported being beaten while pregnant. Rape and sexual sadism are a common element of wife abuse. Walker relates that almost every one of her subjects reported being sexually abused by her mate, often in painful and horrible ways. Many women report being beaten or strangled to the point of unconsciousness. It is not at all uncommon for battered women to be so badly injured that they require not only a doctor's care but hospitalization. Nor is it all that uncommon for women to be killed by their batterers. Sociologist Marvin Wolfgang's monumental study of homicides in Philadelphia revealed that of the total number of female homicide victims, 41 per cent were killed by their husbands and 21 per cent were killed by boyfriends. One-quarter of the female victims died by means of the killer's hands, fists, and feet. Indeed, Wolfgang concluded that, statistically, a woman homicide victim was most apt to meet her fate by being beaten to death by a man in the bedroom.

It is important to bear in mind, too, when considering the seriousness of the harm inflicted by unarmed husbands and lovers, that battering episodes typically encompass a number of different kinds of violence and can sometimes go on for hours. It is not unusual to read a report of a woman being pushed, slapped, punched in the face, thrown downstairs or against the walls or furniture and then—when she is on the floor—kicked and stomped until the man finally quits out of sheer exhaustion or she loses consciousness, and sometimes not even then. Moreover, such episodes are almost never isolated incidents but are repeated over and over again, with cumulative physical and emotional damage being inflicted, and often a new beating occurring before the injuries from the last one have even healed.

Yet despite all of this indisputable suffering, the case law in many states continues to assume that the harm inflicted by an unarmed assailant's hands or fists is not sufficiently "grievous" to give rise to a right of self-defense. And the beaten women who know better and who, in desperation, resort to weapons to defend themselves against beatings that they cannot defend themselves against any other way, are convicted of criminal homicide and sent off to prison.

Theresa Jones, for example, had been beaten frequently by her husband, LeRoy, during their marriage. On the night of his death, during an argument, he said he was going to beat her up again after the children were in bed. He picked up a table knife, threatening to throw it at her, and then took several steps toward her with the knife upraised in his hand, telling her he was going to kill her. Believing that he meant what he said, she reached into the buffet, grabbed a .22 caliber pistol she had hidden there, fired two warning shots into the ceiling, and told him not to come any closer. When he kept coming, she aimed the gun at him and shot him. At her trial, she told the jury, "I was afraid he was going to jump on me or kill me or beat me or something, and I just couldn't take no more beating." Charged with murder, Theresa was convicted of manslaughter. In affirming the conviction the California Court of Appeal said, "When the character of the crime and the manner of its perpetration do not reasonably create a fear of great bodily harm, as they could not if defendant apprehended only a misdemeanor assault, there is no cause for the exaction of a human life. A misdemeanor assault must be suffered without the privilege of retaliation with deadly force." In other words, in that court's view, a woman's fear that she is about to be injured or killed by an unarmed man is *never* reasonable, no matter how genuine her fear might be, because an unarmed assault is normally treated by the law as a misdemeanor. Rather than resort to a weapon to defend herself, if her own hands and fists are not sufficient, her only legal alternative is to allow herself to be jumped on, beaten up, and possibly killed.

Ordinarily, it is up to the jury to decide whether the harm threatened in a given case is sufficiently serious or, as it is more often put, if the amount of force that the defendant used was greater than was necessary to counter the threat she faced. Sometimes, however, in his or her instructions to the jury, a trial judge will tell the jurors that, in effect, they *must* find a killing not to have been justifiable where it was in defense against an unarmed attack. For example, at the trial of Lillian Easterling (a Chickasaw Indian woman who stabbed her frequently abusive common-law husband while he was choking her and threatening to kill her, after he had grabbed her by the hair and beaten her on the head and face and back with his fists), the judge instructed the jury that, under the law, "no person has the right to use a dangerous weapon merely to repel a simple assault without weapons." That jury convicted Lillian Easterling of first-degree manslaughter and sentenced her to six years in prison.

Similarly, when Janice Painter was put on trial for killing, not a violent spouse but a violent adult stepson, who objected to her marriage to his widowed father and subjected her to a long campaign of threats and violence, the judge instructed the jury that "great bodily harm means an injury of a more serious nature than an ordinary striking with the hands or fists." The situation at the Painter house had become so desperate that Mr. Painter, blinded and severely disabled by a stroke, insisted that his wife start carrying a gun with her all the time because he feared that he could no longer protect her from his son. The young man, Ted, had been forbidden to come to the house. However, on the day he was killed, he insisted on coming to visit his ill father. A violent family argument arose and Janice, disabled, herself, by a previous injury and on crutches, had tried to get to the phone to call the police. Ted prevented her from reaching the phone by knocking her over backwards, and she fell, striking her back against a table as she went down. Her legs were temporarily paralyzed, and she was unable to get back up. Ted came rushing at her with his hands outstretched towards her throat. She pulled out the gun that she kept in the front pouch of her sweat shirt and fired one shot. When he kept coming, she fired three more. An ambulance was summoned and both Janice and Ted were taken to the hospital, where Ted died of his wounds.

Janice Painter was convicted—not just of manslaughter but, incredibly, of first-degree, premeditated murder—and sentenced to life in prison. Presumably, under the law as the judge interpreted it, she would have been justified in defending herself by punching Ted in the nose or strangling him back with her bare hands. The judge's instruction was tantamount to telling the jury that Janice Painter's only legal course of action was to lie there paralyzed and helpless on the floor and to let Ted do anything he wanted to her, including kill her, as long as he did it without a weapon.

Even when the trial judge doesn't specifically instruct the jury that an unarmed assault will not justify a killing in self-defense, the jury will often act on that assumption anyway. It can do this by convicting the defendant under a rule in many states that says that a person who uses excessive force in an otherwise entirely justified act of self-defense is guilty of manslaughter or by finding that the woman's fear that she was about to be injured or killed was unreasonable. Juries seem to see excessive force in many situations where a woman uses a weapon against an unarmed man, even when it is hard to imagine what alternative she realistically had. Una Bush's case is one example among many. Her husband, Gary, was a wife-beater. His first wife divorced him after enduring three years of violence at his hands; even after the divorce she had to get a restraining order to try to keep him away from her. His second wife Una, unaware of his marital history, learned of his propensity for violence a bare three weeks after their wedding when he slapped her during an argument about whether or not they were going to go to the movies. A week or so later, Una accidentally burned the chicken she was fixing for his dinner. Gary accused her of doing it on purpose to spite him. When she protested, he grabbed her arm, threw her on the couch, and stood over her, trapping her there. Each time she tried to get up he smashed her in the face with his fists and slapped and pummeled her on the face and body, harder and harder with each of her efforts to escape his blows. A few weeks later, when she was two months pregnant, Gary attacked her in a fit of jealousy over an imagined liaison with another man. He slapped her and threw her on the floor, pinning her shoulders down and kneeling on her stomach. Ignoring her repeated pleas not to injure the unborn child, he beat her and beat her, all the while threatening to kill her, until she finally pretended to lose consciousness, and he stopped.

When Una was five months pregnant he beat her severely again, this time because she was ill with the flu and asked him to get his own dinner. He punched her in the abdomen with his fist, so hard that she began to vomit blood and had to be taken by ambulance to a hospital. A month before she finally fought back, Gary attacked her again during an argument about going out. The baby was two months old, and Una hadn't been out of the house in the evening for several weeks. Gary had promised to take her out and then changed his mind at the last minute. When Una tried to leave by herself, he hit her, threw her against the coffee table and, when she was on the floor, kicked and pounded her while promising to kill her and "send her to her grave."

A month later, a little over a year after they were married, Gary came home drunk at three o'clock in the morning and locked the door behind him with a key. He crawled into bed with Una and began to kick her and yell at her, so she got up and went to lie down in the baby's room. When she heard Gary in the bathroom and knew that he was still awake, she went back and tried to talk to him about their problems; but he refused. She took the keys from the dresser so that she could get out of the house if she had to and went back to bed in the baby's room. Gary burst in and grabbed the keys and told her that she was not going anywhere. Una got up and started walking into the living room; but as she passed the bedroom, she looked in and saw the keys lying on the floor. As she reached down to pick them up, Gary grabbed her and flung her onto the bed. She got up and tried to get to the window; but Gary grabbed her again, twisting her arm and taking back the keys. She ran into the kitchen and picked up the phone to call the police; but Gary followed her and took the phone away from her, telling her that she wasn't going to call anyone. He grabbed her around the throat and began choking her until she could no longer breathe; and then, letting go of her neck, he kept hold of her arm and beat her on the head and face while she fought to break free. As they struggled, she told him that if he didn't stop, she was going to hurt *him* someday. His response was to continue beating her, saying, "You're going to hurt me, huh? Bitch, you gonna hurt me? I'm going to send you to your grave." In desperation, Una grabbed a kitchen knife that was lying on the counter and began jabbing at Gary with it, trying to stop his attack; but he kept on threatening to kill her and hitting her as hard as ever until he suddenly sank to his knees, crying out that he was hurt. Una ran to the phone and called the police and then ran next door, sobbing and screaming for help.

Una Bush was charged with first-degree murder. At her trial, the prosecutor argued vigorously that Gary Bush did not deserve to die just "for slapping a woman." Apparently, the jury agreed with him. They found her guilty of involuntary manslaughter (the performance of an otherwise legal act in an illegal or negligent manner). The verdict suggests the jury believed that, in resorting to a weapon to defend herself in that situation, she was criminally negligent in assessing the seriousness of the danger she faced or the amount of force she needed to use to counter it. In other words, what Gary Bush was inflicting on Una, as he choked her and smashed his fist into her face and promised to kill her, was not the kind of serious bodily injury that would justify using a deadly weapon.

Similar problems regarding the seriousness of the threatened harm arise in cases where the assault on the woman was carried out not just with fists or feet but with some object that is not ordinarily regarded as a deadly weapon. Researchers have reported an amazing array of objects that men have resorted to in their assaults against their mates. William Stacey and Anson Shupe, in their study of 542 women admitted to shelters for battered women in the Dallas–Fort Worth area report:

> There were, of course, many women who had been stabbed, cut, shot and pistol-whipped. But in family violence the definition of a weapon embraces a virtual inventory of household objects that otherwise might seem perfectly harmless. During our research we began keeping an unofficial tally of the weapons that women reported their men had used. This list, which obviously does not exhaust all the possible weapons in a household "arsenal" that could be used to hurt included pistols, shotguns, knives, machetes, golf clubs, baseball bats, electric drills, high-heeled shoes, sticks, frying pans, electric sanders, toasters, razors, silverware, ashtrays, drinking glasses and beer mugs, bottles, burning cigarettes, hair brushes, lighter fluid and matches, candlestick holders, scissors, screwdrivers, ax handles, sledgehammers, chairs, bedrails, telephone cords, ropes, workboots, belts, door knobs, doors, boat oars, cars and trucks, fish hooks, metal chains, clothing (used to

smother and choke), hot ashes, hot water, hot food, dishes, acid, bleach, vases, rocks, bricks, pool cues, box fans, books, and, as one woman described her husband's typical weapons, ''anything handy.''

No matter how much damage common sense tells us that an enraged man can do to a woman with an ordinary object, if it is not something that is *usually* regarded as a dangerous weapon, it is very hard for a jury to perceive it as something that might cause death or serious injury. In case after case, women have been convicted for defending themselves against men who were assaulting them with these kinds of objects. Euberta Jackson, for example, stabbed a man named Tom Mims who was beating her with a chair. Mims was very drunk and much stronger than she. He had her trapped in a tiny house trailer and told her that he would not let her leave. Standing between her and the trailer's only door, he picked up a chair and began hitting her with it. She tried to ward off the blows with her arms and, when that didn't help, she tried to grab hold of the chair but couldn't keep a grip on it. Picking up a knife that was lying on the kitchen counter, she began jabbing at him with it, trying to get him to back off but to no avail. Finally, she stabbed him in the chest, which stopped him long enough to let her get past him and out of the trailer. She ran across the street and called an ambulance, but Mims died of his wound. Euberta Jackson was charged with murder and found guilty of voluntary manslaughter. A beating with a chair in an enclosed place from which she could not escape was not considered, by her jury or by the Georgia Court of Appeals, to present a threat of serious bodily harm sufficient to justify her resorting to a weapon to defend herself. Trapped in the tiny house trailer and unable to fend off the blows with her bare hands, her only legal course of action was to submit to the beating and pray, one supposes, that he would stop before he maimed or killed her.

In Washington state, Linda Thompson was convicted of second-degree murder in the shooting of her husband when he attacked her in a parked car with his fists and a wine bottle. Wayland Thompson had begun to abuse alcohol and prescription drugs while recovering from injuries he received in an automobile accident. During the two years of their marriage, his problem with drugs and alcohol became steadily worse; and he developed a pattern of violently abusing his wife when he was high. The night he was killed, he had been drinking heavily and had taken a large injection of Nembutal. Wayland, Linda, and two friends spent the evening together. Late in the evening, Wayland insisted on driving the car although he was clearly in no condition to do so. He took them all on a terrifying ride, swerving all over the road at 90 miles-an-hour and forcing an oncoming car to pass them on the right at least once. When their friends begged him to drive more carefully or to let his wife drive, he became angry and abusive and threatened to kill them all. At several points during this episode, Linda tried to turn off the car's ignition; but every time she did, he hit her with his fists or with the wine bottle. Even so, she did not fight back but kept trying to calm him down and find a way to get the car stopped.

Finally, Thompson drove back to their house, and the two friends got out at once and left. Linda and her husband remained in the car. She testified that he continued to abuse her and began to threaten to take the car out again and kill everybody. She continued to try to calm him down and get hold of the car keys. He kept on beating her with his fists and with the bottle. Finally, she took out a pistol which she carried in her purse. When he began to beat her again, she shot him. Apparently, the jury did not consider either the fists or the bottle to constitute a serious threat. Linda was convicted of second-degree murder, and her conviction was upheld by the Washington Supreme Court.

In North Carolina in 1980, Cynthia Brooks was convicted of manslaughter for shooting her estranged husband when he attacked her with the stick end of a broom. They had been separated for a week when he came to her house and assaulted her. During the melee, he put his hands around her throat and tried to strangle her; and then, letting go of her, he pulled out his knife and threatened her with it. He started to leave but then suddenly returned to the house, picked up the broom, and came at her with the handle end. Terrified, she ran to her son's room, grabbed the gun that was kept there just inside the door, turned, and fired blindly. The jury evidently believed that her resort to the use of a firearm was reckless in the face of such a threat and found her guilty of involuntary manslaughter.

In cases where a woman kills a man who has beaten her frequently in the past, another kind of problem involving the seriousness of the threatened harm sometimes arises regardless of what the man chooses to beat her with. This is the assumption that, since he had beaten her regularly before and hadn't killed her, there is no reason to assume that the outcome would be any different this time. Apparently, once a man has established himself as a nonlethal wife-beater, some judges and juries will presume that he will always be a nonlethal wife-beater. No matter how serious the harm he was threatening to inflict upon her on the present occasion, it could not be serious enough to justify her use of a deadly weapon to defend herself against it because she knew from past experience that she would (probably) survive. This is an assumption that all of the research on domestic violence has repeatedly shown to be erroneous. Where battering is chronic, the most common pattern is for the beatings to get progressively more violent. When violent men do kill their wives, it is not apt to be out of the blue but at the end of an escalating series of assaults. Nevertheless, the presumption hangs on.

Verneater Chapman, for example, had lived for five years with a violent man named Robert Rice. During that time, he beat her as often as every other weekend. He lost his job at the place where they both worked, for bursting in to the women's locker room and beating her up there. Three times she had him placed under a peace bond to try to prevent him from injuring her. The night she killed him, she had been asleep on the couch in the apartment they shared when he came in and started hitting her on the head. He yelled at her to gather her possessions and get out because he was replacing her with another woman; but when she tried to get up from the couch, he trapped her there and began kicking her in the stomach. Robert had insisted that she sleep with a .22 revolver under her pillow for her own protection; and when he raised his foot to kick her again, she pulled out the pistol and started shooting. Verneater Chapman was convicted of voluntary manslaughter. Her case was appealed; and in its opinion upholding her conviction, the Appellate Court of Illinois said, "In this case, the defendant testified she was in fear for her life when Rice beat her on the head and kicked her in the stomach. However, the circumstances do not indicate that Rice was using deadly force upon her. She testified that Rice beat her frequently, and she had him placed under peace bond on three occasions. The evidence does not establish any reason which would require the court to believe that this assault was more serious than the others." It is hard to see how a woman in Verneater Chapman's shoes could overcome this presumption of once a nonlethal wife-beater, always a nonlethal wife-beater, short of letting herself be beaten to death—surely an unreasonable length to require a woman to go to prove herself right.

About one-third of the states have statutes that permit another basis for the use of a deadly weapon in self-defense. These statutes allow a person to defend himself or herself against someone who is committing a violent felony. These laws, unfortunately, have been of little use to battered women in self-defense cases where the issue is the seriousness of the harm threatened by the beatings. Wife-beating, when it does not involve a dangerous weapon, is not a felony in most states. No matter how savage a beating may be, it will almost universally be treated by the police and the courts as a misdemeanor assault. And even where it is a felony, this may be of no avail to a beaten wife who kills her husband.

At the time Theresa Jones' case was tried, California, a state which permits the use of deadly force to defend oneself against a violent felony, had a law that provided that, "any husband who willfully inflicts upon his wife corporal injury resulting in a traumatic condition...is guilty of a felony." The defense requested that the judge instruct the jury that Ms. Jones had the right to use deadly force to resist a felony, and that wife-beating was such a felony. The judge refused this request and, on appeal, the California Court of Appeal upheld his ruling. The appellate court (in a triumph of circular reasoning) held that although wife-beating was indeed a felony, it was not the *right sort* of felony because (despite the legislature's sticking a felony label on it) it was still just plain old wife-beating, which everybody knows is a misdemeanor, and does not constitute serious bodily injury.

"In creating the statutory felony of wife beating," said the court, "the purpose of the legislature was not to issue a license for a wife to kill her husband but to provide a means of dealing with a particular family situation...A misdemeanor assault must be suffered without the privilege of retaliating with deadly force...The fact that the assault is committed by a husband should not alter the rule. The existence of the matrimonial status should be an additional reason to forgo resort to a homicide. The legislative purpose in enacting section 273d, Penal Code, was to reduce domestic conflict, not to promote resort to violence in the household."

It is hard to understand by what logic a single act can be a felony for one purpose and a misdemeanor for another. It would seem, in this court's view, that the proper way for a woman to "reduce domestic conflict" is to allow herself to be beaten at her husband's will. It would also seem that, in this court's view, the mere fact of being married to her assailant leaves a woman with a lesser right to self-defense than any other citizen.

Although many women who kill men in self-defense are battered women who kill their husbands or boyfriends, this is not the only self-defense situation where the issue of the seriousness of the threatened harm creates problems for women. The question of whether rape, by itself, constitutes a bodily injury sufficient to justify killing a rapist in order to prevent its occurring presents another whole series of difficulties. The problem revolves around the legal issue of whether rape, alone, is harm enough or whether a woman who defends herself against a rapist must prove she believed that, in addition to "only" raping her, the man was going to seriously mutilate or kill her.

Sixteen states, as we have seen, permit a person to kill in order to prevent the commission of a violent or forcible felony, without defining in the statute which felonies it covers. Courts in these states have gone both ways on the question of whether a woman who uses a deadly weapon to stop a man from raping her can avail herself of such a statute, although rape (in every state) is classified as a felony, and it is unquestionably a forcible one.

As long ago as 1924, the Supreme Court of New Mexico ruled that rape was a felony covered by that state's statute and that a woman had a right to kill "in defense of chastity." The case involved a virtuous wife named Hilaria Martinez, who lived with her husband and children in a cabin in a remote part of the state. The man she killed, Andres Lopez, was building a cabin nearby and had twice come to her house when her husband was away and tried to molest her. On one such occasion, he had grabbed her and tried to drag her into the bedroom and only desisted when she picked up a rifle and threatened to shoot him. The day she killed him, she had gone with her children to the creek that ran between the two cabins to wash clothes, taking the rifle with her because she was afraid that Lopez would try to assault her again. As she was bending over the washing, Lopez came up behind her and grabbed her. She broke free, seized the rifle, and told him to get away; but he raised his axe in a threatening gesture. When he ignored a second warning from her and continued to brandish the axe at her, she fired.

She was indicted for murder, and the jury returned a verdict of voluntary manslaughter. On appeal, the New Mexico Supreme Court overturned her conviction, ruling that the jury should have been told that Hilaria had a right to kill Lopez to prevent an assault with intent to commit rape, a felony under New Mexico law. In addition, the court held that rape, by itself, constitutes the "great personal injury" that is required by the general self-defense statute in New Mexico and that the jury should have been told that by the judge as well.

By contrast, in Los Angeles in 1959, a woman named Elizabeth Taylor was assaulted by a man who was a tenant in her house and stabbed him with a butcher knife. It was not the first time that he had tried to molest her. Just the week before, she had only managed to escape him by running out of the house; and she had asked her brother to warn the man to stop bothering her. She testified at her trial that the night she stabbed him, he came into the kitchen and asked if she were alone; then he grabbed her and ran his hands under her dress. She jumped away, but he pulled her into the bedroom, telling her he would have her that night or kill her. She was still holding a knife that she had been using in the kitchen. They struggled over it, and she stabbed him. She was charged with murder; and at her trial, the defense argued that, under California law, she was permitted to kill to resist an attempt to commit a felony, and that rape was such a felony. The judge disagreed and left it up to the jury to decide—on whatever basis it chose or on no rational basis at all—whether it thought that the act of rape inflicts great bodily injury on the victim. This jury apparently felt that it did not. Elizabeth was convicted of manslaughter, and the California Court of Appeals upheld the trial judge's ruling and her conviction.

Fifteen states permit the use of deadly force in self-defense against an assortment of specific felonies and every one of them includes rape on its list. Presumably, in these states, a woman who kills a man in the course of an actual or attempted rape would not have to prove to the jury that she suffered, or was about to suffer, any injury beyond the rape itself. This does not mean, however, that when a woman kills a rapist in one of these states, and is charged with homicide, that an acquittal is a foregone conclusion. She still must meet the other requirements of the law of self-defense, such as that the threatened harm was imminent, that she had no opportunity to retreat from the situation, and that her perception of the danger she was in was reasonable. She must also convince the jury that she is telling the truth about the episode; and her credibility is just as subject to the jury's doubts and prejudices on that score as any rape victim's in an ordinary rape trial. In other words, if she is anything less than a perfect virgin, she is going to have a very hard time of it.

Shirley Mae Thomas, for example, a young black woman from Houston, Texas, was picked up by four young white men on their way from Georgia to the Cotton Bowl game in Dallas. She testified that they abducted her in Houston and took her forcibly by car to Dallas, where they literally held her prisoner in a motel room. During the trip in the car and later in the motel, she was repeatedly raped and sodomized by all four of them. In a desperate attempt to escape, she managed to get a .22 pistol out of her purse and began firing wildly, injuring two of the men and killing a third. One of the injured men managed to get the gun away from her, but she was able to get out of the motel room door, stark naked, and escape.

The prosecution's version of the events was that the four young men were solicited by her in a bar in Dallas and that she willingly agreed to come with them to the motel because she was a prostitute. When there, she cold-bloodedly set about to murder and, presumably, rob all four of them. In fact, she was so self-assured in her plan that she didn't even bother to put her clothes on before she fired the shots, since she confidently expected to kill them all and would have no need to escape quickly.

The judge instructed the jury that, in addition to her right to defend herself against a threat of death or serious bodily injury, under Texas law she had a right to use deadly force against the felonies of rape and kidnapping. Clearly, according to her story, she was in the process of being kidnapped when the shooting took place and, having already been raped several times, she was in obvious danger of being raped again. Unfortunately for her, however, Shirley Thomas did not measure up to the jury's idea of a credible rape victim, and they chose not to believe her story. They found her guilty of first-degree murder and two counts of attempted murder and sentenced her to a total of eighty years in prison.

The remaining one-third of the states have no statute specifically permitting the use of deadly force in defense against rape or against the commission of a felony. In these states, whether a woman is legally justified in using deadly force against a rapist will vary with the case law of her state and the whims of the judiciary. In some she may be obliged to convince the jury that rape, or at least the particular rape that she faced, constitutes a sufficiently serious bodily injury to justify her using deadly force to prevent it. In others, she will have to demonstrate to the jury that, in addition to "only" rape, she reasonably feared that she was in danger of death or serious physical injury.

Cases involving women who kill rapists in the act of the rape are understandably few. Consequently, this is still an open question in a great many states because the appellate courts have not had an opportunity to rule on it. An interesting light is thrown on one state's view of the seriousness of the injury inflicted when a woman is "only" raped, by a series of cases in California that culminated in the controversial *Caudillo* decision in 1978. These were not justifiable homicide cases but rather involved a trio of statutes that provided a much stiffer minimum sentence if a person inflicted "great bodily injury" in the course of committing burglary, robbery, or rape. Since the legislature did not define "great bodily injury" in the statute, it was left to the appellate courts to do so. In the first two cases to raise the question, California courts of appeal ruled that the injury inflicted must not be trivial or insubstantial or even moderate in nature but "significant or substantial." Both of these cases involved physical assaults, not rapes, committed in the course of a robbery. A few years later, three cases were decided that did involve rapes committed in the course of other crimes; and in all three the appellate courts held that rape alone, without the infliction of additional damage, could constitute great bodily injury for the purposes of these sentencing statutes. In other words (in California at that time), if a person raped his victim in the course of robbing her or burglarizing her home, he would have to serve a considerably longer sentence for the burglary or robbery, in addition to any sentence he must serve for the crime of rape itself.

However, in the *Caudillo* case, the Supreme Court of California overruled these three cases and specifically held that a rape alone does not amount to great bodily injury. Therefore, when a robber or burglar commits a forcible rape (or sodomy or forcible oral copulation) in the course of his crime he will not face the ten-year stiffer sentence that he would face if, instead of raping his victim, he stabbed her or broke some of her bones. The court particularly relied on its perception that the injury from rape is primarily psychological and emotional and that the adjective "bodily" cannot have been meant to cover such injuries.

In a pained and reluctant concurring opinion, Chief Justice Rose Bird almost begged the legislature to correct this result by amending the law; and a bill to that effect was proposed in the legislature the following year but never went anywhere. The *Caudillo* ruling is therefore still law in California. While the decision was limited to the meaning of the language in the sentencing portion of the three statutes that it addressed (and would not necessarily apply to any others, including self-defense), it is important to note that the California justifiable homicide statute is written in precisely the same language, "great bodily injury." It remains to be seen whether the courts will someday apply the *Caudillo* reasoning to self-defense and rule that a woman is not entitled to kill to defend herself against forcible rape but only against some felony that involves greater bodily harm, whatever that may be.

It is hard to imagine anything much worse than what the California Supreme Court, in its wisdom, ruled did not constitute serious bodily injury in the *Caudillo* case. Here is that court's own description:

> She was pushed inside and blindfolded. After taking her to the bedroom, defendant led her to the living room, where she heard him unzip his pants. He ordered her to undress. Defendant allowed _____ to keep on her panties, pantyhose and shoes; he directed her to "turn around slowly." Then defendant, seated on the living room sofa, pulled _____ toward him, pushed her to to her knees and inserted his penis in _____'s mouth. _____ gagged; she felt like vomiting. Then he ordered her to completely undress.
>
> Defendant compelled _____ to stand, and inserted his fingers in her vagina. He asked her if she could become pregnant; she said she did not think so. Defendant then raped the victim...
>
> Defendant then inserted his penis in _____'s rectum. _____ pulled away, telling defendant she was going to be sick. _____ had diarrhea, and evacuated her bowels twice. Defendant kept insisting that _____ satisfy him.
>
> Defendant again forced _____ to orally copulate him; she gagged and spit...
>
> Defendant raped _____ for the second time, but could not ejaculate. He again forced her to orally copulate him, and ejaculated in _____'s mouth; _____ gagged, spit and vomited. Still not content,

defendant again inserted his penis in ____'s mouth, wiping away his victim's vomit.

II

The seriousness of the threatened harm is not the only obstacle that the law of justifiable homicide places in the path of a woman who kills a male assailant. Another equally formidable one is the requirement that the threatened harm be imminent. Ordinarily, this means that the assault is already actually taking place or so close to beginning that there is nothing the intended victim can do to avoid or prevent it. A killing is not justifiable if it comes too soon, in response to a bare threat to do future harm, if the person making the threat does not accompany it with some action that would give the threatened person reason to believe the threat was about to be carried out immediately. Conversely, a killing is not justifiable if it comes too late, after the assault is over, because then it will be regarded not as self-defense but as revenge.

We see here once again the law of self-defense functioning as a guide to manly behavior in dangerous circumstances. A real man, a brave man, faces his adversary in a fair fight. He does not sneakily lie in ambush or shoot an enemy in the back or kill him while he is asleep. He does not panic and kill someone who is just blustering and making threats. He does not avoid a showdown by indulging in a pre-emptive strike, getting his adversary before the latter can get him. These are the acts of cowards and villains, and the law has always declined to excuse or jutify them. Not without reason, of course.

These rules of manly behavior apply quite sensibly to most of the situations giving rise to self-defense pleas in which men have historically found themselves. A perusal of earlier American cases (decided when the law was still developing and which still influence courts' decisions today) leaves one with the impression that the single most common problem that led to killings and claims of self-defense was a dispute between rural neighbors about fences, water holes, and straying livestock. Frequent, too, were cases involving town bullies and groups of rowdies, as well as the expectable fist fights that begin over insults or women and escalate into deadly confrontations. In situations like these, a requirement that the threatened death or serious injury be immediate and unavoidable makes perfectly good sense. The actors in these dramas come together only briefly.

The "imminence requirement" restricts the possibility of taking a life to the moment of an actual confrontation. People are discouraged from going gunning for their enemies before such a confrontation takes place or after it is all over. Both before and after, presumably, they are in different places, leading their separate lives, and of no real danger to one another.

The situation of a battered woman and her attacker, however, could not be more different. Far from the single brief episode that the law assumes, domestic battering (as we shall see) is ongoing, and the essential factor in it is that the woman cannot, or believes she cannot, leave. All of the research on domestic violence shows that men who beat their wives seldom do it just once. Battering becomes habitual, and over time the beatings tend to become more frequent and more serious. Women who are trapped in violent relationships are painfully aware of the inevitability of the next beating, although they have no way of knowing when it will come or what kind of an incident (often astoundingly trivial) will trigger it. In circumstances like these, it is not at all an exaggeration to say that the threat of death or serious injury is *always* imminent. It is not psychologically realistic to regard such a relationship as a series of brief confrontations separated by periods of calm with no threat and no risk, as though these were antagonists who occasionally run into each other in the same bar or neighbors who periodically squabble about barking dogs. These antagonists live with each other. The threat of violence is a permanent and ongoing part of a battered woman's life. The question is not *whether* he will beat her up again but *when*, and not whether he will injure her but how badly or whether he will kill her this time.

Similarly, the physical and psychological realities of ongoing domestic violence are ignored when the imminence requirement is interpreted by the courts to mean that "mere" threats are not sufficient justification for acting in self-defense but that an overt act must first take place to indicate that the person making the threat is preparing to carry it out. There is an enormous difference between a death threat by a stranger in a bar and a death threat by somebody who has already extensively and painfully demonstrated his willingness to carry out his threats and inflict serious harm. Research has shown that when men do kill their wives, the homicide is frequently preceded by "mere" threats. When a man who has beaten her up before says to his wife, "This time I really am going to put you in your grave," it is hardly reasonable (or just) to expect that woman to wait, for the sake of the imminence requirement, until his hands are around her throat and she is losing consciousness before she acts to save herself.

The scenario envisioned by the law of self-defense as it developed was a face-to-face confrontation between two reasonably equal combatants prepared to settle their differences with their fists if need be. Unless the parties actually squared off against each other in this way, the possibility of death or serious injury was not sufficiently imminent. Although many self-defense killings by battered women do take place during such face-to-face struggles, many do not. Not infrequently, they take place when the man is sleeping, or when his back is turned, or by a shot through a door that he is threatening to break down. These are the cases where the imminence requirement causes the most trouble for women defendants.

A battered woman and her assaultive spouse are seldom equal combatants calmly facing each other down. The batterer, larger and stronger, is a man who has learned to vent his frustration and anger or enforce his authority by causing pain to another human being. He is not interested in "fighting fair." What he is engaging in is not fighting at all; it is terrorism. The battered woman learns from her experience that there is nothing, literally nothing, she can do to stop a beating after it has begun and that struggling or fighting back will likely only make his assault more furious. Helpless, her only option is to take what measures she can to minimize the damage and endure the beating until her assailant decides to stop. It is small wonder that such a woman, knowing that another beating is inevitable and that she will be helpless to defend herself against it once it has begun, may seek, or seize, an opportunity to defend herself that will have some chance of success.

Consider, for example, the story of Hazel Kontos. After twenty-five years of a happy marriage, Mrs. Kontos' husband died, leaving her a substantial amount of cash that she kept in the house, as he had. A few months after his death, Hazel, a lonely fifty-six-year-old widow, met and married a man named James Cooner. Although she didn't know it, Cooner had been married four times before and had beaten at least two of his former wives. Her marriage to him was miserable, violent, costly, and brief. Hazel left him three months after the wedding and divorced him three months after that. Even the divorce didn't end the situation, however. Cooner constantly threatened and harassed her; she was unable to keep him out of her house, and eventually she even went so far as to pay him a considerable sum of money to leave her alone. One day, three months after the divorce was final, Cooner came to the beauty salon where Hazel worked and threatened her again. He said he was going to "perform kidney surgery" that night, and then he was going to go to Hawaii and never have to work again. Hazel became so frightened that she left through a back door and went home. Later that night he came to her house and (after gaining entrance) terrorized her for two solid hours, holding a cocked pistol to her throat, slapping her around, and constantly threatening to kill her. Finally tiring of these activities, he went into her bedroom, undressed and lay down, keeping the pistol with him. Hazel took another gun from a drawer, crept into the bedroom, and shot Cooner in the head.

Was Hazel Kontos acting in self-defense? From her point of view, most assuredly. The man had a gun and had repeatedly threatened to kill her. At any moment he might get up and come after her again. It was one o'clock in the morning; she had no place to go if she let this intruder drive her out of her own house. Even if she had left on this occasion, it would not have lessened the danger she faced from the man one iota. Leaving him hadn't stopped him, divorcing him hadn't stopped him, even paying him off hadn't stopped him. From where she stood, alone in her house with an armed killer in her bedroom—a man who had been diagnosed by two doctors as a chronic paranoid schizophrenic—the threat of death or serious injury could hardly have been more real or more imminent. The only way she could defend herself against him was to catch him off guard. He was too strong and mean to confront head on. But the law was otherwise. Hazel Kontos was convicted by a jury of first-degree premeditated murder and was sentenced to life in prison.

The imminence requirement was a major legal obstacle in two similar cases that we have already looked at. Bernadette Powell— whose ex-husband had kidnapped her and her child at gunpoint and held them prisoner for hours, driving aimlessly and alternatively threatening to kill her and to have her held down and shot full of heroin so that she would lose custody of the boy—took advantage of a chance to escape when he fell asleep and shot him in the process. Alene Collier, whose boyfriend had driven her out of her house into the night three times and repeatedly threatened to kill her, finally fired a shot at him from outside a window where he couldn't reach her with his knife. Both of these women had been threatened and injured by these men in the past. Both knew that there was no way for them to defend themselves in a face-to-face confrontation. Both seized the only available opportunity to save themselves from serious violence and quite possibly death. But in neither case was the danger sufficiently imminent to meet the law's requirements.

The imminence requirement can sometimes turn a life and death situation into a macabre game of timing, as in the case of women who shoot men who are about to burst through a door. Sharon Crigler, for example, shot her angry, gun-toting former boyfriend as he tried to unlock the door to her apartment with a key he wasn't supposed to have. Sharon and Keith Rolland had lived together in her apartment for several months. During that time he had beaten her frequently and severely. Finally, no longer willing to put up with his brutality, she made him move out and return his set of keys to her. This was followed by a series of attempted reconciliations. During one of them, Sharon went to Keith's apartment and found another woman in his bed. She angrily put a foot through one of his paintings and turned over his stereo set. Then she went home and, fearing that Keith would be furious at her for what she had done and come after her, she called the police for protection. They arrested him on some old traffic warrants, but he was released on bail a few hours later. He went to Sharon's building and got a key to her apartment from the manager. Sharon was in the apartment with her niece and a friend. The unit had only one outside door, and there was no telephone. She heard the keys jingling in the door lock and called out, "Keith, if it's you, get away, back off." There was no response, and she still heard Keith fumbling with the keys in the lock. She had a pistol, with one bullet, that she had borrowed from her mother after Keith's arrest. She fired at the door and shot Keith, who was on his knees outside it, through the heart. Sharon was convicted of manslaughter.

Similarly, Lucille Valentine was charged with murder when she shot her estranged husband through the door of her house trailer. He had beaten her up a number of times during their marriage and had twice stabbed her with a knife in unprovoked attacks. After they separated, he came to her place very early one morning and began pounding on the door. He was yelling obscenities and threatening to kill her. When she heard him trying to pry open the door, she fired two shots from a .22 pistol at it. One of the bullets struck and killed him. She was convicted of voluntary manslaughter and sentenced to two years in prison.

Presumably, if either of these terrified women had waited until the violent threatening man outside had actually gotten the door open and assaulted her and then she had shot him face-to-face, her act would have been legitimate self-defense—provided, of course, that he didn't kill her first. Sandra King's timing was off, too. Her boyfriend came to her house, drunk and abusive, at two o'clock in the morning. He threatened to smash a window with a brick, come in, and kill her and her seven-year-old son. She shot him as he climbed up onto the porch with a brick in his hand.

And Roberta Shaffer's timing was just as bad. After she fled to the basement following an argument, the man she lived with, John Feruzzo (who had beaten her severely and threatened to kill her in the past), came to the top of the stairs; and he told her that if she didn't come up, he would come down and kill her and her children, who were in the basement with her. Five minutes went by, during which she started to call the police from the basement phone; but she stopped and hung up when Feruzzo promised to leave the house. Instead of leaving, however, he returned to the top of the stairs. He had come down "only" two or three steps when she shot him. The Massachusetts Supreme Court, in affirming her conviction for manslaughter, said that there was sufficient evidence for a jury finding that she was not in immediate danger of death or serious injury at the hands of the deceased. Just how much closer she should have let him come before she would have been justified in pulling the trigger, the court did not say. Halfway down the stairs? The bottom of the stairs? Within grabbing distance of the two toddlers? Until his hands were around her throat? There is no justice in a criminal law that can require that sort of cold-blooded calculation of a terrified woman desperately trying to save the lives of her children and herself from a man whose avowed intention was to kill them.

Helen Young learned about the consequences of her bad timing directly from the judge who found her guilty of voluntary manslaughter and sentenced her to serve four to twenty years in the Ohio State Reformatory for Women. Calling her crime only a "technical" voluntary manslaughter, he said that if she had not shot her boyfriend when she did but had waited until he was actually beating her (as he had done frequently in the past and was undoubtedly about to do again) her action would probably have been self-defense, and she would have been found not guilty. The difference between nearly a quarter of a century behind bars and walking out of court a free woman hinged on her having pulled the trigger a few seconds (or at most a few minutes) too soon.

This illustrates another way in which the imminence requirement frequently causes problems for battered women defendants. A woman who has been repeatedly beaten by the same man learns to recognize the signals that he is building toward another assault. She may believe that her life literally depends on being able to read these cues and take evasive action before it is too late. Sometimes, when a woman kills a man who has beaten her in the past it is because she knows he is about to beat her again although he has not yet made an overt move toward her. However reasonable and necessary her act may have been from her point of view, she is liable to be found not to have acted in response to an imminent danger.

Betty Hundley's case is an excellent example of this. Betty and Carl Hundley were married for ten years. During that time Carl's abuse of Betty had been constant and severe. He hit her, kicked her, and choked her. He had broken her nose at least five times and had knocked out several of her teeth. He had repeatedly broken her ribs, and he frequently pushed or kicked her down the stairs. She was a diabetic; and a number of times Carl hid her insulin or diluted it with water, causing her to go into diabetic coma. He threatened to cut her head off and cut her eyeballs out. His pattern was to indulge in this sort of violence whenever he was drunk.

Many of his assaults were in front of witnesses. Her sister testified that she had seen Betty beaten so badly by Carl that blood poured from her face, and her injuries required stitches. Betty's niece, Angela, testified that when Betty once hid from Carl at Angela's home, Carl came there, dragged Betty by the hair from her hiding place, threw her to the ground, and repeatedly kicked her until the police arrived. Betty's brother-in-law stated that Carl had threatened other members of the family as well and that his threats were taken very seriously by all of them.

Six weeks before Carl was killed, Betty moved out and went to live in a motel. She had just been discharged from a stay in the hospital when Carl beat her up again, and she could take no more.

Her moving out did not stop his abuse, however. He began to harass her constantly, telephoning her night and day and threatening to kill her and her whole family. She began to carry a gun.

On the day of his death, Carl saw Betty in the morning and told her he was going to come over later and kill her. That night, while she was in the bathroom, she heard him pounding on her motel room door. He broke the lock and came in, hitting and choking her and threatening again to kill her. He forced her to take a shower with him, shaving off her pubic hair in a rough and painful fashion, and then he raped her.

Afterward, Carl stayed in the room and continued to threaten Betty, who was crying and terrified. He picked up a beer bottle and pounded on the night table with it, demanding that she go and buy him some cigarettes. Since Carl had beaten her with beer bottles many times in the past, she was frightened that he was about to do it again so she got her gun out of her purse and told Carl to leave. He laughed at her, saying, "You are dead, bitch, now!" and reached again for the beer bottle, turning away from her as he did so. Betty closed her eyes and pulled the trigger, firing five times. She then hobbled, bruised and sobbing and barely able to walk, to the motel office where she asked the manager to call the police.

Betty Hundley was charged with second-degree murder. At her trial the State did not present a shred of evidence that contradicted her story. The prosecution's entire case rested on convincing the jury that according to Betty's own evidence she did not face an immediate threat from Carl. They were convinced; Betty Hundley was convicted of involuntary manslaughter and sentenced to serve two-to-five years in prison.

The imminence requirement reaches the point of complete absurdity in the rape situation. If she acts too soon, before the man has actually initiated any specifically sexual activity, there is often a question about whether rape was precisely what was imminent when he approached her in a sexually menacing way. If she acts too late, after intercourse is completed, she is presumed to be indulging in vengeance. The only point at which she can act in her own defense is the one at which she is least able to do so, when she is pinned down and the rape is actually taking place.

The celebrated Inez Garcia case illustrates this dilemma with painful clarity. Inez Garcia was a young, married, Hispanic woman who had been strictly raised in the traditions of her religion and culture. Far from her home and family, she was living in Soledad, California, in order to be near her husband who was serving a term in prison there. One night, two men came to her door, looking for the young man with whom she was temporarily sharing living space. They beat him up and drove him out of the house and then turned on Inez, dragging her out into the alley where one of the men raped her while the other stood guard, laughing. They left her then, but a few minutes later the second man, Miguel Jimenez, called Inez on the telephone and told her they were going to come back and do something even worse to her. She picked up a rifle and went out onto the streets. When she came upon the pair a few blocks from her house, Jimenez drew a knife. Inez fired a shot at him. He kept coming toward her, and she kept firing until the gun jammed. The man who had actually raped her was uninjured. Miguel Jimenez was dead. A period of about twenty minutes had elapsed between the rape and the shooting.

At her first trial, Inez Garcia's defense attorney, Charles Garry, did not argue self-defense at all. The fact that the shooting came some time after the rape, not during it or just before, appeared to eliminate self-defense as a viable legal theory because of the imminence requirement; the defense presented to the jury was that of impaired consciousness, a variation of temporary insanity. Most of the media coverage and controversy that surrounded the case at the first trial centered on the question of whether a woman who has been raped is justified in seeking revenge against her rapist. Feminists, including Inez' many supporters, were divided on the issue. Some were clearly disturbed by the implications of what appeared to be vigilantism, but many others were angered and dismayed at a legal system that required Inez Garcia to be painted as crazy and hysterical for acting in a way that appeared to them to be rational and understandable.

Inez Garcia's conviction of second-degree murder was overturned on appeal on the basis of an error in the judge's instructions to the jury about reasonable doubt, and she was granted a new trial. At this second trial, Inez was represented by a skilled feminist defense attorney named Susan Jordan who decided to abandon the mental impairment approach. She tried to make the jury see that, from Inez' point of view, she was indeed acting in self-defense—not against the rape that had already taken place but against the threat of death, the "something worse" than rape, that Miguel Jimenez had threatened her with in his phone call. This, of course, presented a different sort of timing problem, not that the shooting had come too late but that it had come too early, before the threatened harm was really imminent. This legal obstacle, along with a number of others, was overcome by a carefully orchestrated strategy of educating the jury and the judge about the devastating effect that rape has upon any woman—and in particular on a woman of Inez Garcia's cultural background—and the way that this could affect her perception of both the seriousness and the immediacy of the danger she faced. Her actions were presented to the jury as completely reasonable under the circumstances. The jury was finally able to see the situation from Inez' point of view and she was acquitted.

The requirement that the threatened harm be sufficiently imminent has proved to be a major obstacle in framing self-defense pleas for female defendants who have killed violent men. It has been the frequent cause of convictions of women who saw the immediacy of the harm they faced in a different way than the law expected them to. It is still one of the most common reasons why women defendants, and their attorneys, decide against raising a self-defense argument at trial, although such women clearly believed that they were acting to save their own lives.

Some, like *The Burning Bed*'s Francine Hughes, who poured gasoline over her sleeping ex-husband and then set the house afire (after years of relentless abuse and fruitless attempts to get away from him), raise an insanity defense despite the very real risk of years of mental commitment that very well may be worse punishment than a prison term. Others plead guilty in exchange for a reduction of the charge from murder to some form of manslaughter that carries a much lighter sentence and the possibility of probation or a suspended sentence and, thus, no time in prison at all.

Eileen Bartosh, for example, pleaded guilty to a charge of voluntary manslaughter after shooting her husband in the back with a shotgun. In a textbook case of wife-battering, her husband began beating her very shortly after their marriage, with steadily escalating violence that included a severe scalding with boiling water. He demanded that she quit her job, cut her off from family and friends, and kept her a literal prisoner in the house, never letting her out of his sight except for trips to the bathroom. She was not allowed to get medical treatment for the injuries her husband inflicted on her; and when the police came to the house at the request of Ms. Bartosh's concerned sister, to inquire into her welfare, she was forced—with a gun in her back—to assure the officer that everything was fine. The night she shot her husband, he had beaten her unconscious, all the while screaming at her that he was going to kill her. When she came to, she took a shotgun, went into the bedroom where her husband was getting undressed, and fired. When she was arrested, she had bruises covering her entire body; her face was permanently disfigured with a scar across one eye, and her ears were almost beaten completely away. All of this had happened in a mere eighteen months of marriage.

The fact remained, however, that she had gone into the bedroom and shot her naked husband in the back. Whatever threat she had reason to believe he posed to her at that juncture, it was not a sufficiently imminent one in the eyes of the law to justify her shooting him. So she pled guilty; and at the hearing at which her sentence was to be decided, the prosecutor stood before the judge and urged him to impose a substantial sentence, saying that she deserved some time in prison for taking a human life. "She should have sought help," said he, ignoring the fact that she had virtually been held prisoner for a year and a half; "I don't know why she didn't." Fortunately, the judge disagreed and, while he imposed a ten-year sentence, five years of it were suspended, and the other five were to be on probation. The fact remains, however, that in addition to the horrendous physical and emotional scars she bears, Eileen Bartosh must also carry with her the stigma of a felony criminal conviction for the rest of her life.

III

Of all the technical requirements of the law of justifiable homicide, none has caused the courts more perplexity than the question of retreat. As we saw in the last chapter, English common law from very early times required a person to back away from a fight, retreating "to the wall," before he was justified in standing his ground and killing his assailant. This retreat rule was adopted by many of the eastern states and later by some others. But in the west and south, the idea of a law that required a man to turn tail and run from a fight went so against the regional grain that the rule never took hold in many of those states. This division still exists today, with somewhat more than half of the states requiring retreat, at least in some circumstances, and the rest not. Although the common law historically distinguished between fights that were mutually entered into (where retreat was required) and unilateral assaults by strangers (where it was not), that distinction has vanished from the modern law. Where retreat is required, it is required across the board.

Although the rationale for requiring an assault victim to retreat where possible (rather than stand and kill his or her adversary) is usually identified as "a reverence for human life," the debate on the question in fact has historically focused on whether retreat was "manly" behavior. Indeed, the state court decisions that rejected the retreat rule collectively embodied what came to be known as the "true man doctrine," after a case decided in Ohio in 1876 in which the Ohio Supreme Court announced that "a true man, who is without fault, is not obliged to fly from an assailant, who, by violence or surprise, seeks to take his life or do him enormous bodily harm." As we have seen, Professor Beale, in his extremely influential Harvard article in 1903, which argued for the universal adoption of the retreat requirement, felt constrained to couch his arguments in these same terms, asserting in effect that a *true* true man will have the courage to restrain his passions and spare the life of his adversary no matter how sorely provoked he may be.

The whole debate about whether it is reasonable for the law to require a man to retreat from a potentially deadly encounter is based, once again, on the assumption that the kind of situation involved is a face-to-face, fist-to-fist encounter between two equally matched combatants, both of whom are spoiling for a fight. Where this is, in fact, the case, the retreat rule makes a certain amount of sense. Fist fights that are mutually entered into clearly should not escalate into life or death confrontations. A rule of law that puts a burden on the participants in such encounters to back off, at whatever cost to masculine pride, rather than kill each other can hardly be argued with. The problem, for women, is that this rule of law is applied to them in situations that are in no way analogous to ordinary fist fights but are, in fact, unilateral physical assaults by men upon women.

Where two men (or two people of either sex, for that matter) mutually enter a physical fight, there are many ways for one to signal to the other that he, or she, wants to de-escalate the proceedings. He can back away, smile, make conciliatory gestures, say he doesn't want to fight, offer to buy his adversary a drink and talk things over, apologize for his own words or behavior, or concede that the other guy is right. Usually something from this repertoire will work, and violence will be avoided. It takes two willing participants to make a proper fight. But where one person flat out attacks another—not to settle differences but as a means of acting out rage, frustration, self-hatred, or to punish that other person for some real or imagined transgression—conciliatory or submissive gestures are unlikely to have a defusing effect. In fact, it is just the opposite; these gestures can often merely make things worse by underlining the difference in power that made it possible for one person to start using another as a punching bag in the first place and to continually get away with it. Backing down, in that kind of situation, is not a way of saying, "Let's not fight." It is a way of saying, "Go ahead and beat me; I won't resist."

Whatever its original connotation, the duty to retreat has come to mean more than just this backing away from an adversary or refusing to fight. It also includes an affirmative obligation to escape, or try to escape, where there is an opportunity to do so. In some states that follow the retreat rule, one is only obligated to flee from an attacker when one can do so "safely" or "with complete safety." In others, the obligation applies unless, by running away, one would actually encounter greater danger than would have been faced by staying put. Either way, the law in the "retreat" states requires the victim of an assault to look for an avenue of escape, coolly assess its risks relative to the immediate danger faced, and (if warranted) utilize it. Failure to do so can mean that the assault victim's right later to claim self-defense, should she stay where she is and kill her attacker, is completely forfeited. The fact there was arguably an opportunity to run away, which she did not seize, is not just one of a number of circumstances that go into a jury's assessment of the reasonableness of her actions. Instead, the obligation to retreat is an absolute one. Her reasons for not running, however valid they may have appeared to her, are irrelevant. All that matters is whether the jury, in retrospect, believes that she could or should somehow have gotten away. If she conceivably might have run and didn't, her otherwise entirely justifiable killing of her attacker is a criminal homicide.

The problems that this requirement raises for battered women who strike back at their batterers are many. Most wife-beating takes place in the home and, like other violent crimes, it occurs most often at night. A battered woman is frequently isolated, with no friends or support systems in her community, no money of her own, no transportation. She often has young children for whose safety she feels responsible and whom she dares not leave behind to bear the brunt of her husband's anger. She may well have sought protection from the police, friends, family in the past and learned that they are unwilling or unable to provide it. She may also have tried to run from her husband in the past, only to have him come after her and drag her back by force, and punish her severely for it. Almost certainly she perceives that—even if she does escape this time—when the storm blows over, she will have to return to the only home she has and that, inevitably, she will be beaten again. Such a woman's decision not to run out into the night—often with no money or clothes, leaving her children behind, with no place to go, and with a violent and possibly homicidal man in pursuit—is often the most reasonable one she could make. A rule of law that says that none of these circumstances matter—that despite everything, there was a door, and she didn't run out of it, and that is the only fact that counts—serves neither reason nor justice.

Not only does an absolute retreat requirement fail to take relevant circumstances into account, it also allows no consideration of the influence of fear on the person's actions. It is indeed striking that in all of the dozens of court opinions over the decades that have discussed the duty to retreat (some approving it and some rejecting it) the subject of fear is almost universally ignored. Certainly this is once again the result of the role of self-defense law as an arbiter of "manly" behavior in the face of danger. A "true" man is cool and calm and rational no matter how great the peril. A "true" man doesn't succumb to fear or panic when his life is threatened. To acknowledge that he might would be to reward cowardice, which is the most distinctly unmanly behavior of all.

But where does all this nineteenth-century hairy-chestedness leave women (or, for that matter, many men)? One fact emerging from studies of battered women with remarkable consistency is the constant fear with which they live. It is a fear that can be so pervasive that it often becomes the single most important element in a woman's life, controlling all her actions and decisions: all of her waking hours are spent in fear that anything she says and anything she does, no matter how trivial, may trigger more violence. A woman living in such circumstances can be quite literally paralyzed by fear, too scared to run. And yet her inability to do so can turn an otherwise completely justifiable homicide—the harm sufficiently serious and sufficiently imminent, her perception of her peril and her response to it reasonable—into a crime for which she may be punished by many years, or her entire life, in prison.

The obligation to retreat, of course, only applies to the actual confrontation during which a person is killed. It has nothing whatsoever to do with the question of why the woman didn't leave the relationship long before. However (as we shall see in later chapters), the question, "Why didn't she leave him?" is one that troubles juries in these cases perhaps more than any other. I suspect that failure to escape from a beating and failure to have left altogether before things reached such a deadly pass often get muddled in the jurors' minds. Certainly, the same ignorance that leads many people, including jurors, to assume that battered women are *always* free to leave their violent situations, can also lead them to assume that a woman who is *in the process of* being beaten or threatened by her mate is also free to simply turn and walk out the door. Indeed, battered women seem to be expected to escape from situations in which escape, for anyone else, would clearly be seen to be impossible. In case after case, in which the obligation to retreat was an issue at the trial or on appeal, women have been convicted for killing men who were holding them with one hand and beating them with the other or who had them pinned down on the floor or trapped in a corner or were menacing them with a knife or a loaded gun.

Emelia Lenkevich, for example, was standing at the kitchen sink fixing dinner when her husband came up behind her with a knife in his hand and said to her, "You are not going to get a divorce... I'll kill you first." Unarmed, Emelia grabbed her husband's hand and fought to get the knife away from him. Their struggle moved into the adjacent dining room where her husband, still holding the knife, began slamming her head against the door that led to the bedroom. Then he grabbed her around the throat and started to strangle her. She was still struggling to free herself or to get hold of the knife. She had seized him with both hands and was holding on with all her might when she suddenly lost her balance and fell forward. Somehow, as she fell, she stabbed him through the heart with his own knife.

There were two doors in the kitchen leading outside but both were locked. It is hard to see how she could have escaped, or even tried to escape, from her husband's sudden armed onslaught. Nevertheless, the judge told the jury that she had an obligation to retreat. They found her guilty of second-degree murder and sentenced her to life in prison.

Similarly, after an evening spent out drinking together, Edna Marie McGrandy stood in her kitchen facing her husband who was in the doorway aiming a cocked rifle at her and threatening to kill her. In desperation, she picked up a butcher knife and slashed at him, trying, as she testified, to "get him out of my way so I could get out." The prosecutor at her trial made much of the fact that there was a second kitchen door which led to an outside porch with a stairway to the ground, and he argued vigorously that she should have tried to escape that way. The judge told the jury that she was obligated to retreat if any way appeared to her. In convicting her of manslaughter, the jury apparently felt that she should have tried to get out that porch door despite the fact that her husband had her covered with the gun, and she obviously couldn't outrun a rifle bullet.

The law has always recognized an exception to the requirement of retreat when the assault being defended against takes place in the assault victim's home. This stems from the ancient idea that a man's home is his castle, the place where he has a right to expect safety. In fact, it is sometimes still referred to as the "castle doctrine." It was unthinkable that the law would require a man to flee from a homicidal threat in his own home and thus abandon his castle (and his possessions, including his women) to his enemy. Since an assault against a woman most often takes place in what ought to be regarded as *her* castle, one might expect that this major exception to the retreat requirement would work to the advantage of battered women, but too often that is not the case because the courts over the years have developed several exceptions to this exception. Not surprisingly the large majority of the cases, where it has been held that one *must* retreat from one's own home, involve defendants who are battered women. In fact, these exceptions to the castle doctrine have been applied so exclusively to such defendants that the courts over the years appear to have developed these new rules specifically to prevent women who kill their husbands from "getting away with murder."

In the most troublesome of these exceptions to the castle doctrine, some courts have held that although one need not retreat from an attack in one's own home by an intruder, the obligation to retreat *is* applicable when the attack is made by a co-tenant, someone who has as much right to be on the premises as the victim of the attack. Although this rule has occasionally been applied to such people as fellow rooming house tenants, it is most frequently applied to cases of domestic assault: a woman, who would have been entirely justified in standing her ground and defending herself against a physical attack in her home by a stranger, is held to have been obligated to flee from an identical attack by a man who lives with her. The courts and legislatures of a few states are beginning to acknowledge the pointlessness of this rule and the unfairness of its results, but the notion that somehow a woman shouldn't be permitted to kill her homicidal husband in *his* castle, but should flee from it instead, is a very persistent one. Edna McGrandy's and Emelia Lenkevich's cases were just two in a series of cases involving battered women who killed their batterers in which the Michigan courts struggled with this question. It took sixteen years of expensive and harrowing litigation to finally establish, in just that one state, that a woman in her own home has the same right to defend herself against her homicidal husband as she does to defend herself against a homicidal stranger. However, a similar series of cases in Florida has led that state's highest court to the opposite conclusion. In Florida, a woman who is attacked in her home by a man she lives with must try to run away before she can defend herself. Ironically, another Florida Supreme Court decision established that the woman does not have to try to escape from her own home if the man she is defending herself against is her lover who does not live with her. The absurd result is that a woman in Florida has a greater right to kill her boyfriend than to kill her husband if she is assaulted by either one *in her home* even if all of the circumstances of the attack are otherwise identical.

The question of whether a woman has the right to stand her ground and defend herself in her own home against an assault by a man she knows and has been intimate with but does not live with, such as a boyfriend or an estranged or former husband, has vexed the courts in the "retreat" states considerably. Logically, under the castle doctrine, she should have a right to. Since such a man is not a co-tenant, the exception for co-tenants does not apply. However, Florida to the contrary, that is not a result that many state courts are willing to accept, and so they have created yet another exception to the castle doctrine. This one says that although one need not retreat from an assault in one's home by an *intruder*, one must retreat from an assault by someone who is there by permission. Once again, it appears that most of the instances in which this rule is invoked are cases involving defendants who are battered women. The result has been one bizarre case after another in which a woman's right to defend herself—and quite literally whether she would go to prison or go free—hinged not on whether she reasonably believed her life was in danger but on whether the man she killed had a key to her apartment, slept over, or kept clothes in her closet, and thus had implied permission to go there when he wished.

The New Hampshire Supreme Court, for example, held that Florence Grierson did not have the right to stay put and defend herself against Charles Peabody when he attacked her with a knife in her kitchen. She and Peabody, who were both divorced, had been seeing each other for about two years. Their relationship was a rocky one. He had beaten her severely a number of times and had threatened to kill her. Once when she fled her home to escape one of his assaults, he stayed behind breaking the windows and smashing her furniture. Although Ms. Grierson lived alone, Peabody often spent the night at her house and came and went as he pleased.

The night she killed him, they had been out drinking together; and when they came back to her place, he began accusing her of seeing another man. She denied it and, enraged, he lunged at her with a small paring knife, cursing her, and threatening to "fix" her. Like Emelia Lenkevich, she tried to get hold of the knife to keep him from stabbing her. As they struggled he began to beat her on the face with his fist, still holding the knife with his other hand. As she pushed back against his hand, she managed to turn the knife and fatally stab him.

She was convicted of manslaughter. During her trial, the prosecutor argued to the jury that there were three doors leading out of the kitchen that afforded her an opportunity to escape and she should have tried to do so. In its opinion upholding her conviction, the New Hampshire Supreme Court held that she indeed had an obligation to flee from her home rather than defend herself in it. Although Peabody was not, strictly speaking, a co-tenant, he was not a trespasser either; and the rule that one need not retreat from an attack in one's home was only meant to apply to attacks by trespassers. He was there by invitation; the fact that he had free access to her home and had spent the past two nights there made him something like a temporary co-tenant. In all of the legal debate about her obligation to retreat, of course, it was overlooked that she realistically had no opportunity to retreat once Peabody's knife assault had begun.

By contrast, the Supreme Court of Pennsylvania, in Carol Eberle's case, held that she was not obligated to retreat from an assault by a man who lived elsewhere but had a key to her apartment, kept his clothes there, slept over frequently, and was free to come and go in her absence. Carol worked nights. One evening while she was at work, her boyfriend, Charles Dilks, called to tell her that he would meet her at her apartment when she got off. She got home at 4:00 A.M., but Dilks didn't show up. She sat on the sofa and ate some salami, slicing it on the coffee table with a knife, then went to sleep on the sofa. Around six that morning, Dilks, extremely drunk, let himself into the apartment. When Carol asked him where he had been, he became violently angry and yanked off the top shelf of a bookcase across from the sofa and ripped down a shelf that was fixed to the wall directly over the sofa where Carol was sitting. Alarmed, she stood up in the narrow space between the couch and the coffee table. Dilks lunged at her, and she stabbed him with the salami knife that she had left on the coffee table.

She was charged with murder and convicted of voluntary manslaughter. At her trial the prosecution argued that she might have been able to escape from the apartment despite the facts: it was a tiny, cluttered studio with only one door; she would have had to maneuver around several pieces of furniture and dodge around a corner to reach that door; and she was essentially trapped between the sofa and the coffee table. The judge, who tried her case without a jury, agreed with the prosecutor. He held that her social arrangement with Mr. Dilks made him the equivalent of a co-tenant and that she had failed in her obligation to try to run away rather than defend herself there. The Pennsylvania Supreme Court, however, saw the facts differently. Although Dilks had the run of the place and was there by invitation, he maintained a separate residence and was therefore not a co-tenant. Consequently, Carol Eberle was within her rights to fight back where she was, and the court vacated her conviction and set her free.

The status of an estranged husband causes even more confusion on the issue of retreat and seems to revolve more around property rights than any rationale of justification. After three years of marital unhappiness punctuated by frequent beatings, Sarah Lamb decided to separate from her husband, Larry. After an argument over who should get the apartment, during which he beat her up and threatened to kill her with a knife held to her throat, Larry moved out. A few days later, following a reconciliation attempt by Larry that culminated in another threat to kill her, Sarah agreed to move in with her parents and let Larry have the apartment until he could find a new place to stay. Several days later, Larry removed all of his belongings and went to live with his new girlfriend. Sarah and her cousin Charlene then moved back into the apartment.

A short time later, Sarah and Charlene and another friend, Ricky McCullough, were out together at the local bar when Larry came in. He asked Sarah to go out with him, and she said no. Then she and Charlene and Ricky went back to the women's apartment. Charlene left again soon after, but Sarah and Ricky stayed there to play some records. The phone rang; it was Larry, drunk, angry, and accusing her of having another man in her apartment. A few minutes later after furiously pounding on the door, Larry broke it open and burst in. He attacked Ricky and they ended up wrestling on the bed. Sarah tried to pull Larry off Ricky, but Larry punched her so hard in the face that she was slammed against the wall. Ricky fled into the living room leaving Larry to turn on Sarah. He grabbed her, threw her on the bed, and put his hand around her throat, saying, "Bitch, I'm going to kill you before I leave here. Before I leave here tonight." Ricky came back into the room at that point, and he and Larry began fighting again. Sarah ran into the kitchen, got a knife out of a drawer, and ran back into the bedroom. Larry broke off his fight with Ricky to come after Sarah again. She jumped up on the bed; when Larry swung at her with his fist, she closed her eyes and slashed out with the knife. Then, she testified, "When I opened my eyes Larry was standing there and he looked at me. He said, 'Jean you stabbed me.' Like that. So I said, 'Oh my God, no I didn't.' Then I seen the blood start flowing. And he fell to the floor. When he fell to the floor then I said, 'Oh God please don't let him be dead,' like that."

Sarah was charged with murder. At her trial the judge ruled, incredibly, that Larry was not an intruder despite the fact that he no longer lived in the apartment and had clearly not come there with Sarah's permission. Because he and Sarah were still married,

Larry had as much legal right to be in the family home as Sarah had. Consequently, she was obligated to try to escape from her home rather than stay there and defend herself. She was convicted of second-degree murder and sentenced to twelve-to-fifteen years in prison. An appellate court upheld the judge's ruling on her obligation to retreat. The case was appealed further, however, and the New Jersey Supreme Court finally decided that under the circumstances Larry was indeed an intruder. Sarah had had no obligation to retreat after all but was within her rights to defend herself in her home. Her conviction was reversed, and she was granted a new trial.

For Sarah Lamb, Carol Eberle, Florence Grierson, and many other women who have killed men in self-defense, the difference between having committed a serious crime and having committed no crime at all revolved around the absurd and totally irrelevant question of who had a right to be on the premises and not whether the woman was in fact acting to defend herself. Even more absurd, there is no way in the world any one of these women could possibly have known that the law of self-defense was different for her than for other people because of the legal technicalities of her marital status or living arrangements. It is hard to imagine that any system of criminal law could really expect that a woman who is facing a homicidal assault by a violent man—desperately seeking to save herself—will stop to analyze their comparative claims to the property and then conclude—despite his knife or his gun or his hands around her throat—that she is legally obligated to try escaping from him; and thus, although there is a weapon at hand, which she *could* use to defend herself, she *should not* choose to use it. Unfortunately however, in many states, that scenario is exactly what our law requires.

IV

The *seriousness* and *imminence of the harm threatened* and the *requirement of retreat* constitute the three major areas of the law of self-defense that cause problems for women, although they are not the only ones. Two others merit mention here: the requirement that a person who resorts to deadly force in self-defense be free of any responsibility for provoking the confrontation and the prohibition against firing more shots than may have been necessary to disable an assailant.

The law of self-defense in virtually every state provides that a person has no right to use deadly force in self-defense if he or she was the initial aggressor or the one who provoked the conflict that escalated into a life-threatening situation. This is a rule that developed to discourage bullies from picking fights and then hiding behind the law of self-defense if things got out of hand. It is also intended to prevent people who are bent on murder from setting up a phony self-defense situation by provoking a fight with the intended victim. Both, of course, are laudable goals, but this element of the law has sometimes worked very unfairly against defendants who are battered women, especially those whose experience with their batterers tells them that a serious assault is imminent and that they should get a weapon in case they need to use it.

A woman who is the first to resort to a weapon in a final confrontation is apt to be characterized as the aggressor even if her purpose is purely defensive. This happened, for example, to Loretta Branchal, who lived for six years in New Mexico with a man named Benjie Romero. Romero had persistently abused Loretta and her children. He had beaten her with his fists and with a board, threatened her with knives, shot at her with a high powered rifle, held a gun on her to force her to eat, and had once threatened her with a knife and a gun to compel her to handle a dead rattlesnake. He was a satanist who believed the devil gave him powers; when he communicated with the devil, he always wore a fingerless glove. Loretta, who was a religious woman, found this behavior of Romero's especially terrifying. In addition to his abuse of Loretta, he abused her children, once placing her daughter in extreme danger by throwing her into a pigpen with a grown pig. He had broken out all the windows in Loretta's mother's house and was known to the police for beating up and robbing old people.

Benjie Romero was particularly prone to violence when he was drunk. Sometimes, to avoid his drunken rages, Loretta would take her children and go sleep in old cars or abandoned houses. She had tried calling the police once, but they told her there was nothing they could do and that the family must find ways to solve their own problems.

The night she killed him, Benjie came home drunk and belligerent. He began to work at repairing a light, and Loretta could tell by the way sparks were flying and the way Benjie was ignoring the risk of electrocuting himself that he was very drunk. He insisted on rousting one of the children out of bed to bring him a screwdriver, calling the child a bitch (*cabrona*). Loretta was afraid he was working up to one of his rages. Telling him to leave the children alone, she went outside to his truck and got a gun, which she put in the pocket of her housecoat.

A friend of Benjie's arrived at the house, and he and Benjie started talking about the devil. Disturbed by this talk, Loretta went into the kitchen to avoid them, but they followed her and stayed there drinking beer and smoking marijuana. Loretta finally went to bed, taking her baby with her, and placing the pistol on the mattress beside her. Benjie kept coming into the bedroom and harassing her, pestering her for food and blankets for his friend. He grabbed the baby and shook it awake, and Loretta angrily told him that if he were not so near to the baby she would kill him. Benjie began bragging to her about his list of people he intended to kill: her baby, her mother, and her two brothers. Then he began to sing: *"El rey, yo sago el rey, no chinges con migo porque yo sago el rey."* (The king, I am the king. Don't fuck with me because I am the king.)

Loretta finally got out of bed, put the gun back in her housecoat pocket and went into the kitchen. Benjie went outside and Loretta locked him out but when he began to beat on the door and threaten to break it down, she let him back in. Benjie was furious and advanced on Loretta with an expression of anger on his face more extreme than she had ever seen before. Her terror was increased by the fact that he was once again wearing the fingerless glove. She warned him to stay away from her and backed away but he kept coming. She fired a single shot at him, killing him. She testified:

> I was thinking that I didn't want to kill him. I just wanted to get him scared like he used to get me scared. But it didn't work out. He just showed anger and more anger. That's when I figured that if I didn't shoot at him he was either gonna kill me, take the gun away from me or kill one of the kids, or kill me, or something. I just got so scared that I didn't know what to think. I just had to shoot.

Loretta was charged with murder. Her first trial ended in a hung jury: they acquitted her of first- and second-degree murder but were unable to agree on manslaughter. She was tried again, this time only for voluntary manslaughter, and was convicted. The judge at that trial refused to instruct the jurors on self-defense, thereby preventing them from even considering her argument that she was defending herself. The judge ruled that because she had provoked the encounter and because she was not in immediate danger of death or serious injury from an unarmed man, she was not entitled to raise a claim of self-defense. Because the judge found that there was no issue of self-defense, the jury was permitted to hear none of the evidence about Benjie Romero's past acts of violence toward Loretta, the children, or other people. A psychologist was prepared to explain to the jury why Loretta stayed with Romero, how she recognized a predictable pattern in his drinking and violence, and why his invocations of the devil and wearing of the glove were significant to her, but he was not permitted to testify. The jury had no way of knowing why she had good reason to fear for her life or why she felt she had to draw a gun on an unarmed man. The prosecution throughout had portrayed Loretta as an angry and vengeful woman, and the judge later explained his ruling by stating that he did not want to condone shootings by angry spouses in retaliation for past abuse.

The case law in some states has developed a presumption that where a gun is used in self-defense, the firing of one shot that hits the attacker and presumably disables him is justifiable. The firing of one or more subsequent shots, however, is not deemed necessary for self-defense and constitutes the use of excessive force under the circumstances, which in most states is manslaughter, or even evinces an intent to kill, which can be murder.

Dathel Shipp's was such a case. Ms. Shipp had known her ex-husband, Robert, since she was a young girl; and their long relationship had given her every reason to fear his proclivity for violence. Twenty years before she had married him, he had killed his first wife, for which he served ten years in the Illinois penitentiary. When he was released on parole, he recruited her as a prostitute, and she worked for him for three years. When she decided to leave that way of life and went home to live with her parents, he went to their home, broke in and pulled a gun. He shot Dathel in the shoulder. When her mother tried to intervene he told her, "Shut up or else I'll kill you too." He shot Dathel again, in the hip, and dragged her out of the bedroom where she was cowering, although her mother put up a monumental struggle to protect her. As Robert dragged Dathel and she struggled to get away, he shot her a third time, in the face. Dathel then managed to break away and ran outside and down the street, with Robert running after her still firing. She found refuge in a tavern and locked herself in the restroom. Robert tried unsuccessfully to break down the door and then fired two shots through it but missed her because she managed to flatten herself against the wall. Finally, the Chicago police arrived and arrested him. He was convicted of attempted murder and sentenced to serve eight to fifteen years in prison.

During the seven years he was in the penitentiary, Dathel corresponded with him and visited him. After his release he moved in with her, and a year later they got married. It was a violent marriage: Dathel was beaten frequently and was hospitalized at least once with broken ribs. After only two years, she divorced him.

Following the divorce, Robert harassed her constantly. He threatened her with guns, raped her, and struck her hard enough to leave a scar on her face. She got a restraining order against him, but it did not stop him. He told her in no uncertain terms that if he ever caught her with another man he would kill her.

Ten days before their final encounter, she ran into him at a tavern; and he followed her outside. They argued, he pulled a knife and threatened to cut up her face so thoroughly that nobody would be able to recognize her. He told her that he would "just cut [her] throat and go back to the penitentiary." Then he grabbed her by the arm and tried to force her into his car but the police arrived at that point and arrested him for assault. After this episode, Dathel began carrying a revolver in her purse.

Ten days later, Dathel went back to the tavern, checking the parking lot to be sure his car was not there. When she got inside, however, Robert was sitting at the bar. She stayed and talked to several women friends. Then, apparently to show Robert that she could be with another man if she wanted to, she propositioned a man in the bar and left with him. They went to a nearby house and went upstairs to the bedroom. Robert arrived soon afterward, burst in, and rushed upstairs. The man Dathel was with, who had known Robert Shipp for many years, was so terrified that he hid under the bed. Dathel began reciting the terms of the restraining order. Robert started toward her, and she picked up the revolver that she had placed on the dresser. She cocked the gun and told him not to come any closer. Telling her to go ahead and shoot him, he kept coming toward her, and she kept backing away until she was trapped in a corner of the room. His hand was in his pocket where he usually kept his knife or his gun. When he was within six feet of her and still advancing, she began firing—fearing that if she didn't kill him, he would take the gun and kill her. She testified at her trial, "I remember pulling the trigger, and he kept coming, so I kept shooting."

She fired five shots in all. The first hit Robert in the stomach and the second in the groin. After that shot he spun around and began to fall. She fired twice more, hitting him in the side as he went down, and one final shot into his back. One of the shots fired into his side, severing his aorta, killed him. Only a few seconds elapsed between the first shot and the last.

Dathel Shipp was charged with murder. The jury found her guilty of voluntary manslaughter. As the appellate court observed, "In view of the verdict, it is conceded by both the State and the defendant that the jury found that the defendant actually believed that her employment of deadly force was necessary to prevent her death or suffering great bodily harm, but that belief was unreasonable." The prosecutor had argued at trial that Dathel had "overreacted" by firing all five shots at Robert. The prosecution's position was that even if Dathel's belief was reasonable when the first two shots were fired, after he was hit in the groin and began to fall, he had been effectively disabled; and the last three shots, including the fatal one, were unreasonable and unnecessary. Despite the speed with which the whole episode unfolded—and the fact that she had every reason to believe that he was armed and no reason to believe he was any more seriously disabled by the second shot than by the first—this argument apparently convinced the jury which convicted her.

This presumption (about the ability of a person acting in self-defense to disable rather than kill an assailant) is another holdover from frontier times when men were presumed to be handy with firearms, and it is one more example of the outdated masculine standards of behavior that have become embedded in the law of self-defense. A woman who, terrified, unfamiliar with firearms, having no confidence in her ability to hit the broad side of a barn, starts firing and doesn't stop until the gun is empty, can find herself facing a homicide conviction although her actions met all of the other requirements of self-defense law. The difference between a serious crime and no crime at all can be the panicked firing of just one bullet too many.

4

The Question of Reasonableness

The ultimate question in a self-defense case is whether the defendant's act was a reasonable one. Even if she can successfully negotiate the legal hurdles of seriousness, imminence, retreat, and the like, she must still convince the jury of two things: that her belief that she was in imminent danger of death or serious injury was reasonable under the circumstances and that her reponse to that perceived danger was a reasonable one, not an overreaction. This has nothing to do with the genuineness of her belief: in most states it is not enough that the woman defending herself was utterly certain that she was in mortal danger when she struck back and killed her attacker if her certainty does not appear reasonable to the jury. Nor does it matter that she sincerely believed that the only way that she could save herself was to pick up a weapon and inflict fatal damage on the man if the jury feels that her conviction about the need for such an extreme reaction was unreasonable. Although logically separate, these two considerations tend to blur together into the general question of whether the woman's act was reasonable.

The self-defense law of almost every state includes some kind of reasonableness requirement. At first glance, of course, imposing a standard of reasonableness on acts of self-defense seems itself to be eminently reasonable: one would hardly expect the law to excuse unreasonable behavior that results in someone's death. However, the requirement that the jury must find the defendant's action reasonable before it can acquit her presents another major source of problems for women in self-defense cases. The jurors are invited—indeed obligated—to substitute their judgement for hers in a situation that most of them can barely imagine being in and seldom understand.

The question of reasonableness is the point at which our society's ambivalence about violence against women and all of our collective prejudices and stereotypes about women who are victims of male violence are apt to be injected into the jury's deliberations. Every juror enters the jury box with deeply held, if unconscious, ideas about human nature and how reasonable people behave and about marriage and the proper roles of men and women within it. These beliefs, and many others (as well as individual jurors' own life experiences) will naturally color the way the jury evaluates the reasonableness of a woman defendant's claim of self-defense. A juror who shares the old stereotype of women as irrational, emotional, inherently unreasonable creatures will not be receptive to a woman's argument that what she did when she took someone's life was reasonable. A juror who accepts the widespread myths—that battered women are masochists who want to be hurt or nagging shrews who drive their long-suffering mates to violence—will not be inclined to find any defense against such "invited" beatings reasonable. A juror who has grown up with our society's centuries-old conspiracy of silence about domestic violence, and cannot believe that men who appear to be normal and nice ever kill or injure their wives, will have a very hard time seeing a woman's fear that she was about to be killed or seriously hurt as reasonable. A juror who believes that acquitting any woman who kills her husband will give all wives a "license to kill," and will result in an "open season on men," will surely not find any such killing reasonable, no matter what the circumstances. The reasonableness requirement, above all, allows those many jurors—who, for no very clear reason, are appalled or frightened by the idea of a woman taking a life; or who simply believe that no woman is ever, under any circumstances, justified in killing her husband—to act on those feelings by finding the woman guilty because her action was not reasonable.

It may seem an overstatement to assert that juries are unwilling to find an act reasonable purely and simply because it was committed by a woman. Where self-defense is involved, however, it is difficult to avoid the conclusion, looking at convictions, that jurors frequently are unwilling to believe that it is *ever* reasonable for a woman to kill her mate.

How else, for example, can one explain a case like that of Una Bush, who stabbed her husband as he held her and beat her and repeatedly announced his intention to kill her? Or that of Odessa

White? Ms. White had lived with George Butler for five years. Although he treated her well when he was sober, he was a mean and violent drunk. During the course of their relationship, Butler had frequently injured her seriously enough for her to require medical care. He had broken her ankle, beaten her on the head with a tire jack (causing permanent scars), and thrown her into a piece of furniture so violently that she broke four ribs. He had smashed her face so viciously with a bottle that surgery was required to repair the damage, and another time she had to be operated on to remove a growth caused by a blow to her breast. He had twisted her right arm so severely that she again required surgery, resulting in a three-inch-long scar. While that injury was still healing, he assaulted her again (kicking her arm and dislocating the elbow, which had to be put into a cast) and beating her so brutally that her eyes and face were so swollen she could not see or eat. Shortly before she finally killed him, he had injured her right arm again, this time breaking her wrist and requiring another cast.

Not long after this attack, Butler got drunk again; and during an argument about whether he should go out and buy more liquor, he grabbed Odessa by the injured arm and told her he was going to whip her again. She broke free and ran into the bedroom where she hid for a few minutes. She picked up a pistol from the top of the dresser as she heard Butler coming after her, walking fast from the kitchen through the dining room toward the bedroom where she was trapped. She fired one shot hoping it would stop him; instead he ran toward her, and she fired again, killing him.

If ever there was a situation in which it was reasonable for a woman to believe she was about to suffer serious bodily injury—and that there was no way she could prevent it without using a weapon against the drunk and brutal man who was lunging toward her— Odessa White's would appear to be it. The jury, however, found her guilty of voluntary manslaughter. In its opinion upholding the jury's verdict on appeal, the Appellate Court of Illinois said, "The jury determined beyond a reasonable doubt that the defendant's belief that the use of force was necessary to prevent her own death or great bodily harm was not a reasonable belief. We cannot say that the evidence of guilt here is so improbable as to justify a reasonable doubt of guilt. On the contrary, the guilt of defendant and the absence of any legitimate right to self-defense has been proved beyond any reasonable doubt."

Similarly, the jury did not believe Sheral Lynch acted reasonably when she shot and killed a man named Jimmy Dyess. Sheral was only nineteen when she killed him and had been living with him since she was sixteen. Jimmy was over twice her age and had a long history of violence in his relationships with women. As his former wife testified at Sheral's trial, he was a violent man who had beaten all the women he had ever had, and "he had quite a few of them." Jimmy was a logger and was very fit and strong. During the time he and Sheral were together, he had beaten her twenty or thirty times, sometimes very severely. A few weeks before their final confrontation, he had beaten her so savagely with a baseball bat that she was unable to walk for two weeks.

The night she shot him, they had been arguing. Dyess had hit her and thrown her on the bed, telling her, "I'm going to beat your goddam ass and make you tell me the truth." Fearing another brutal beating like the awful one with the bat, she got away and ran out the back door, grabbing a gun out of the dresser drawer as she went. She didn't get far, however, because Jimmy came after her and cornered her in the yard. She backed away from him, warning him to stay away from her. He told her, "You ain't going no damn where," and came toward her. She kept backing away and warned him at least two more times to keep away from her, but he kept moving forward. Finally, unable to stop him any other way, she pulled the trigger, not aiming but firing blindly.

Three eye-witnesses corroborated her story. Nevertheless, the jury found she had not acted in self-defense and found her guilty of manslaughter. There was no appeal, and she began serving her twenty-one year prison term in the fall of 1978. Subsequently, long after the time for appealing her conviction had run out, she was successful in getting the Louisiana Supreme Court to consider an appeal anyway. Happily, that court saw the situation differently than the jury had. Concluding that "in view of the past beatings inflicted on her and other women and Dyess' dangerous character, her fear and apprehension were reasonable," that court finally, in the spring of 1983, overturned her conviction and set her free.

Jurors are not alone in their visceral resistance to finding that a woman acted reasonably in defending herself against a violent mate. When judges (at the defendant's request) try cases without juries, they often have the same problem, as, for example, in Barbara

Watson's case. Barbara and her common-law husband, Matt Black, lived together for ten years and had three children. Their relationship was a rocky one, marked by his frequent assaults on her that were apt to be triggered by arguments over trivial or nonexistent things.

The evening of August 7, 1978, had been a particularly volatile one. Early in the evening, as they were walking down the street together, she had asked him a question; his response had been to turn on her and hit her, knocking her to the ground with sufficient force to injure her forehead, hand, and knee. Later, back at the house, he had threatened to beat her with a baseball bat. A short while later, Barbara and Matt and two friends spent some time together visiting one friend's daughter. When they all left, Barbara and her husband were walking together some distance ahead of the other couple when Black suddenly attacked her again. As Barbara told the judge:

> So we was walking, you know, up the street. And he just hauled off and grabbed me around the neck and shoulders and started choking me. And he had me down on the ground. And I was scared. And he said, "You black bitch, I should have killed you a while ago when we was at the house."
>
> And I was scared. It was me or him. I didn't know what to do, I was so scared. I was scared he was going to kill me, because he told me he was going to kill me.
>
> So that's why I shot him. I don't know how I managed to get the gun. I was just scuffling down on the ground. It was me and him.

She also testified that the only reason that she had a loaded gun in her purse at all was that she had found it in a vacant lot next door to her home and had put it in her purse so that her children would not find it in the house. The other couple, who witnessed the assault from about thirty yards away, confirmed her version of what happened: she was on the ground, Black's hands were around her throat, and he was choking her when she shot him.

The Philadelphia judge who heard this testimony ruled that she had not acted in self-defense and found her guilty of voluntary manslaughter and possessing a concealed weapon with intent to employ it criminally. In his ruling, he specifically found that her fear that she was in imminent danger of death or great bodily harm was unreasonable, not only because her husband was unarmed but because he had beaten her so many times before without killing her.

The trial judge also seems to have suggested that by staying with a man who beat her she consented to the abuse and in effect waived any right to defend herself against it.

The difficulty that judges and juries have with finding that a woman's fear that she will be injured or killed by her husband is reasonable is compounded by the traditional test of reasonableness. Jurors in self-defense cases are usually told to assess the reasonableness of the defendant's act by asking themselves whether what he or she did was the sort of thing that would have been done by a reasonable man in the same circumstances.

The "reasonable man" is a mysterious figure who has lurked about in the shadows of English and American law for almost two centuries. He was invented by English judges who were baffled by the problem of how to fathom, in each individual case, whether the defendant actually possessed the state of mind—negligence, for example or recklessness—required by the law for civil or criminal liability. The behavioral sciences were in their infancy, and it was generally agreed that only God himself could really know what was in a person's mind and heart. Moreover, every person is different from every other: some are cautious, others are impulsive; some are bright, others are dim-witted; some are hot-tempered, others are slow to anger; some are calm in a crisis, others panic. English common law judges, and their American followers, were disturbed by the proposition that these infinite variations in human personality should have to be taken into account every time a court considered whether an individual should be held morally and legally culpable for his or her actions. Not only would the courts be required to know the unknowable about the defendant's state of mind but, worse, they would be obliged to apply a different standard of behavior to different people who committed essentially the same act, depending on the strengths and weaknesses of each individual's intellect, judgement, and character. This was a disorderly state of affairs that the courts were unwilling to tolerate. As Oliver Wendell Holmes put it, "The law takes no account of the infinite varieties of temperament, intellect, and education which make the internal character of a given act so different in different men. It does not attempt to see men as God sees them, for more than one sufficient reason."

What was wanted was an objective, universally applicable standard by which everyone's actions could be measured and this was provided by the "reasonable man." If a reasonable man would have seen a particular danger, for example, and taken measures to prevent it, then the defendant in a suit for negligence should have too; and if he failed to, he would be liable for damages. The reasonable man has long been the standard by which acts of self-defense are measured. If a reasonable man would have believed (facing the particular kind of assault the defendant did) that he was in danger of death or serious injury and that he could only save himself by killing his assailant, then the defendant was reasonable in so believing and the killing was justified.

Once again we see the law imposing a masculine standard against which to measure a woman's behavior. The reasonable man is really none other than our old friend the "true" man wearing a different hat. A judge's instruction that tells the jurors to evaluate a self-defense situation according to what a reasonable man would have done in the circumstances inevitably invites them to look at the incident as though it were a fight between two men. And that image carries with it, as we have seen, all of our society's rules about how a true man—who is of course a reasonable fellow—behaves in a fair fight. He stands and faces his adversary, meeting fists with fists. He isn't frightened or provoked to violence by mere threats; he doesn't use a weapon unless one is being used against him; and he doesn't indulge himself in cowardly behavior such as lying in ambush or sneaking up on an enemy unawares.

Women aren't brought up to behave this way. They aren't expected to fight—quite the opposite, in fact—and they carry with them none of the cultural baggage that men do regarding the elaborate rules of this quintessentially masculine game. As one commentator has observed, the reasonable man standard fails to recognize "...the crucial fact that a standard is inappropriate if it will permit self-defense only where the battered-wife defendant responds in a manner foreign to her acculturation...Essentially, requiring that the battered-wife respond in a 'manly' manner in order to justify the homicide, virtually precludes that defense from the battered woman defendant." It is absurd for the law to demand that a woman who is assaulted conform her actions to a code of manly behavior on pain of imprisonment if she fails. And it is equally absurd for the law to say that a woman's behavior is only reasonable when she behaves like a *man*.

Even if the jury instruction is framed in terms of a "reasonable person" rather than a "reasonable man," as some more enlightened courts have begun to do, this problem will not be cured. Fighting has always been defined by our society as a masculine activity. We automatically tend to impose male rules of behavior on violent confrontations because those are the only ones we have. There are no rules governing women's responses to male violence that a hypothetical "reasonable person" could be expected to recognize and share, because we as a society have so resolutely refused to acknowledge that such violence exists. A jury's assumption is bound to be that, in these situations, a reasonable person would do what a reasonable man would do.

It should come as no great surprise to anyone that a woman might react to a male assault differently than a man would. Obviously most men are bigger than most women, both taller and heavier, and proportionally more of their body weight is in muscle. On the basis of the difference in size and strength alone, a woman's perception that she cannot defend herself against a man without using a weapon to equalize the situation is often perfectly reasonable. But the fact that her opponent is bigger and stronger than she is not the only thing that influences a woman's perception of her ability to defend herself. Almost everything she learns about her body and how to use it, as she grows up in our society, works against her developing confidence in her physical ability to counter a violent assault.

Although significant differences in size and strength between boys and girls don't really become apparent until adolescence, a woman's training for membership in the "weaker sex" begins virtually at birth. Baby girls are expected to be little and delicate, baby boys to be strong and vigorous. These expectations are so ingrained that parents will see "appropriate" physical characteristics in their newborn babies when those characteristics are not really there at all. In one study, parents were asked to describe their babies within the first twenty-four hours following the birth. Both mothers and fathers described their newborn girls as smaller, weaker, softer, more awkward and delicate than boys. Conversely, parents of both sexes described their newborn boys as stronger, firmer, hardier, more alert, and better coordinated than girls. In fact, the babies did not differ in size, weight, or Apgar general health scores. The parents saw what they wanted to see: delicate little girls and big brawny boys.

These parental perceptions of the relative strength and vigor of boy and girl babies lead to different treatment of boys and girls from a very early age, even by parents who believe themselves to be free from sex bias. Researchers have found, for example, that parents touch, handle, and talk to their girl babies more than their boy babies; parents of boys on the other hand manipulate their arms and legs more, handle them in ways that stress their musculature (such as sitting or standing them up) and play more roughly with them. There is no evidence that baby boys are in fact stronger or more vigorous than baby girls. On the contrary, on most scales, infant girls appear on the average to be slightly hardier and more physically advanced than boys. But the tendency of parents is to treat baby girls as though they were the more delicate sex. Once begun, it is a hard habit to break. And little girls who are treated as though they are weak and delicate tend to grow up thinking of themselves that way as well.

As children grow, boys are encouraged to develop their physical capabilities. Girls often are not. Parents expect and tolerate far more physical activity, rowdiness, and noise from their preschool sons than from their daughters who are expected to be quieter, neater, and more docile. From quite an early age, boys and girls are encouraged to develop strikingly different play patterns. Boys spend far more of their time than girls in active play that involves use of the large muscles. They are pushed towards participation in team sports such as baseball, basketball, and soccer that permit the development (over a period of years) of increasingly complex physical skills, from the toddler kicking or tossing a big soft ball to the adolescent seriously engaged in competitive athletics.

Girls, on the other hand, spend far more of their time indoors. One study of fifth graders found that 40 percent of the girls spent more than three-quarters of their playing time indoors, compared with only 15 percent of the boys. This indoor play, typically with one or two friends rather than a group, is usually quiet and unphysical, involving dolls, jacks, and board games. Even outdoors, girls' games like hopscotch tend to involve far simpler physical skills than boys' sports and offer no scope for developing increasing physical competence. In unstructured outdoor play, the differences between boys and girls is just as striking. One researcher, for example, who observed children's use of outdoor space in a New England town, found that there was a significant difference not only in the size of the area that boys and girls are allowed to roam about in but also in the use that they made of outdoor spaces. Boys were far more apt to manipulate their environment, changing and building things.

Girls, restricted in how far they could go by parents who feared for their safety and concerned with not getting dirty, tended to stay in one place, pretend they were indoors, and furnish make-believe rooms with household items. Already well before the age of twelve, they were convinced that they were not competent to build and manipulate things the way the boys did, a belief the boys were all too happy to encourage by ridiculing and sabotaging the few efforts in that direction that the girls did make.

These doubts about physical competence are common in girls and usually have no basis in objective fact. There is no reason at all why a girl can't hammer a nail or dribble a ball or climb a tree every bit as well as a boy. But many girls grow up believing that they can't. Girls learn early and well that physical competence is not expected of them, and they have no reason to expect it of themselves. They are not encouraged to develop confidence in their ability to use their bodies, and when they are successful in performing a physical task, they are far more apt to attribute it to luck than to skill or effort, which boys typically do. In one study, a group of first graders were asked to throw a ball and evaluate their own and each others' performance. Even though, in fact, the girls performed every bit as well as the boys, the researchers found that both girls and boys evaluated the girls' performance as inferior. As early as six or seven, it appears, girls have begun to expect to fail at physical tasks and have learned to regard themselves, and be regarded, as physically incompetent, even in the teeth of evidence to the contrary.

Even if a girl manages to avoid or resist this early training in helplessness and seeks to develop her natural physical abilities through athletics, she may be met with obstacles and discouragement at every turn. Organized athletics have always been for boys. The suggestion that girls should be allowed to play on Little League teams was met with howls of outrage; and despite successful lawsuits by a few determined female would-be players, youth sports such as baseball, basketball, hockey, and football are still effectively closed to girls in many places. The sports that girls have traditionally been encouraged to pursue—if they insist on being athletic—are tennis, swimming, and gymnastics. Although these all are excellent athletic endeavors that require the highest level of physical skill, they are not sports that give their participants any experience or competence with violent physical contact. Indeed, it is the fact that these are not contact sports that makes them so widely accepted as appropriate for women.

The same is true for the sports girls are offered in school athletic programs. Congress passed legislation in 1972 that was designed to eliminate unequal treatment of the sexes in education and explicitly included athletics in the coverage of the law. Title IX, as it is known, requires schools to provide equal athletic opportunities to boys and girls, including co-ed physical education classes; and the law has brought about considerable improvement in the level of athletic experience now available to girls. However, the law specifically excludes the contact sports—boxing, rugby, ice hockey, football, basketball, and other sports the purpose or major activity of which involves bodily contact—which would teach girls to use their bodies offensively and defensively. Schools are permitted to substitute other sports that are considered more appropriate for girls in both physical education classes and interscholastic team programs, and they routinely do so. Even with this major exception to completely equal treatment of the sexes, the athletic provisions of Title IX have been far and away the most controversial section of the statute and are constantly threatened with repeal.

Clearly, the message that growing girls receive is that physical prowess is not as important for them as for boys and that they need, and deserve, to be protected from the rougher aspects of sports. Most girls never have the experience of testing themselves physically against other people and finding out how strong and tough and able they are. Nothing in their school experience is designed to give them confidence in their ability to fend for themselves in dangerous situations.

Nor do girls usually get any direct physical training in self-defense. Every girl and woman is aware of her vulnerability to rape. Girls are admonished, almost from infancy, to beware of strange men and deserted places. Their freedom is often severely curtailed out of concern for their safety, and they learn early that the world is a more dangerous place for them than for their brothers. Yet, they are not routinely taught how to defend themselves. At most, they are apt to be offered a short course in "self-defense" that teaches them to avoid dark streets and provocative behavior and to blow a whistle or scream if they are attacked. The assumption is that girls and women can't really defend themselves and might as well not try. If they can't avoid the danger altogether, then the most they can do is try to attract the attention of someone, presumably male, who will come and defend them.

Boys in our society grow up with infinitely more exposure to physical conflict than girls, and they are expected to learn to deal with it as just one ordinary aspect of their lives among many. Little boys roughhouse, fight, and play-fight. Little girls do not. Development of physical toughness is seen by our society as an important part of the growing up process for boys. They are encouraged toward independence from toddlerhood; they learn very early that just about the worst thing a boy can do is be a sissy or "act like a girl." One study of children's playground behavior revealed that even in the early grades boys tend to form "toughness hierarchies," so that all of the children on the playground can usually reliably tell an observer who, among the boys, is tougher than whom, even though no actual fighting has gone on to settle the question.

Boys receive far more physical punishment than girls, and it is made clear to them that they are expected to "take it like a man." Boys learn to deal with forceful or even painful physical contact in the games they play. They tackle each other, hit and block, and bowl each other over sliding into second base. They punch each other, mock wrestle, and play "hurting" games where the object is not to acknowledge pain or give in to it and cry. Even those boys who have no taste for this sort of thing often participate in it vicariously through spectator sports, mentally playing the game along with the players and sharing the knocks they take.

Above all, boys fight. Fighting, or the possibility of fighting, is an integral part of the masculine experience in our society. Sociologist Murray Straus and his colleagues cite research indicating that three-quarters of the respondents of a national sample felt that when a boy is growing up it is very important for him to have a few fist fights. Even though the majority of men in this country have, no doubt, lived their whole lives without actually exchanging blows with another male in anger, every one of them grows up knowing that if he is pushed too far, if his body or his pride is sufficiently threatened, he can and will resort to his fists. And there are very few men or boys in this country, however pacifistic, who have not spent some time thinking about how they would react to a punch in the nose or worse.

A code of conduct surrounding fighting (much of which we have already examined) is so much a part of the culture that boys simply grow up knowing it. Part of this code is the mutual understanding that fighting is merely a form of communication of last resort. When words run out, when threats don't work, or a bluff has been called, men fight. When it's over, they can shake hands and be friends again. Among men, physical violence is not always to be taken personally.

The expectation of being made a soldier and bravely fighting for one's country is also an integral part of being male in our society. Even without a draft, and even given the reaction against things military in the aftermath of Viet Nam, every young man in this country knows he could be subject to a military call-up; and every young man must grapple with the question of how he will comport himself in the face of a violent death.

None of these things are part of a woman's ordinary experience. Women are not supposed to be tough. Girls aren't knocked around on the playground or the playing field because they know that the boys know that they should never, ever hit girls; and girls know that they aren't supposed to hit each other. Although girls can be abysmally nasty and spiteful, we very carefully channel their aggressiveness into verbal rather than physical forms of expression. For most girls, the very idea of a knock-down-and-drag-out fight is so alien that it isn't even a hypothetical possibility for settling a dispute, much less as establishing status among their peers. They don't grow up with the expectation that, like it or not, they may someday have to fight—even to defend themselves—because they don't grow up expecting that they might be forced to fight physically with someone.

Nor do girls grow up expecting that they will someday find themselves on a battlefield, fighting for their lives, or dying for their country. I believe it is safe to say that if there has been a consensus in this country about any military policy through the years, it is that, draft or no draft, women cannot, should not, and will not serve in combat. *In our culture, men fight. Women don't.*

We raise our daughters to have little confidence in their physical abilities. We give them no training in how to defend themselves. We protect them from any experience with physical confrontation. When a woman who has grown up in our society suddenly finds herself the victim of a violent assault, she is almost certainly going to read the situation differently from the way most men would. She is likely to feel utterly helpless. Fighting back with her fists will probably appear to her to be a completely futile gesture. Indeed, it may very well not even occur to her at all. Certainly she will not see what she and her attacker are engaged in as a two-sided fight where both combatants give it their best, fight fair, and the best "man" wins. All that her lifetime of training in physical helplessness and incompetence prepares her to do, if there is no one to protect her, is let herself be raped or beaten and try to stay alive until her ordeal is over.

It is clear that women in our society are not raised to be fighters. On the contrary, in many subtle ways women are raised to be *victims*. A woman often comes into a violent confrontation burdened not only by a sense of physical helplessness but by psychological helplessness as well. Although we have come a long way in the last twenty years, our society still has very different expectations of men and women based on deeply ingrained beliefs about their inherent differences. Our culture's picture of woman's true nature—indeed our ideal of femininity—has always included strong elements of passivity, submissiveness, and dependence.

In a pioneering series of studies designed to identify sex-role stereotypes, Dr. Inge Broverman and her colleagues found that there is widespread agreement in our culture about the "typical" characteristics of men and women. The researchers identified forty-one bipolar characteristics (such as "not at all agressive—very agressive") about which there was such broad consenus as to whether they were masculine or feminine that they could confidently be labeled stereotypical sex-role items. A partial list of stereotypical feminine characteristics:

- Not at all aggressive
- Not at all independent
- Very emotional
- Very submissive
- Very excitable in a minor crisis
- Very passive
- Not at all competitive
- Very home oriented
- Not at all adventurous
- Cries very easily
- Not at all self-confident
- Very uncomfortable about being aggressive
- Very dependent
- Very gentle
- Very religious
- Very quiet
- Very strong need for security

These views were expressed by people of both sexes and all ages. They did not vary with educational background or socio-economic status and were shared by such diverse groups as college students, mental health professionals, and nuns and priests. Both men and women accepted the stereotypes as desirable attributes of each sex and believed that they themselves possessed the appropriate ones for their own gender. According to the authors, "The sex-role definitions are implicitly and uncritically accepted to the extent that they are incorporated into the self-concepts of both men and women."

As the authors of the study point out, these are not just widely agreed-upon characteristics of typical women. They are also widely agreed-upon characteristics of *ideal* women. They are not failings that women should be thankful to overcome but ideals that women should strive to achieve. At the same time, all but the last four were found to be at the less socially desirable end of the pole. When respondents were asked to rank the list of stereotypes in terms of the social value of each characteristic, it was clear that stereotypically masculine characteristics are more highly valued in our society than stereotypically feminine ones. So that, all the time a young girl is learning what it is to be feminine and how important it is to become feminine, she is also learning how inferior it is to be feminine. The more she reaches the ideal that society sets for her, the less society will value her and the less she is apt to value herself.

In the fifteen years since these initial studies were done, a number of psychologists have turned their attention to sex-role research and have made similar findings about sex-role stereotypes. Several instruments have been developed to measure (among other things) the extent to which people adhere to sex-role stereotypes; and they all generally agree about what those prevailing stereotypes are. The widely used Bem Sex Roles Inventory of characteristics that are considered to have positive social value, includes on the feminine side of the scale: yielding, shy, affectionate, sympathetic, eager to sooth hurt feelings, soft-spoken, childlike, and gentle. Stereotypically male are: self-reliant, independent, assertive, forceful, willing to take risks, self-sufficient, dominant, aggressive, and competitive.

Janet Spence and Robert Helmreich, in their *Personal Attributes Questionnaire* (another widely used instrument that asks respondents to grade themselves or others on a scale between two extremes, one masculine and one feminine), place on the stereotypically feminine side such items as "not at all aggressive," "not at all independent," "very emotional," "very submissive," "very excitable in a *major* crisis," "very passive," "very gentle," "cries very easily," "not at all self-confident," and "goes to pieces under pressure." Similarly, Alfred Heilbrun's *Adjective Check List* includes on its Femininity Scale such characteristics as "dependent," "emotional," "excitable," "fearful," "submissive," "timid," and "worrying."

It should be emphasized that sex-role stereotypes are just that—stereotypes. They are broadly held and mostly *unexamined beliefs* about the fundamental nature of men and women and reflect a widely shared assumption that there are, in fact, significant innate psychological differences between males and females. In fact, modern psychological research is almost unanimous in its conclusion that there are few, if any, inborn differences in the psychological functioning of the two sexes. In the most exhaustive review of the literature of sex differences, Eleanor Maccoby and Carol Jacklin of Stanford University found that the only differences that were consistently supported by research data are greater aggressiveness in males, superior visual-spacial acuity in males, greater verbal ability in females after puberty and greater mathematical ability in males after puberty. Of these four, the authors suggest that there is some evidence of a biological basis only for the first two, although it is far from conclusive.

There is still debate among social scientists about these few possible exceptions. However, there can be little doubt that Maccoby and Jacklin have laid to rest the idea that there are significant *inborn* differences between the sexes in the way that they behave and think and feel. And yet, the sexual stereotypes remain as potent as ever, telling people how they are *supposed* to behave and think and feel, and they exert a continuing influence on how men and women perceive themselves and each other.

Experts disagree on exactly how we learn sex roles. The social learning theorists believe that children are taught appropriate sex-role behavior by parents and other adults who provide models for them to imitate, who praise and reward desired behavior and discourage what is undesired. Cognitive development theorists believe that children develop a mental concept of maleness and femaleness and, after learning what gender they are, attempt to fit their behavior to the concept. Still others advocate a psychoanalytic approach by which a child gradually comes to identify with the parent of the same sex and learns appropriate sex-role behavior by imitating that parent. However it happens, all the experts agree that by the time children are of preschool age (about four or five) they know not only what gender they are but, more important, that it makes a difference. They know that different behavior is expected of boys and girls and have begun to act in sex-typical ways. They have, in short, begun to be socialized and, for girls, this means that their lessons in the appropriateness of helplessness and dependency are under way.

We have already seen that parents have different expectations of sons and daughters from the day they are born, based on the parents' own stereotyped notions of typical sex-linked characteristics and behavior. Several other studies illustrate just how much adults can be influenced by sex-role stereotypes even when they deal with very young children. John and Sandra Condry showed a group of college students a videotape of a baby reacting to the sudden popping up of a Jack in the Box. The baby's first reaction was to be startled. The second time the Jack jumped out of the box, the baby reacted with tears and screams. Half of the observers had been told that the baby was a boy and half that it was a girl. Those who believed they were watching a boy attributed the baby's tears and screams to anger. Those who believed they were watching a girl attributed ''her'' crying and screaming to fear. As the authors of the article observed, the sex differences were entirely in the eye of the beholder. In another study, a group of male and female adults was asked to observe and play with a three-month-old baby. Half believed that the baby was a boy and half that it was a girl. All of them ascribed sex-stereotyped behavior to the baby based on the sex they believed it to be. When they played with the baby, they also tended to offer it toys that were stereotypically appropriate to its presumed sex, the doll to the ''girl'' and the football to the ''boy.''

Although there is considerable debate about the exent to which parents overtly enforce sex-role stereotypes in very young children, there can be no doubt that, at least in the clothes and toys that parents choose for their children and the type of play they encourage, parents are a child's earliest teachers of appropriate sex roles. Despite the ubiquity of blue jeans, many little girls are still dressed in dresses a good deal of the time and discouraged from playing games that will cause them to get dirty or accidentally expose their underwear. A study of the way that parents furnish their children's rooms revealed that girls were given primarily domestic toys like dolls and household objects that encourage quiet, passive, home-centered play, while boys' rooms contained far more action-oriented objects like blocks, toy vehicles, sports equipment and action-figure dolls like G.I. Joe. We have seen these early influences result in very different play patterns as children get older that seriously hinder girls' development of physical competence and contributes to their perception of their own helplessness.

Even when children are very young it appears that peers— playmates and older siblings—are some of the most potent enforcers of sex-role stereotypes. Evelyn Pitcher and Lynn Schultz made an extensive study of children between the ages of two and five in a variety of nursery schools; the study was undertaken in part to learn whether a fifteen-year period of feminist concern with sex-role socialization has had any significant impact on children's perception of sex-appropriate roles. They found that boys and girls, observed in unsupervised play with each other rather than in their interactions with adults, had begun by age three to play quite differently. Girls were already tending, or being pushed, toward increased "domestication" in their play, learning to inhibit their assertive impulses and develop nurturant ones. Boys, on the other hand, by about four, were clearly headed in the opposite direction, with teasing, rough-and-tumble play, and competition for dominance being the central focus of their activities. By age five, the authors noted that children "are becoming uncompromisingly stereotyped in their sex-role attitudes and quite forceful in the sex-typing pressure they exact from peers: they are quite ready to ridicule children without mercy for deviations from sex-appropriate behavior..." One of the aspects of their behavior that the researchers found most marked was the sex difference in the children's response to conflict or aggressive behavior by a playmate. The boys tended to initiate such aggressions and to react to them directly, by hitting or fighting back. Girls, on the other hand, tended to use more indirect, passive tactics, ignoring the unwanted behavior or withdrawing from it.

> This sex difference in mode of conflict, with boys favoring direct and girls indirect means of regulating their peer interactions, reflects a basic difference in male and female sex roles, and is a recurring theme of this book. Sex differences in negative social contacts during boys' and girls' play seem to be forerunners of basic dichotomies in their adult role behavior. We conjecture...that the initiation-response differences are related to sex differences in dominance, with boys' negative

initiations representing dominant strategies and girls' negative responses representing submissive behaviors.

These stereotypes of dominance and submission, active boys and passive girls, are bolstered by the other sources of sex-role stereotyping that all little girls are exposed to. The picture books they are given and the stories they are read present them with a parade of helpless girls and women as role models. Traditional folk tales, many of them popularized by Disney cartoons that are carefully re-released so that children growing up in America will have an opportunity to see most of them in their early years, offer such paragons as Cinderella, trapped in her cruel household, Rapunzel in her tower, Snow White in hiding, Little Red Riding Hood terrified in the woods, and Sleeping Beauty as good as dead. All of them are victims, all are helpless to protect themselves from the evil people who threaten them, all have no hope at all except to be rescued by a stronger, abler, braver male.

When she is not being encouraged to play princess-in-the-tower by old fairly tales, the young girl is led into the weird half-world inhabited by little girls, usually little sisters, in many picture and story books. In a pioneering study of these books, Professor Lenore Weitzman and her colleagues analyzed the sex-role stereotypes found in all of the preschool books that had been awarded the prestigious Caldecott Medal, as well as a representative sample of Newbery Award winners, Little Golden Books, and etiquette or proper-behavior books designed for preschool children. They chose to study picture books because, along with televison, they give most young children their first view of the world outside their home, showing them what other children do and what behavior is appropriate for boys and girls their age. Picture books are particularly influential because they are shown and read to children over and over again and, unlike television, they are usually directly presented by a parent so that the values and models they convey appear to come with direct parental sanction.

Weitzman found that, in the first place, girls and women were seriously underrepresented in the books she studied. Almost all of them featured male characters, human or animal, with girls and women on the periphery when they were there at all. In these books, it is the boys who are the actors and the doers. They have adventures, take risks, and make things happen. Little girls mostly sit and watch what the boys do. They are almost always dressed in frilly girl clothes, clean and neat. They spend most of their time indoors. When little girls do go out of the house, they get in trouble and have to be rescued. Boys and men are always the rescuers. Girls in these books seldom act with courage or resourcefulness. They are helpless, hopeless, and passive. Only girls and women cry.

Weitzman's study was done in 1972, and one might hope that children's books have come a long way since that benighted time. However, when Shirley St. Peter did another survey of 206 picture books for children aged three to six, in 1979, she found that the situation had in some ways actually gotten worse. She divided her books into three groups: those published before 1965, those published since 1965, and a third group drawn from a feminist list of nonsexist children's books. Between the first and second groups, there was a substantial increase in the proportion of books with male central-characters, male title-characters, and those with a male picture on the cover. In the second, more recent group, fully three-quarters of the instrumental activities described in the books—making, doing and building things—were carried out by the male characters. Things were much more balanced in her third group of books (and it is encouraging that a parent who wishes to make the effort to seek out nonsexist books for young children can now do so), but the randomly selected book off the rack or the library shelves is still apt to hold stereotyped role lessons for little girls.

If the preschool girl is not learning about her powerlessness from her picture books, she is probably watching television where the lesson is repeated *ad nauseam*. Saturday morning cartoons contain the same dreary stereotypes. Boys have adventures, solve problems with their cleverness and daring, and conquer all manner of enemies domestic and extraterrestrial. Girls watch, cheer from the sidelines, and get into all sorts of stupid scrapes from which they have to be rescued. In one study of the effects of viewing such programs, Emily Davidson and her colleagues wished to show a group of five- and six-year-old girls three cartoons, one sex-stereotyped, one consciously nonstereotyped, and one neutral. They found that stereotyping is so pervasive that the best that they could come up with as a neutral cartoon was an episode of "Scooby Doo," in which four kids (two boys and two girls) solved a mystery. Of the two girls, the pretty one was stereotypically dumb and passive and the smart, sensible one was stereotypically homely. Despite this problem, their research showed that little girls who watched the more stereotyped cartoon exhibited more sex-stereotyped behavior in a subsequently administered test.

The adult programs that young children watch are not very different, although some progress has certainly been made by the networks in recent years in presenting a more varied image of adult women than the dumb/happy/devious housewife of the fifties and sixties. Even so, unless women have magic powers, helplessness is still the commonest characteristic of women in dramatic shows. Women are the victims. Women get into trouble and have to be rescued. The beautiful-woman-in-peril is still one of the commonest plot staples for television shows and movies. Where a woman character moves the plot forward, it is apt to be in an indirect way. She will be used as bait or as a decoy, snatched from the jaws of disaster at the last possible moment. Or she will be dressed up (as scantily as possible) as a hooker, a model, a call girl, or a wet T-shirt contestant in order to infiltrate the bad guys and get information. When her ruse is discovered, she will yell for help and be rescued by her male boss or partner just in the nick of time. It is very rare indeed to see a woman on television—even a trained police-officer—directly confront a male antagonist unless she is armed. Almost the only women on prime time television who are not helpless victims are the occasional murderess and the recent crop of beautiful, manipulative bitches on the nighttime soaps, and it is clear how we should feel about *them*.

Studies like Davidson's (referred to above) and many others have confirmed that television does convey sex-role messages that are absorbed by young viewers. The more television they watch, the more stereotyped their view of sex roles is likely to be. Although there is some dispute among researchers about whether television teaches children new stereotypes or merely reinforces the ones they have already picked up from the culture in other ways, there is no question that it is an extremely important medium of sex-role socialization—and that a major part of that medium's message is the helplessness and vulnerability of women.

The other great socializing institution in our society is the school; and as a girl enters the school system, she gets the same message. Teachers are themselves products of our society's socialization process and frequently have different, stereotyped, expectations of boys and girls. They expect girls to be neater, quieter, more docile and obedient than boys; and in myriad ways (some blatant and some extremely subtle) they elicit and reinforce the behavior that they expect. Also, as we have seen, children's peers play a role in reinforcing stereotypical, sex-role behavior (particularly aggressiveness in boys and passivity in girls). Throughout the elementary school years, boys and girls spend most of their time with friends of their own sex. In addition to providing a comfortable forum for trying out gender-appropriate behavior, these single-sex groupings impose a considerable amount of conformity on individual members. Girls do things they perceive as "girl things" and boys do "boy things." To deviate too far from these stereotypes is to risk ridicule and social ostracism.

Until quite recently, schools overtly and purposefully treated boys and girls differently as they guided them toward divergent adult lives. Fortunately, much of this has ceased. The blatant sex-stereotyping that once marked readers and other textbooks is much less prevalent although there is a rising clamor from the far right to put the stereotyping back in. Following the passage of Title IX of the Civil Rights Act, schools—especially high schools—have stopped designating certain courses as for "boys only" or "girls only," counsellors are less prone to automatically discourage girls from pursuing careers or steer them into "feminine" jobs, and expenditures for boys and girls sports programs is more even handed. It is ironic and sad, however, that as officially sanctioned enforcement of sex roles has been dwindling in the schools, the kids themselves (adolescents and preadolescents) have been assiduously developing a teen culture based on savage embrace of traditional sexual stereotypes. Male rock stars strut on stage and in videos bristling with leather-and-spikes symbols of macho virility, singing songs and acting out dramas of male domination and contempt for women. Female rock stars, the few that there are, are caricatures of the traditional subjects of men's pornographic fantasies, sluts and "boy toys," not people but objects to be used or abused. Movies by the hundreds are cranked out for teen audiences that revolve around these same stereotypes of "randy boys" and "sex-object girls." More disturbing, for what they teach, are the scores of teen movies that depict young women being pursued and terrorized by crazed or monstrous males—with the camera always putting the viewer in the shoes of the terrorizer. Boys in the audience get to experience the "thrill" of abusing and mutilating women, and girls in the audience graphically experience their helplessness to resist or escape such *inexorable* male violence. Both get the message of which role, victimizer or victim, is appropriate to which sex; both are encouraged to enjoy that role because these stories are presented—often very effectively— as entertainment.

By the time she comes to adulthood, the ordinary American woman has had twenty years of schooling in passivity, dependence, and physical and emotional powerlessness. She also has had twenty years of schooling in fear. One of the most constantly repeated lessons that every woman has heard from her earliest childhood is that she *must* be afraid. The world is an especially dangerous place for women because lurking out there, everywhere, are men who may do her harm. Young girls (and young boys too, of course) are warned over and over not to talk to strange men or accept offers of candy or money from them or get into cars with them. We have seen that girls' physical freedom to roam about is often restricted by their parents out of fear that they will be molested. As they get older, young women learn that they must adjust their behavior to accommodate the danger and the fear. American women keep what has, with good reason, been called a "rape schedule," severely limiting their movement in public after dark. Every woman knows the terror of hearing a man's footsteps behind her when she is walking alone, the little flutter of fear when a man gets into the elevator or subway car that she is in alone, the worry that her car will break down when she is driving alone through a strange neighborhood, even the panic that a ringing phone or an unexplained noise in the small hours of the night can engender.

It is women who are warned not to go out alone at night; violent men are not made to stay home. It is women who are warned not to walk in woods or parks or down deserted streets alone; violent men are not prohibited from frequenting isolated areas. The twofold message is clear. A woman, just because she is a woman, is a potential victim of male violence all her life. And the only realistic, "reasonable" way of dealing with this fact is by avoiding the danger because a woman is powerless to defend herself against a physical assault by a man.

We raise women to be different from men. We expect women to be different from men. How can we, in fairness, turn around and penalize them for not acting like "manly" men when they are threatened with violence? Every time a woman faces an assault by a man, her response, without question, is going to be colored by her experience of growing up and living in our society. A woman—who has spent twenty, thirty, or fifty years absorbing the message that she is, and ought to be, gentle and weak and helpless; that she needs to be protected from pain and injury; that she cannot really rely on her own strength to save her from danger; that male violence is profoundly to be feared but cannot be defended against—is bound to view a violent assault differently than would a man whose own training in these matters is likely to have been so very different. A response to violence that might be unreasonable in a strong, healthy, "real" man may well be perfectly reasonable in a woman.

That women in our society develop a unique perspective on male violence and their ability to defend themselves against it is unquestionable. The problem is how to fashion a law of self-defense that will take this perspective into account and not apply an inappropriate *masculine* standard of reasonableness to a woman's behavior. Obviously, a different law for men and women is an unacceptable answer. What is needed is a law that is sufficiently flexible that the actions of each individual defendant, female or male, can be judged fairly in the light of her or his own *actual* ability to have defended against the attack in a nonlethal way.

Feminist attorneys were encouraged by a decision of the Supreme Court of Washington state in 1977 that appeared to offer a solution to this problem. The case involved Yvonne Wanrow, the Indian woman who shot and killed a man who broke into the house where she was staying, threatening both her and her children. Earlier in the day, the same man had attempted to molest Wanrow's young son, dragging him off his bicycle and towards his house while the boy was in the care of Yvonne's friend and babysitter, Shirley Hooper. The boy ran to Hooper's house; and shortly afterward the man, William Wesler, appeared at Hooper's door, whereupon Hooper's seven-year-old daughter identified him as the man who had sexually molested her a few months previously. When Shirley Hooper learned from her landlord that Wesler had reportedly molested at least one other child and had at one time been committed to a mental hospital, she called the police and asked them to arrest him. When the police arrived, however, they told her they could not get an arrest warrant until the following Monday. Shirley was very frightened, especially since someone had twice attempted to break into her house the previous week, and she suspected that it had been Wesler. She called Yvonne Wanrow and Yvonne's sister and brother-in-law, and they all sat up together in the house that night, watching out for prowlers. About five o'clock in the morning, Wesler burst into the house, obviously drunk, and refused to leave. There was a considerable ruckus, during which Yvonne, who was on crutches with her leg in a cast, turned and found Wesler looming directly behind her. Terrified, she fired at him and killed him.

Yvonne Wanrow was put on trial and convicted of second-degree murder. Her conviction stirred up a lot of anger among the feminist community in Washington state; and attorneys Liz Schneider and Nancy Stearns, of the Center for Constitutional Rights in New York, were enlisted to assist Wanrow's local attorney, Carol Schapira, in mounting a vigorous appeal. In a ground-breaking brief submitted to the state supreme court, the Wanrow defense team argued that, because women have been discriminated against for so long in their access to sports and self-defense training and have been socialized to equate femininity with helplessness and being protected by others, the only fair standard by which to measure the reasonableness of a woman's actions in defending herself is one that incorporates the woman's own perspective on the danger that she faced.

The Washington Supreme Court agreed. In its opinion over-turning Wanrow's conviction and granting her a new trial, the court said that "the defendant's actions are to be judged against her own subjective impressions and not those which a detached jury might determine to be objectively reasonable." It went on to state:

> The impression created—that a 5-foot 4-inch woman with a cast on her leg and using a crutch must, under the law, somehow repel an assault by a 6-foot 2-inch intoxicated man without employing a weapon in her defense, unless the jury finds her determination of the degree of danger to be objectively reasonable—constitutes a separate and distinct misstatement of the law and, in the context of this case, violates the respondent's right to equal protection of the law. The respondent [Wanrow] was entitled to have the jury consider her actions in the light of her own perceptions of the situation, including those perceptions which were the product of our nation's "long and unfortunate history of sex discrimination". . .Until such time as the effects of that history are eradicated, care must be taken to be sure that our self-defense instructions afford women the right to have their conduct judged in light of the individual physical handicaps which are the product of sex discrimination. To fail to do so is to deny the right of the individual woman involved to trial by the same rules which are applicable to male defendants.

What the Wanrow decision did was affirm that, in the state of Washington, while a person who kills in self-defense must have acted reasonably, that reasonableness is to be judged not by an *objective* standard—what would a reasonable man or a reasonable person have done in the same circumstances—but by a *subjective* standard—was what *this* particular defendant, with her unique viewpoint, did in these particular circumstances reasonable?

The Wanrow decision was a breakthrough in women's self-defense cases because of its stunningly explicit recognition of the unfairness of applying an essentially masculine standard of reasonableness to a woman's actions. The jury in a self-defense trial in Washington would henceforth be told that it must put itself in the defendant's shoes and view the situation as she did, knowing what she knew and seeing what she saw. This was unquestionably a fairer approach. However, a quick glance at the cases in Washington that have arisen since the Wanrow decision reveals that it hasn't made as much difference in the actual outcome of cases involving women and self-defense as many people had hoped.

Since 1977, at least fifteen women in Washington have been convicted of some degree of homicide or assault for using deadly force to defend themselves against men who were assaulting them. In 1977, as we have seen, Sharon Crigler was convicted of manslaughter when she shot her former boyfriend through the door of her apartment as he was trying to unlock it with an illicitly obtained key. In the same year, a jury returned a second-degree murder conviction against Dorothy Savage, who having endured twelve years of violence, shot her husband after he attacked her without provocation. While she was cooking dinner, he began beating her on the head with his fists; and when she ran into the bedroom, he dragged her across the bed by her hair and beat her again. When she saw that he had taken their pistol from its customary hiding place in the base of a bedside lamp, she feared that this time he intended to kill her and grabbed the gun and shot him. In November of 1977, a jury convicted Claudia Thacker (a French G.I. bride who had been a battered wife for twenty years) of second-degree murder when she shot her drunk and furiously violent husband as he threatened to kill her and all of the children. The fourth conviction in 1977 was that of Janice Painter for first-degree murder in the killing of her hostile and violent stepson after he knocked her off her crutches and came at her as she lay paralyzed on the floor.

In 1979, LaVonne Bailey was convicted of second-degree assault when she stabbed her husband with a hoof-trimming knife, collapsing his lung. After only two months of marriage, the Baileys were already discussing divorce. He had been on an increasingly abusive four-day drunk and she armed herself with the knife because she feared he would injure her. He had told her that he was leaving town but she didn't believe him so she went around to the taverns to see if he was still there. He jumped her as she walked into a tavern, swung at her, and they both fell to the floor; as they struggled, she stabbed him.

In 1980, three more women were convicted in Washington state. We looked at Elizabeth Knott's story in Chapter One. Married to a man stationed at a Washington state Navy base, she had been a frequent victim of his brutality, as had her three children. She had left him once but returned out of concern for her youngest child whom she had had to leave behind with him. The day she returned and found the daughter badly injured, she told her husband that she wanted a divorce. Enraged, he attacked her and, in fear for her life, she shot him. She was sentenced to ten years for manslaughter. In December of 1980, Ivy Kelly, a fifty-eight year old grandmother, was convicted of second-degree murder and sentenced to twenty years for the shooting of her husband, an ex-policeman, who had beaten her in the past and was threatening to kill her when she shot him. The third woman convicted in 1980 was never actually tried but pled guilty to second-degree murder on the advice of her attorney who apparently did not believe she had a chance for acquittal. As we have seen, Alice Keyes, a black woman, was sexually assaulted by her white employer who broke into the room she lived in at the cafe where she worked. During the ensuing struggle, she shot him with his own gun. She was sentenced to thirty years in prison.

The following year, another rape victim who shot her attacker, Messaline Perry, was convicted of assault pursuant to a guilty plea. Also in 1981, Sherry Allery was convicted of second-degree murder in the shooting death of her ex-husband. After a five-year marriage during which she was frequently pistol whipped, threatened with knives, and once beated so badly with a tire iron that she was hospitalized, she filed for divorce. Twice she had gotten restraining orders from the courts to keep him away from her, but he persistently stalked and harassed her, lurking in doorways near her parked car and leaping out from the dark to assault her. The night she killed him, he had been bothering her on the phone at work. She went home early and locked herself into her apartment to escape him only to find him hiding there in the dark. When he told her that he was going to kill her and seemed to be groping in a kitchen drawer for a knife, she shot and killed him. She was sentenced to twenty years in prison.

There were three more convictions in 1982. Charlene Hall was convicted of first-degree manslaughter for shooting her boyfriend who had beaten her many times and who she thought was going to kill her. Stella Ford, convicted of manslaughter, shot her husband with his own gun when he threatened to kill her. She had been a battered wife for twenty years. Lily Tomerlin was convicted of second-degree assault for slashing an extremely drunk man in the face with a broken beer bottle. He had been harassing her viciously on the street, and she was afraid he was about to assault her.

In February of 1984, Paula Three Stars pled guilty to first-degree manslaughter in the shooting of the man she lived with, who had frequently beaten her. Originally charged with first-degree murder, she feared that as an Indian woman she would not receive a fair trial although she acted in what she believed was self-defense. She agreed to plead guilty in exchange for the prosecutor's recommending to the court that she serve only a year in jail. The judge, however, ignored the recommendation and sentenced her to ten years in prison.

In March 1984, Bonnie Weiss pleaded guilty to first-degree assault after she shot and wounded her estranged husband as they sat in his truck arguing about custody and visitation in their divorce. Bonnie had left her husband after nine violent years and had obtained a restraining order against him. As they sat and argued, he threatened to kill her; and when he seemed to be reaching under the seat where he usually kept a gun, she shot him. She was sentenced to twenty years in prison. At this writing she is attempting to persuade the courts to allow her to withdraw her guilty plea and have a trial.

A subjective test of reasonableness is certainly better than an objective one, since under it a woman defendant is at least not held to an irrelevant or unrealistic standard of reasonable behavior. It is without question an interpretation of the law that is worth working for, especially in those states where reasonableness is an element of self-defense law imposed by statute. Since self-defense statutes rarely specify what standard of reasonableness is to be used, this is almost everywhere a matter of judge-made law and is thus a reform that can be pursued through the appellate courts. Such courts in at least four other states—Illinois, Michigan, Arizona, and North Dakota—have adopted a subjective test of reasonableness. However, as this string of convictions of women in one state that employs a subjective test of reasonableness indicates, it is far from being the whole solution. In fact the author of the Wanrow opinion, Washington Supreme Court Justice Robert F. Utter, has stated that the legal direction charted by the Wanrow case, "simply has to continue, to be broadened. Society's not there yet on women's defense issues."

Objective and subjective tests of reasonableness are not the only possible standards by which to judge an act of self-defense. A third alternative, which has been followed by several states and the American Law Institute's Model Penal Code, is to dispense with the reasonableness requirement altogether. Under this purely subjective standard, the only question is whether the person claiming to have acted in self-defense did *in fact* believe in the necessity of using deadly force. The jury's task is to look at all the evidence and determine whether the defendant's belief that she or he was about to be killed or seriously injured was genuine, not whether the defendant should have believed as she or he did or whether some hypothetical other person in similar circumstances would have.

This divergence among the states reflects a debate about the nature of criminal liability that has occupied American and British legal theorists throughout this century. The idea that it is appropriate to employ an external, objective standard, such as the "reasonable man," in determining whether an individual is guilty of a crime has come under attack almost from the time the courts first began adopting it. The objections tend to follow two lines of reasoning.

The first is that the fundamental bedrock of our system of criminal law is the concept of *mens rea*: the guilty mind or, roughly, criminal intent. A person can only be held criminally responsible for an act if he or she possesses the necessary mental state that renders the act criminal. Thus, when a person takes another's life, his criminal liability will depend entirely on his mental state. If he harbored a malicious intention to kill the other, he will be guilty of murder. It he was so provoked by his victim that he was unable to form such an intent but rather acted in the heat of passion, he will be guilty of manslaughter. If he intended to kill the other but acted not maliciously but in self-defense, he is guilty of no crime at all. It is the jury's responsibility to determine an accused person's actual mental state in order to determine moral culpability and thus criminal liability.

An objective standard of criminal liability, such as the reasonable man test, does just the opposite. Rather than looking to the accused individual's actual mental state, it predicates criminal guilt on whether the accused individual's behavior met some external theoretical standard. Whether the individual in question was, for whatever reason, incapable of meeting that standard is irrelevant. A person can be found guilty although he or she in fact had no criminal intent. Many legal scholars have argued that it is fundamentally unjust to determine criminal liability by a standard that completely ignores the actual mental state of the person accused.

The second line of objection to the use of an objective standard in criminal law, arising from the "legal realist" school of the early twentieth century and continuing on with the modern critical legal theorists, points out that legal rules like the reasonable man standard ignore the social reality of people accused of crimes. They argue that there is great potential for injustice when the law assumes that all people are alike and will respond to identical situations in identical ways, and when it imposes criminal liability on their failure to do so. Such legal rules lead to unjust outcomes by refusing to acknowledge the real differences between the way people of, for example, different sex, economic class, or ethnic background might perceive a situation and their available options in responding to it; at the same time they serve as a potent force in perpetuating the social inequities that they ignore.

The arguments against the use of an objective standard to determine criminal guilt obviously go far beyond the question of whether the reasonable man standard is an unfair one to impose on women. However, cases involving women who kill in self-defense point out with stunning clarity just how unjust such a standard can be in operation. Over and over, as we have seen, such women have been found guilty of crimes because they have not measured up to an abstract masculine standard of behavior although they *absolutely* believed that they had to kill their assailants to save themselves.

5

Reasonableness and the Battered Woman

I

Physical differences in size and strength, lack of athletic training and self-defense skills, and socialization into passivity and helplessness affect all women in our society to a greater or lesser extent. However, for most women who kill in self-defense, these experiences are only a part of what influences their assessment of danger and the options available to them to counter it because most such women are battered women, and the men they kill are their batterers. Such a woman's past experiences with her assailant and her first-hand knowledge of his violence and his willingness to inflict injury on her, inevitably influence the reasonableness of her assessment of the likelihood that he is about to seriously injure or kill her and whether or not she can prevent that from happening without seriously injuring or killing him first.

The proposition that a battered woman's past experience with her batterer affects the reasonableness of her perception of the peril she is in when he commences to beat her up again would appear so obvious as to hardly require discussion. However, as we shall see, the greatest burdens a battered woman defendant faces at trial are, first, finding a way to explain to the jury how living constantly with violence and the threat of violence affected her view of her situation, and, second, convincing them that her fear of serious injury or death was reasonable.

Fear is a battered woman's constant companion. She wakes up afraid and goes to bed afraid. When she is home alone, she is afraid of what will happen when her man returns—that he will be drunk and angry, that he will beat her for something, often some household chore she has failed to do or for something he has imagined she has been doing in his absence. When he is with her, she is afraid that anything she might do or not do or that something someone else might do that she cannot control—an admiring glance from a man on the street, a phone call from a friend, a whining child—may trigger an episode of violence. Even sleep brings no respite, for she never knows when she might awaken to find herself being raped or beaten. Her sleep is interrupted by nightmares and sudden cold-sweat awakenings. There are women who sleep with their shoes on in case they must run for their lives in the middle of the night.

Everyone has experienced fear at some time, and we all know the feeling of a racing heart, clammy sweat, dry mouth, spinning thoughts and frozen legs that a panic of fear can bring. What we all have difficulty imagining, however, is the effect of living constantly with such fear. In their study of battered women who were referred to a rural mental health clinic, psychiatrist Elaine Hilberman and her colleague Kit Munson described it thus:

> The variety of initial complaints and diagnoses notwithstanding, there was a uniform response to the violence which was identical for the entire sample. The women were a study in paralyzing terror which is reminiscent of the rape trauma syndrome...except that the stress was unending and the threat of the next assault everpresent...Agitation and anxiety bordering on panic were almost always present: "I feel like screaming and hollering but I hold it in." "I feel like a pressure cooker ready to explode." They talked of being tense and nervous by which they meant "going to pieces" at any unexpected noise, voice or happening. Events even remotely connected with violence, whether sirens, thunder, people arguing or a door slamming, elicited intense fear. A woman who had been shot by her husband panicked at any loud noise. There was a chronic apprehension of imminent doom, of something terrible always about to happen. Any symbolic act or actual sign of potential danger resulted in increased activity, agitation, pacing, screaming and crying. They remained vigilant, unable to relax or sleep. Sleep, when it came, brought no relief. Nightmares were universal, with undisguised themes of violence and danger: "My husband was chasing me up the stairs...I was trying to escape but kept falling backwards." "There was a man breaking in the house...trying to kill me." "Snakes were after me...in my bed."

These women are not experiencing hysteria. There is nothing irrational about their fear. On the contrary, it is all too firmly grounded in reality. A battered woman, by definition, lives with a man who has repeatedly demonstrated both his willingness to inflict pain on her and his ability to do so. The kinds of injury and pain that such women are subject to fairly boggle the imagination.

In their study of 542 women admitted to shelters in the Dallas–Fort Worth area, sociologists William A. Stacey and Anson Shupe tell of women rammed against walls by cars; burned with cigarettes crushed on their backs, necks, faces, and arms; splashed with acid; forced to drink bleach; and burned with butane lighters held to their hair and flesh. "...One husband poured a can of drain cleaner into his wife's open palm and forced her to hold her hand under the running kitchen faucet. Another drenched his wife's clothes with gasoline during an argument and stalked her through the house with matches, threatening to 'torch' her."

Lenore Walker tells of women being stomped until their backs are broken; scalded with boiling liquids and hot foods; burned with cigarettes and hot irons; shot; stabbed and mutilated with knives and other sharp objects; and sexually tortured, having objects and substances forced into their vaginas and being made to have sex with animals and, at gunpoint, strangers, as well as suffering vaginal and anal rape.

Even in the more common battering situation, where the man uses "only" his hands and fists and feet in his assaults, as we have seen, the pain and injury that his victim suffers can be devastating. The studies present an endless litany of broken bones, smashed jaws, shattered teeth, yanked out hair, bruises, eyes and mouths swollen shut for days and weeks, chokings, smotherings, damaged internal organs and, over and over, miscarriages and deformed babies caused by kicks and blows to pregnant abdomens.

In 1983, Dr. Angela Browne of the University of New Hampshire did a study which compared a group of forty-two battered women who had killed their mates with a larger sample of two-hundred and five abused women who had not. The purpose of the study was to isolate the variables that seemed most to differentiate the two groups. Looking at the violence that both groups of women experienced, she found that the kinds of violent acts they faced were not significantly different. "Typical battering incidents involved a combination of violent acts and verbal abuse or threats. Types of physical abuse described ranged from being slapped, punched, kicked or hurled bodily, to being choked, smothered or bitten. Women reported attacks in which they were beaten with an object, threatened or injured with a weapon, scalded with hot liquid, or held underwater."

Although the kinds of violence were the same for both groups, several other crucial variables were not. The homicide group reported that the assaults came far more frequently than those suffered by the abuse-only group. Over 63 percent of the women who ultimately killed their husbands reported being beaten more than once a month, compared with 45 percent of the others. Even more telling, nearly 40 percent of the women who committed homicides were (by that point in the relationship) the target of this kind of serious brutality more often than once a week. Only 13 percent of the battered women in the control group reported such frequent assaults.

The women who killed their batterers also suffered significantly more severe and more frequent sexual abuse. Both groups experienced a high incidence of rape (forced sexual intercourse) by their spouses: 76 percent of the homicide group and 59 percent of the control group reported that this happened to them. However, the homicide group suffered a much greater frequency of spousal rape than the comparison group; 40 percent of them reported being raped "often," compared with only 13 percent of the battered women who did not kill. This forced sex often was part of, or the culmination of, a serious beating, inflicted upon a woman who was already injured, bruised, and bleeding. It also tended to be brutal and violent, accompanied by pinching, biting, choking, and bashing the woman's head against solid objects. Apparently intended less for sexual gratification than to inflict pain and humiliation, such episodes often went on for hours and resulted in serious injury to the woman.

Forced intercourse was not the only form of sexual abuse that both groups of women were compelled to endure. Well over half (62 percent) of the women in the homicide group, and 37 percent of the comparison group, reported that their husbands had forced or urged them to perform other sexual acts that the women considered abusive or unnatural. "Sexually abusive acts reported by the women in the homicide group included the insertion of objects into the woman's vagina, forced oral or anal sex, bondage, forced sex with others, and sex with animals. One woman reported being raped with her husband's service revolver, a broom handle, and a wire brush. As with other types of violence, sexual abuse by partners typically involved a variety of assaultive behaviors. . . ."

A third significant difference in the nature of the violence suffered by women who killed their mates was in the severity of the injuries that they sustained. They were injured far more seriously than their nonhomicide counterparts.

> Injuries to women in the homicide group ranged from bruises, cuts, black eyes, concussions, broken bones, and miscarriages caused by beatings, to permanent injuries such as damage to joints, partial loss of hearing or vision, and scars from burns, bites or knife wounds. Interestingly, although the number of abusive acts reported by women in the homicide group was not significantly higher than the number of acts perpetrated against comparison-group women, these acts were apparently done with much more force. When asked about four specific incidents, women in the homicide group were much more severely injured in both the second (a typical) and the worst (or one of the most frightening) incidents and, overall, sustained more, and more severe, injuries than did the women in the comparison group.

A woman who is being beaten and tortured and sexually abused several times a week or even several times a month lives a life that is a blur of pain and fear. One injury follows another with no time for healing. New bruises fall on old bruises, stitches are ripped out as old wounds reopen, half-knit bones are broken again. When the man who has proved himself to be so brutal, so inexorable in his cruelty, begins to assault her yet again, it is hard to imagine that anyone could doubt the genuineness and reasonableness of her fear or question whether her belief that she is about to be seriously injured yet again is a reasonable belief. Even so, prosecutors and judges and juries do so over and over again.

A battered woman's fear of her husband springs from her first-hand experience of his violence. Actual injuries suffered, however, are not the only thing that contributes to a woman's fear of her violent mate. Far from being merely the accidental fallout of the batterer's violent behavior, her fear of him is often the intended result of conduct specifically calculated by the man to keep her constantly cowed and terrified. The techniques of psychological abuse that violent men use to intimidate and control the women in their lives are as varied as the human imagination. Verbal harassment is usually a large part of it. The woman is bombarded with constant criticism and deprecation. Everything she does is wrong. Everything she says is stupid. She is a terrible housekeeper, a worse bedpartner, a totally incompetent mother, a whore, a bitch, and a slut. She is so ugly that no other man could possibly want her. Everything that goes wrong is absolutely her fault. If he beats her, she has only herself to blame. Years of this kind of treatment can do devastating damage to a woman's self-esteem and have the insidious effect of bullying her into accepting *his* view of his violence, that it is justified by her own failings as a woman and as a wife.

This is apt to be reinforced by isolation, another common form that psychological abuse often takes. Battered women are frequently intentionally cut off from contact with other people. Sometimes this is the result of the almost pathological jealousy that many battering males exhibit; but it is not only limited to keeping her from having contact with men. Many battered women tell of being cut off from their families and friends, forbidden to socialize with their fellow workers or to work at all, even prohibited from going to church. They often must account for literally every penny of their money and every minute of their time. Their men believe that they have the right to control and monitor every aspect of their women's lives.

The more isolated a woman is from the outside world, the more dependent she must be on her husband. His constant attacks on her competence and value, combined with her ever-diminishing sources of support or help, make the possibility of standing up to him or leaving him unimaginable. His power over her begins to appear invincible.

For some batterers, however, the control over their wives that verbal harassment and social isolation — enforced by sporadic bouts of serious physical violence — gives them is not enough. These are the ones who resort to acts of real terrorism to maintain the upper hand. Angela Browne reports that two of the most commonly reported examples of this kind of behavior are forcing the woman to play Russian roulette with a loaded gun and making her watch while the man tortures or kills a pet animal. Many women tell of being stalked or tormented with guns and knives or splashed with gasoline and threatened with lighted matches or lighters. Much sexual abuse is specifically calculated to cause as much psychological devastation as physical pain. Many batterers seem to delight not merely in making death threats but in detailed and gory descriptions of exactly how the woman will be tortured and killed and how slowly and painfully he will cause her to die.

The pattern that a man's abuse typically follows is also a crucial contributing factor to the reasonableness of a battered woman's fear of death or serious injury at the hands of her abusive husband.

There are probably many marriages in which a man resorts to physical violence once and never does so again, perhaps because he is genuinely appalled at his own actions or because his wife makes it absolutely clear that she will leave him if he ever does it again. Much research indicates, however, that once a man develops a pattern of hitting or beating his wife it is highly unlikely that he will ever voluntarily stop. Physical violence, and the threat of physical violence, become for him an increasingly easily resorted-to technique for controlling his wife, imposing his will, getting his way, winning arguments and (some would argue) dealing with stress elsewhere in his life.

Virtually every study shows that the common pattern is for the man's violence to increase steadily over time, both in frequency and severity. Stacey and Shupe found, for example, that *"as the frequency of battering episodes increased, the more severe they became. [sic]* Likewise, the longer that violence continued over months and years, the more serious and dangerous it became. In other words, over time situations usually progressed from verbal abuse to punching the woman often to using weapons. Moreover, such violence began to occur more frequently. Several women told us that they were somehow able to stand back one day and review how the pattern of violence had been intensifying; they then suddenly felt more afraid than at any time during a single beating.*"

There is more to the usual pattern of violence than repetition and escalation, moreover. Dr. Lenore Walker has pointed out that in the majority of cases in her studies of battered women, the battering followed a distinct three-stage cycle: a tension building phase followed by a major explosion of violence which is followed, in turn, by a period of contrition and attempted reconciliation. It usually does not take a battered woman long to come to recognize the pattern and anticipate its phases. Battering is not just a series of unconnected ordinary arguments that sometimes get out of hand and result in violence. On the contrary, battering is an ongoing, constant phenomenon in a relationship that is merely acted out in different ways at different stages in the cycle. A battered woman's fear is no less acute and her perception of being in serious danger is no less reasonable because she is not being actively beaten at any particular moment.

According to Walker, the first or tension-building stage is characterized by an ongoing series of minor incidents and assaults. He may push or shake or slap her, throw things, dump the dinner on the floor or smash up the furniture. He is likely to accompany this with a barrage of verbal criticism and complaint, berating her for her housekeeping, her cooking, her ability as a mother, her looks, her family and friends. He may begin to make accusations that she is cheating on him with such unlikely partners as the mailman or the carry-out boys at the market or even her own relatives or women friends. If he is one the many batterers who is most violent when he is drunk, he may start on a round of increasingly heavier drinking. He may also begin to make threats about what he will do to her if she doesn't mend her ways.

These are all things that, taken one by one, tend to seem relatively minor. A woman would feel absurd calling the police, or even her own mother, to complain that her husband had shoved her into a wall or punched her on the arm or thrown a plate of meatloaf at her. So she often copes with these "little batterings" as best she can, denying her anger, soothing and placating and agreeing with her husband's accusations that his rage is caused by her own failures. What she knows, though, after she has seen the whole cycle through a couple of times, is that this first-stage tension-building behavior leads inevitably to stage two, an explosion of serious violence.

The terrifying thing about major battering episodes, where the man is completely out of control and is apt to go on pounding and smashing until his victim is unconscious or he himself drops from exhaustion, is that they are, at the same time, both predictable and unpredictable. A woman who is trapped in such a violent relationship knows she will be beaten again and that the next serious beating may well be worse than the last one. She knows, too, that the commencement of tension-building behavior signals a major explosion's inexorable arrival. She does not know, however, when it will happen or what might trigger it.

One of the most striking characteristics of the stories that battered women tell about their lives is the incredibly trivial nature of the things that often touch off major, even life-threatening, assaults. Del Martin relates:

> In my own conversations with battered women, I have discovered that however a batterer may rationalize his actions to himself, those actions never seem warranted by the actual triggering event. For example, one woman told me she was beaten unmercifully for breaking the egg yolk while cooking her husband's breakfast. Another said her husband blew up because at their child's birthday party she instructed the youngster

to give the first piece of cake to a guest, not to him. Another wife was battered because her *husband's* driver's license was suspended. Other women reported these reasons: she prepared a casserole instead of fresh meat for dinner; she wore her hair in a pony tail; she mentioned that she didn't like the pattern on the wallpaper.

Richard Gelles relates two grotesquely similar stories of serious assaults stemming from the issue of who would get the first piece of cake at a child's birthday party. Stacey and Shupe mention beatings set off by such trivialities as "the woman's habit of biting her nails, her particular choice of lipstick, or what happened to be served one night for dinner." Lenore Walker tells of a woman doctor who was beaten so badly she was hospitalized and lost a kidney all because she had been delayed by a patient and arrived home half an hour later than she had said she would.

Frequently, violent assaults are triggered by things that happened only in the batterer's imagination. Many violent men are tormented by sexual jealousy and imagine their wives are unfaithful at every conceivable opportunity with an unbelievable variety of men—landlords, elevator operators, bartenders, store clerks, neighbors, his relatives, her relatives, even total strangers. The most innocent and casual contact with a man can trigger a tirade of accusations of imagined infidelities, embroidered in pornographic detail, while he tries to beat or browbeat her into a confession and then beats her brutally because she finally does confess or because she doesn't.

A battered woman lives in a state that Dr. Elaine Hilberman has described as "constant anticipatory terror." As the tension builds and the danger signals increase, more and more of her energy must go into trying to anticipate what might set him off. She tries to control every minute detail of the household and her own behavior in the desperate hope of avoiding that one unpredictable trigger. Such women talk about walking on eggshells or living life on tiptoe. Everything she does, from frying an egg to expressing an opinion, becomes literally a life and death matter. The strain of it, and the emotional and physical toll it takes, are terrible and are made the more so by the inevitable failure of her efforts. While she knows that her physical safety, and quite possibly her very life, depend on trying to stave off the impending beating as long as possible, she also knows that she cannot ultimately prevent the explosion that her mate is building himself up to. He may blame his beatings on her failures and shortcomings, and he may sucker her into assuming that blame herself; but the fact is, what the woman does or does not do has virtually nothing to do with whether or when her husband will beat her.

Once an acute battering episode begins there is nothing she can do to stop it and very little she can do to control it. As Emerson Dobash and Russell Dobash point out, the usual techniques that people resort to, to avoid violent confrontations, do not work for battered women. The two primary techniques that sociologists have identified are withdrawing from the situation and agreement with the accusations that the aggressor is making. Withdrawal, however, as we have seen, is often impossible for an abused woman. Unlike a confrontation in a bar between two strangers, the problem isn't that he is feeling mean and might hit someone. The problem is that he specifically intends to hit *her*. There is seldom any place of refuge in a house or apartment from someone in determined pursuit; and even if she does manage to lock herself in the bathroom, she will eventually have to come out, and he will still be there. Fleeing out the door is seldom an option either. He can easily prevent her from leaving and can and will come after her if she does. Most of these serious assaults take place late at night when the woman has no place to go; and even if she can get away, she will often be reluctant to leave her children behind in a dangerous situation.

Agreeing with her husband's accusations is no more likely to succeed for, as Dobash and Dobash observe, "...there may be circumstances in which acceptance of the potential aggressor's definition of the situation will precipitate a violent reaction. Men described as 'norm enforcers'...actually see themselves as acting in a righteous and appropriate manner. They are carrying out justice in their eyes. A woman who agrees, either truthfully or falsely, to her husband's accusations regarding her supposed infidelity or failure to meet his needs may actually guarantee a violent punishment."

Other possible responses seem to be equally ineffective. Richard Gelles points out, in *The Violent Home*, that it seems to make no difference whether or not the assaulted woman fights back. Far from serving to diminish the violence, a woman's failure to fight back can leave her passively at the man's mercy for as long as he has the strength to keep on hitting her. Conversely, if a woman does try to fight back, she is likely to be punished for it with an even more vicious beating. The battered women in Eisenberg and Micklow's study who tried to defend themselves unanimously reported that the more resistance they put up, the more severely they were beaten.

Similarly, Walker's subjects indicated that arguing with the man often only enrages him further while, on the other hand, withdrawing into total silence may have exactly the same effect. Screaming or even crying or moaning likewise can make an attack more severe. Even raising her arms or hands to ward off blows may just result in their being twisted or broken. Study after study has revealed that, where escape is impossible, the only thing that a woman can do once a violent assault has begun is passively submit to it, protecting her most vulnerable parts as best she can by rolling herself into a ball, and just try to stay alive until it is over. As Lenore Walker succinctly points out, "According to reports from the battered women, only the batterers can end the second phase."

The third phase of the battering cycle consists, in some relationships, of a kind of honeymoon period, where the man is contrite and apologetic and often attempts to make amends with flowers and gifts and loving behavior. This seems to be particularly characteristic of the earlier years of an abusive marriage, when the man may still be genuinely remorseful and may be afraid that he has really gone too far this time and that his wife will leave him if he cannot manipulate her into forgiving him. Later in these marriages, and from the beginning in many others, the abusive man demonstrates no contrition whatsoever and either justifies his brutality as appropriate or insists that the whole family pretend that it never happens at all. In these relationships, it may be more accurate to characterize the third stage of the battering cycle as "an absence of tension or violence" and a return to apparently normal married life.

The third stage of the battering cycle may provide the woman a respite from immediate danger, but it does not necessarily bring any relief from her fear and anxiety. At the same time that she is trying to convince herself that this time the tranquility, and even happiness, will last she is constantly looking out for warning signs that the tension is beginning to build again toward its inevitable violent climax. Moreover, the fear generated by a serious beating does not just dissipate when the assault is over. It can continue to exist and effect the woman's outlook and behavior for a long time afterwards. She does not have to be facing an imminent second assault or even overtly threatening behavior to be constantly gripped by an utterly reasonable fear of her husband's violence.

Studies have found that battered women are nearly unanimous in their belief that their batterer is capable, physically and psychologically, of killing them. They have no doubt at all that their lives are in danger during serious assaults. For the battered woman who knows she is quite literally in a life or death situation, her very survival depends on her becoming extremely sensitive to cues. She must learn to read the danger signals of an impending attack, so that she can take whatever protective measures the situation permits: getting the children away, stashing a car key where she can grab it quickly, staying out of cul-de-sac rooms where she can be trapped, maneuvering to keep herself on the other side of large pieces of furniture. The earlier she is able to read the danger signals, the greater the likelihood that she will be able to keep herself alive and uninjured. Unfortunately, what may seem an obvious warning flag to her may later seem to be a lame justification to a jury. It is not at all unusual for a battered woman who kills her husband to explain that she knew that he was about to harm her seriously because he had the same expression on his face or look in his eye that he had when he hurt her badly in the past.

Similarly, a battered woman has no choice but to take her batterer's threats seriously. Threats of violence to come are frequently part of the tension-building period that precedes a serious assault, and she often has had painful first-hand experience of his willingness to carry out those threats. Death threats too must be taken seriously. Despite the arguments frequently made by prosecutors, the fact that he has made them before and has not actually killed her yet does not mean that she can or should assume that such threats are bluffs. She knows that the violence tends to escalate from episode to episode. She knows that he is capable of killing her. A threat to do worse harm to her in the future than he has done to her in the past is, from her point of view, absolutely credible. The death threats that batterers make, unlike the casual ones people sometimes toss into conversations or arguments, are *meant* to be believed. Often taking the form of detailed descriptions of what the man is going to do to her and how, and frequently accompanied by menacing behavior with a knife or gun, these threats are made with the specific intent of causing terror and hence compliance. Many batterers further reinforce the credibility of their death threats by engaging in a terrifying variety of "displaced" homicidal acts, such as killing pets, firing guns into walls and bed pillows, cutting up clothing and other personal possessions, and even digging graves and constructing coffins for their intended victims. The reader may recall Caroline Scott's boyfriend holding her child's teddy bear next to her head and firing a bullet through it. The message of this sort of behavior is always, "You may be next," and a battered woman would be crazy not to take it seriously.

As Hilberman and Munson have observed, "When husbands threaten homicide, they are taken at their word because threats and wishes become a reality with explosive suddenness." Peter Chimbos, in his study of spousal homicides in Canada, concluded that "threats to kill should especially not be dismissed as 'empty bluffs' or 'drunken ravings.'"

When a defendant who is a battered woman testifies that she was afraid her husband was going to injure or kill her, the fear she is referring to is not just the apprehension generated by the man's immediate actions, as though he were a stranger. Her fear is, rather, a reaction to everything that he has done to her before, the things that he has threatened to do, and the things that her experience has taught her he will likely do. The threats and verbal harangues and "little batterings" of the tension-building stage that lead so inexorably to a major beating may seem relatively trivial in themselves. But when they are recognized as part of a pattern they can be seen for what they are and what the battered woman knows they are: signals that worse violence is to come. Since the woman knows from her own painful experience that the next beating may well be worse than the last and that once it starts she will be powerless to stop it, it is not surprising that it is so often during the tension-building stage, when a severe beating looms but has not yet begun, that the woman seizes a weapon and acts to defend herself. What might appear at first glance to be an overreaction is an entirely reasonable response to the situation she actually faces, and indeed, if she cannot get away, may well be the *only* reasonable one.

II

A battered woman knows very well what her batterer has done to her in the past, what he has threatened to do, and what he is capable of doing to her now. But this is not the only part of her experience that affects her perception of the situation and the reasonableness of her response. If she is like the overwhelming majority of battered women, she also knows, first-hand, that she cannot rely on the police, the courts, neighbors, relatives, or anyone else for protection against her violent mate. Every attempt to get help is likely only to reinforce her perception that she has no alternative but to protect herself.

Most of us assume, without ever thinking about it, that if there were someone threatening to do us serious harm, we would have only to call for the police and they would come as fast as they could, arrest the wrongdoer and haul him away. Perhaps we would be right if our assailant were a stranger. But if there is one aspect of the battering experience that women report with more consistency than any other when they tell their stories, it is that calling the police seldom does them any good at all.

Getting the police to respond to a call for help is the first problem. "Domestic disturbance" complaints are assigned a very low priority by most police departments. Many battered women report that a call to the police for help may not be responded to for many hours and, alarmingly often, may not be responded to at all. The United States Civil Rights Commission, in its 1982 investigation of the problems that battered women face in the legal system, found this problem to be widespread. In its report, *Under The Rule of Thumb*, the Commission cited one study from Kentucky that found that police failed to respond at all to 17 percent of all calls they received from battered women. Another police officer testified before the Commission that in his department, police would respond in person to only one out of five or six such calls. If the assault appeared to be already over, it was his department's policy merely to inform the caller of the various social agencies that she could contact the next business day and how to get to the courthouse to file a complaint.

In their study of 2096 battered women in Texas, Stacey and Shupe found that police failed to respond to calls from battered women in an astonishing one case out of three. The problem of getting the police to come when a woman calls for help is so pervasive that some shelter workers and crisis line operators advise battered women not to let the police know when she calls them that the man menacing her is her husband or they advise her to tell them that he is armed even if he isn't.

Even if a battered woman succeeds in getting the police to answer her call, there is often very little the police will, or can, do to protect her. The overwhelming majority of domestic assaults are treated by the police and the courts as misdemeanors, even where quite serious injuries have been inflicted. Unlike a felony, for which the police can arrest a suspect on probable cause, in many states the police must actually witness the commission of a misdemeanor before they can make an arrest. Thus, when a woman calls the police because a man is threatening to attack her or because he has already attacked her, the police may have no power to arrest the man when they get there unless he is foolish enough to assault her again in their presence or to turn his rage against the policemen. Many battered women have pointed bitterly to the fact that the police will not arrest a man for beating up his wife but will haul him to jail without hesitation if he so much as shakes a fist at them.

Another problem is that when the police do answer a "domestic disturbance" complaint they seldom make any official report of it if no one is arrested. This has turned out to be especially troublesome for battered women defendants in self-defense cases. The lack of any police reports about the calls for help she claims she made can lead the jury to believe she is lying, not only about the calls but about the violence as well.

Some states do permit the police to arrest for a violent misdemeanor that they have not witnessed if they have probable cause to believe that the suspect committed it. More and more states are changing their laws to allow this, specifically in response to the urging of advocates for battered women. However, giving the police the authority to make such arrests does not mean that they will actually do so. In fact, arrests in domestic assault cases are relatively rare, despite all of the attention that this problem has received in recent years. The most recent federal government study of the issue, the *Final Report of the Attorney General's Task Force on Family Violence,* published in September of 1984, still points to police failure to make arrests as one of the most serious aspects of the problem of domestic violence.

The police give a variety of reasons for this. One of the most frequently cited is that battered women seldom follow through in pressing charges against their violent mates, so that the police officer's time and risk and considerable paperwork all go for nought. In addition, the police know that a man arrested for a misdemeanor will be released on bail or more likely on his own recognizance almost as soon as he is in the stationhouse, so that arresting him serves very little purpose save buying a few hours time. Many policemen do not regard domestic assaults as criminal matters. They see their role in these situations as trying to get everybody to stop fighting and calm down—in other words, "social work" not "police work." They often assume, with the rest of our society, that if a woman can't get along with her husband, her appropriate recourse is to hire a lawyer and get a divorce, not to expect the police to be marriage counselors. Hence the common practice of the police telling a bewildered, beaten woman that her problem is a civil matter and that there is nothing that they can do.

These attitudes are reinforced by official police department policies in many places. What little formal training officers receive in handling domestic assaults tends to focus on techniques for defusing these situations rather than making arrests in what are apt to be volatile and dangerous circumstances. Many police departments have explicit or tacit nonarrest policies and others have what have come to be called "stitch rules" which specify how serious an injury a victim must have sustained, measured by how many stitches were required, to justify an arrest of her assailant. Some studies indicate that, in fact, the likelihood of an arrest being made in an assault situation is directly related to the degree of acquaintance between the assailant and the victim. Arrest rates are highest where the parties are total strangers, lowest where they are married.

It is quite inaccurate to assume, moreover, that police failure to respond and failure to arrest are merely mechanisms for screening out relatively trivial cases. On the contrary, this combination of police policies and attitudes results too often in all domestic violence complaints being treated as trivial, and it fails to take into account the extreme seriousness of much of the violence that battered women are subjected to and its escalating nature. The consequences can be lethal.

In 1973, the Police Foundation conducted a study in Kansas City to explore the relationship between domestic disturbance calls to the police and the crimes of homicide and aggravated assault. The study concluded that "there appears to be a distinct relationship between domestic-related homicides and aggravated assaults and prior police interventions for disputes and disturbances." Indeed, the study found that in the two-year period preceding the homicides that they studied, the police had responded to at least one disturbance call at the address where the killing occurred in 85 percent of the cases. In fully 50 percent of the cases they had responded to five or more such calls in the same two-year period.

Even in such extreme cases, when police failure to protect a battered woman results in her being killed by her batterer, the courts have upheld the right of the police to exercise their discretion not to make arrests or to answer the call at all. Ruth Bunnell, for example, in the year before her death, had called the police no fewer than twenty times for protection against her violent estranged husband. Her calls had resulted in only a single arrest. The night she was killed, Mr. Bunnell telephoned her and told her he was coming over to her house to kill her. She called the police and begged them to come right away. They refused, telling her to call them back when her husband got to the house. She was never able to make the second call. When her husband got there he stabbed her to death.

Ms. Bunnell's estate brought a wrongful death action against the San Jose police department, but the California courts held that California police departments enjoy absolute immunity from such lawsuits. The state Court of Appeals ruled that despite Ruth Bunnell's repeated calls for protection and Mark Bunnell's previous arrest (from which the police ought to have been on notice that a dangerous situation existed), there was no "special relationship" between her and the police that implied any promise on the department's part to protect her.

For a woman to call the police at all when she is the victim of ongoing violence by a brutal mate is an act of enormous courage and defiance. In seeking outside protection, she may very well be putting herself in even greater danger because the risk of her husband's taking violent retribution against her is very real. Indeed, he may quite specifically have threatened to kill her if she ever tried. It sometimes takes a battered woman years to simultaneously find both the opportunity and the nerve to make that call. One can only imagine, then, how devastating it is for a badly beaten woman to call the police for help only to have them fail to arrive or to arrive and do nothing. She is left, alone, having to face or somehow to hide from a man even more enraged than he was when he assaulted her in the first place. And society's message to both of them is clear: a man can beat his woman up all he wants and not suffer any consequences; a woman who is beaten by her man cannot rely on the police to protect her.

If a battered woman perseveres in her quest for protection and prevails upon the police to make an arrest or else goes down to the courthouse and insists on filing a complaint herself, the results are likely to do little more than reinforce this message. The findings of both recent major government studies, by the Civil Rights Commission and the Office of the Attorney General, confirm the conclusions of many other researchers and observers: the criminal justice system fails the battered woman at every turn.

Decisions about whether criminal charges will be brought against the subject of a complaint, what charges to bring, and whether to pursue the case to trial or settle or divert it are made by the prosecutor. He or she has virtually unlimited discretion in these matters, and any number of studies show that this discretion is far more apt to be exercised to keep domestic assault cases out of the courts than to prosecute them. The Civil Rights Commission identified several reasons for this. Many prosecutors, they found, share with the police and the rest of our society the view that wife beating is not a real crime or not important enough for the criminal courts to bother with. Some also believe that women who file complaints are merely seeking to use the criminal justice system vindictively to settle quarrels or manipulate their husbands. Eisenberg and Micklow suggest, in addition, that prosecutors tend to avoid these cases because of the lack of prestige associated with them in criminal trial circles. As we have seen in the area of police willingness to arrest, the likelihood of a prosecutor filing charges and following through in an assault case is much lower if the accused and his victim are married or involved in a present or past romantic relationship.

By far the most common reason that proscecutors give for declining to prosecute wife-beaters is their belief that the women will subsequently change their minds and drop the charges. This does happen, of course, and probably more frequently than in cases where the accused criminal is a stranger to the victim. The battering husband is usually released on his own recognizance pending a trial date which may be weeks or months away. During that period, whether she has gone back to live with him or not, her batterer is apt to bring intense pressure on her, through threats or protestations of remorse, to drop the charges. Especially if she is still trying to keep the marriage together or if she and her children are dependent on his paycheck for food and shelter, she may well decide that pressing the charges through to trial is not really in her interest. But in those cities where vigorous victim advocate programs provide battered women with support and help in negotiating their way through the often baffling and intimidating criminal court system, the number of complaints dismissed by victims declines dramatically. This indicates that the widely shared assumption of prosecutors that battered women will drop charges is very much a self-fulfilling prophecy. As sociologist Murray Straus observed to the Civil Rights Commission, the explanation that battered women will drop the charges provides

> a ready excuse for the police, prosecuting attorney, and judges to follow their "natural" inclinations of treating wife beating as "domestic disturbances" (i.e. not really a crime) rather than as assaults. This in turn sets up a vicious cycle. Since the cases are defined as not really crimes, or as crimes not likely to be successfully prosecuted, women are discouraged from filing charges and encounter foot dragging when they attempt to pursue such charges. As a result, the many who would bring charges if not dissuaded, or who would follow through if obstacles and foot dragging did not occur, do not.

The obstacles and foot dragging can be formidable. Some district attorney's offices require a "cooling off" period of several days or weeks between the assault and the filing of the formal charges. Others have their own "stitch" rules or will only file charges if the man used a weapon or the woman was hospitalized. Many prosecutors require the beaten woman to convince them that she is a "worthy" victim, that she did nothing to provoke the attack, for example, so that *her* behavior rather than the batterer's becomes the key issue. Some refuse to prosecute unless the woman agrees to file for a divorce. Most district attorney's offices require that the woman actually sign a criminal complaint, a legally unnecessary requirement and one not applied to the victims of violent crimes committed by strangers. Cases that could be filed as felonies are often filed as misdemeanors, and serious misdemeanors are reduced to less serious ones such as "disturbing the peace." Batterers are diverted into inappropriate mediation or counselling programs, and in some cities virtually all domestic violence complaints are turned over to family bureaus or domestic divisions for informal settlement and never get to court at all. Charges are dismissed altogether with no notice to, or consultation with, the victim. By far the most common response to a woman's seeking to get charges filed against her violent husband or boyfriend, however, is a flat refusal by the prosecutor to prosecute him at all.

District attorneys, of course, are interested in winning cases, which they tend to define as obtaining both convictions and stiff sentences for those accused. In domestic violence cases, they are likely to obtain neither one because the same attitudes about the noncriminal nature of wife beating and the sanctity of marriage that police and prosecutors exhibit are likely to be shared by the judges who try them. By one estimate, only one domestic violence case in one hundred ever reaches a courtroom. The few that do get there are treated by judges as relatively trivial matters although the cases that manage to make it through the screening, discouragement, and diversion tend to be the most serious ones. If the man is found guilty at all, he is most likely to be given a suspended sentence or fined a small amount and placed on probation. In many places he can avoid any kind of criminal penalty by agreeing to undertake a mediation or counselling program. Many batterers, perhaps most, are released simply on a promise to the judge not to do it again. Although in most jurisdictions the possible jail time for a serious misdemeanor is as much as a year, jail sentences of even a few days are practically unheard of. Mildred Pagelow reports, for example, that in her sample of 350 battered women, not a single one reported filing charges that were carried through to trial, sentencing, and jail. The U.S. Civil Rights Commission concluded that one of the major problems with seeking to get protection for battered women through the criminal courts is the attitude of so many judges that wife beating is not a serious social problem or a serious criminal offense.

All along the line in her search for protection, a battered woman is apt to be told that her problem is really a civil matter; but civil remedies offer her little more protection than criminal ones. Traditionally, the two main noncriminal remedies available to a battered woman have been restraining orders, which require the abuser to leave the woman alone, and peace bonds, which require the abuser to put up a sum of money that he forfeits if he misbehaves again. Both of these remedies have serious drawbacks. Restraining orders in many states are only available to a married woman who files for a divorce. Consequently, battered women who are trying to keep their marriages together, as well as women who are not married or no longer married to their abusers, have no access to them. Restraining orders can seldom be obtained without the assistance and expense of a lawyer, the payment of filing fees and process servers, and a court hearing ten days after the petition for an order is filed—a dangerous delay.

There is a great deal of confusion about the enforcement of restraining orders. Police are frequently unwilling to arrest a man for violating a restraining order unless the violation occurs in the officer's presence. If the woman has no certified copy of the order to show them, for example because her husband has simply torn it up, there is nothing that the police can do; records of such orders are seldom kept on police computers. Many police departments refuse to treat the violation of such an order as a crime, even where state laws make it so. They will advise a battered woman who calls them and produces a copy of an order that they cannot enforce it. They tell her she should call her lawyer to file "contempt of court" charges—which of course involves more expense, more delay, and another hearing which is unlikely to result in any real sanctions against the batterer anyway.

Although peace bonds are apparently still used quite frequently in a few states, they have fallen into disuse in most places because they raise serious questions of constitutional rights. Under most peace bond statutes, a person who has behaved violently in the past and appears likely to behave violently again is required to post a bond guaranteeing his future good behavior. If he is unable to come up with the money for the bond, he can be jailed until he does. This is a scheme that presents any number of constitutional problems involving both due process and equal protection, particularly in the way that it discriminates against impoverished defendants, and no doubt deserves the relative obscurity into which it has lapsed.

In the last few years, the legislatures of almost every state have passed domestic violence legislation in an attempt to provide a civil remedy to battered women that does not suffer from the problems of these more traditional ones. Most states now permit the issuance of a protective order for a victim of domestic violence, requiring the abuser to cease his abuse; and, in some cases, he must move out of the family home and have no further contact with his victim. Such orders are available to women who have not filed for divorce or are not married to their batterers, although the exact kind of relationships covered varies from state to state. These laws also make very clear who has jurisdiction to enforce them and what the penalties are. Most of them provide for an emergency procedure under which a temporary order can be issued by a judge prior to a full-fledged hearing, so that a woman can have immediate protection.

While protective orders are certainly a better remedy than battered women previously have had in the civil courts, they have not yet proved to be a panacea. The U.S. Civil Rights Commission found that, in many states, resistance by judges has undermined the expected functioning of these domestic abuse laws. Judges were found, in particular, to be unwilling to issue eviction orders and emergency orders although the laws clearly provided for them. Punishments imposed for violating protection orders are often light or nonexistent. The whole purpose of the orders—quick action, sure punishment, and placing the onus of leaving the home on the wrongdoer rather than the victim—has frequently been vitiated.

The simple truth is that our society does not protect battered women from their abusers. Every battered woman who has ever called the police only to have them fail to arrive or fail to arrest the man who has beaten her knows this. Every battered woman who has had her husband arrested only to have him be released an hour later and come home in a rage and beat her again knows this. Every battered woman who has tried to have her abuser prosecuted, only to be talked out of it by a district attorney or threatened with death or disfigurement by her abuser if she doesn't drop the charges knows it. Every battered woman who, against all odds, presses assault charges through to trial, only to have her tormentor suffer no penalty at all and be turned loose in exchange for a bare promise not to hit her again, knows it.

A battered woman's attempts to obtain protection from a violent mate often only serve to reinforce her own sense of vulnerability. No one is going to stop the man from hurting her again. No one will stop him from killing her if he wants to. The knowledge that she cannot rely on society to protect her from the violence that occurs in her own home cannot help but affect a battered woman's perception of the danger she is in when another serious attack is imminent. It is hardly unreasonable for her to conclude that if she is to be protected at all, she must seize whatever means is at hand to protect herself.

III

Perhaps the question most frequently asked about a battered woman who finally resorts to lethal force to defend herself against a violent man is, Why didn't she leave? Why did she stay with someone so awful and allow a situation to develop that could only be resolved by taking a life?

In the context of the law of self-defense, it is essential to understand that there is no legal rule whatsoever that would obligate her to do so. As we have seen, some states require a person to back away from a fight or try to escape from a threatened assault, but this retreat requirement only applies to what takes place at the very moment of a specific confrontation. The law has always been clear, on the other hand, that a person has no obligation to rearrange her or his entire life, or even inconvenience himself, in order to avoid a situation in which the need to act in self-defense might arise. Specifically, one has no obligation to avoid or vacate a place where one has a legal right to be.

The old cases that established this legal principle were concerned with the sorts of situations that men found themselves in. A man had a right to travel down a road, for example, although someone he had quarreled with had threatened to kill him if he travelled along it again. A man who had been threatened by another could strap on his guns and go about his business. He could not be expected to cower at home or curtail his activities to avoid even a lethal confrontation. Modern self-defense cases involving male defendants show no retreat from this principle. As one commentator has noted, a man is never asked to account for the fact that he continued to associate with someone whom he knew to be violent or who had attacked him in the past—nor are men ever expected to justify the fact that they frequent places, such as rough bars, where violent confrontations are likely to arise.

The same principle, of course, must apply to a woman who is threatened with harm in a violent domestic situation. In no way whatsoever does she waive her legal right to act in self-defense because she has chosen, for whatever reasons, to stay in her own home.

Although the question of why she didn't leave her violent mate should not even arise during a trial in which a woman is arguing that she killed her partner in self-defense, it is, in fact, a question that causes jurors a great deal of difficulty when they are asked to find such a woman's actions reasonable. It is often extremely hard for jurors to understand why just walking out the door is not the simple solution to domestic violence that it may appear to be at first glance. Their difficulty is compounded by the tendency of prosecutors in women's self-defense cases to harp repeatedly on the woman's failure to leave, or failure to leave soon enough, or failure to stay gone once she did leave, in order to argue that she was not really afraid or that the threatened harm was not all that serious or that the woman did not mind—or may even have welcomed—the beatings.

Explaining to a jury why many battered women don't leave their husbands and, specifically, why *this* battered woman didn't leave her husband can be one of the most crucial and difficult tasks in the defense of a woman who kills her violent mate, although the question is legally irrelevant. It arises from a fundamental and widespread misunderstanding of the emotional complexity of most battered women's reactions to physical abuse by a partner. To ask, "But why didn't she just leave?" is to assume that leaving, immediately and permanently, is the normal and reasonable response to being battered; that leaving will end the violence; and if a woman fails to leave, her staying with her mate is peculiar behavior that requires explanation or excuse.

Leaving and staying are not simply two cut and dried alternatives, however, but are aspects of a whole range of strategies that a battered woman may employ to try to deal with her situation. A woman who chooses to stay may stay and merely put up with the violence. She may stay and try to change her husband's behavior or develop tactics to avoid or deflect as much of the violence as possible. She may stay and seek outside intervention in the marriage, through counselling or calling the police or obtaining a restraining order. She may stay because she is too terrified to try to get away. She may leave for brief periods to let things cool down and then return. She may go home to her parents or to a friend's for overnight or for a few days, to demonstrate her disapproval of her mate's treatment of her and her unwillingness to tolerate it. She may go to a shelter for a week or two, unsure of whether she will return or try to make a real break. She may institute a legal separation or file for a divorce, either because she really intends to leave permanently or to give her bargaining power as she tries to negotiate a change in circumstances if she comes back. She may leave with no intention of returning only to be hunted down and dragged back by force or at gunpoint or coerced into coming back to prevent the man from harming her children or killing himself. Except for those women who fall at the outer extremes of this continuum—those who helplessly submit to violence from the outset and those who leave at the first blow and never return—most battered women try a number of these strategies, sometimes all of them, during the course of a violent relationship.

It should not be surprising that many women, probably most, choose to stay and try to work things out, especially in the early years of a marriage when violence usually first appears. Most people expect to stay married forever, and battered women are no different. They love their husbands. They care about their homes and families.

They want more than anything to hold their marriages together, not to break them apart. Staying in a marriage that is less than perfect—"for better or for worse"—is hardly deviant behavior. It is what our society still expects of people and what, though perhaps less so than in the past, people still expect of themselves.

When violence first appears in her marriage, a woman's initial reaction is apt to be shock, followed by rationalization. She tells herself that his behavior was an aberration and that it will not happen again. She listens to him telling her the same thing and willingly believes him. Jean Giles-Sims found that fully 93 percent of her sample of battered women were willing to forgive and forget the first beating that they suffered from their partners.

As the relationship goes on and the violence continues and escalates, the woman often engages in a combination of optimism and denial when she regards her situation that keeps her in it despite the pain and suffering she has to endure. The optimism of many battered women about the likelihood of their mate's changing his behavior and everybody living happily ever after is phenomenal. Even in the face of mounting evidence that the violence is not going to stop and nothing that she does or does not do can really affect his behavior toward her, she goes on believing that there must be some magic formula (if she can only find it) that will cause him to stop hitting her and go on loving her.

Along with this unfounded optimism goes a complex system of rationalization and denial that the situation is what it appears to be. Hilberman and Munson delineate four forms that this denial usually takes. The woman may tell herself that violence is a normal aspect of married life. If the woman comes from a background in which there was family violence, either between her parents or against herself, she may be more prone to adopt this view. Some battered women are kept so isolated by their husbands that they have no way to compare their marriages to those of other people and have no friends to talk with who might tell or show them that violence is not something that every married woman must simply tolerate.

Second, a battered woman can find any number of ways to excuse or rationalize her mate's behavior. She can tell herself that the problem is not really his violence but alcohol; if only he wouldn't drink, he wouldn't abuse her. She can blame every beating on some stressful outside event: he had a fight with his boss, got a traffic ticket, lost his job. She can rationalize that he is sick or unstable or mentally ill. She can, in short, buy into his view of his own behavior and blame the violence on anything except him.

Or she can buy into his view of *her* own behavior and blame herself. The third aspect of a battered woman's denial of the reality of her situation is the belief that the violence is justified. He beats her to punish her for her bad behavior, real or imagined. He beats her because she drives him to it, with her stupidity and incompetence and refusal to shut up. If she were only a better person, he wouldn't beat her the way he does.

Finally, a battered woman may tell herself that she really does have the violence under control or will with a little more effort. She need only be perfectly good, totally compliant, utterly silent, and unfailingly sensitive to his every need; and he will not beat her any more.

The battered woman's optimism and rationalizations are ways to cope with her fear. They allow her to minimize and explain away her partner's violence and focus instead on the good times that still come in between the bad ones. Batterers are not subhuman monsters. In between their rages, they are often charming, thoughtful, and affectionate men. Lenore Walker has pointed out how crucial a batterer's behavior following a serious beating can be to convincing a woman to stay in a violent relationship. Many batterers, especially in the earlier years of such relationships, exhibit great remorse after a beating, promising that it will never happen again and lavishing their victims with flowers, gifts, and other loving gestures. Any intention of leaving she may have had fades away in a renewal of optimism that this time he really means it. Even when this kind of extravagant contrition is lacking, many women are able to find the same reinforcement of their optimism simply in the return to what appears to them to be a normal marriage.

As we have seen, once it begins, wife beating usually escalates. Over time, the beatings become more frequent and more severe. As they begin to acknowledge to themselves that the battering is behavior that is not going to change and that (despite the techniques they have developed for coping with the violence) the likelihood of their being seriously injured or killed is increasing, many battered women seem to have one of two reactions. Some begin to work toward leaving the relationship and some, seeing no way out, lapse into passivity and despair.

It is a rare battered woman who simply decides one day that she is leaving, packs her bags, grabs her kids, and walks out the door. Leaving a violent marriage, like leaving any marriage, is likely to be a gradual process rather than a sudden event. In this, a battered woman is no different from anyone else who leaves a relationship in which she or he has a large emotional investment. Walking away from a marriage, even an unhappy one, is not an easy thing to do.

Researchers have observed that a woman's decision to leave, or try to leave, is apt to be precipitated by a number of specific developments. The first is that the violence has become so serious that she can no longer deny that she is in real danger. Another is that her children have begun to be involved, as victims of the man's violence themselves or as potential victims because they have begun to try to intervene on her behalf. Several researchers have noted that learning that a daughter is being sexually abused by the batterer is often the event that triggers a woman's decision to get out. The unfortunate fact is that our society offers far more support for a woman's decision to leave a marriage to protect her children than to protect herself. Jean Giles-Sims has remarked on the key role the presence of some kind of outside support for her decision to leave plays for a woman torn between leaving and staying. In addition, Lenore Walker and others have observed that as a violent marriage progresses, the batterer's loving, remorseful behavior following battering episodes tends to dwindle, so there is less reinforcement for her to stay despite the beatings.

All of the studies agree that leaving a battering relationship is most often a gradual process. The woman leaves and returns and leaves again, often several times before making a permanent break, if she ever does. While this is no different from the pattern that marks the ending of most relationships—breakups, reconciliations, broken promises, breakups again—it is a phenomenon that puzzles and infuriates many casual observers and certainly perplexes jurors. As Russell and Emerson Dobash have noted,

> Surmounting all of these obstacles and making a final break is truly a leviathan task, and even the most determined fail numerous times before succeeding. Yet many people believe that a woman gets only one chance to leave; if she fails, she does not deserve another. Rather than being seen as a necessary part of the process of leaving a marriage and a reflection of the difficulties of doing so, leaving a marriage and

then returning is usually viewed as a sign of capriciousness or lack of sincerity, resolve, or determination on the woman's part.

Even when the woman has gotten past the point of denying or rationalizing her partner's behavior and has come to see that the children would really be better off without this kind of father, there are still formidable obstacles to her getting away and staying away. Some of these are practical. She is likely to have no money of her own, no job skills adequate to support herself and her children, no place to go. She may have relations or friends who will give her shelter for a time; but they are unlikely to take her in permanently, especially if she has children. Many battered women report that the response of their parents to a plea for such help is something like a brusque, "You made your bed, now you lie in it." If her husband has threatened to injure or kill anyone who helps her, she may be unwilling to utilize what help is available in order to protect other people from danger. It takes money to rent an apartment: often the first and last month's rent and a damage deposit can add up to an impossible thousand dollars or more in many cities. And it can take days or weeks of searching to find an inexpensive apartment that will allow children. Waiting lists for public housing are often months or years long. The process of getting on public assistance is often formidable, especially if she is still legally married. Battered women's shelters, which can help a woman solve some of these problems and provide her a safe respite while she plans her future, are few, especially outside the major cities; and they cannot begin to take in as many women as need their services. Most are chronically full, with waiting lists of their own.

Although these practical problems can be daunting, many studies have shown that a primary reason that women don't leave their violent husbands is fear. They are afraid, and with very good reason, that they will be killed if they try to leave. The question, "Why didn't she leave?" implies that leaving is the obvious way to safety, but the gruesome fact is that leaving may be the most dangerous thing a battered woman can do.

It is often difficult for people unfamiliar with the phenomenon to understand that men in violent relationships do not want to let the woman go. It would seem reasonable to suppose that a man who beats his wife over and over again must despise her and would be glad to see the last of her. In fact, the situation is apt to be just the opposite. Although far less is known about the psychological dynamics of men who batter than about women who are battered, one common characteristic of batterers is very clear: they are men who are desperately dependent emotionally on the women in their lives. Often the batterer's greatest fear, ironic though it may seem, is that the woman whom he treats so brutally may leave him. He is apt to punish her mercilessly for any display of independence that might presage a desertion. Many battered women report being hunted down by husbands they have tried to leave and forced at gunpoint to return and face a savage beating for their transgression. It is not at all unusual for a batterer to threaten to kill his victim if she ever leaves him, to kill anyone who helps her if she does, to kill all the children and to kill himself as well.

These threats cannot be dismissed as idle theatrics. In Wolfgang's findings, 41 percent of all women who were homicide victims were wives killed by their husbands, whereas only 10 percent of male homicide victims were husbands killed by their wives. Another 21 percent of women homicide victims were killed by men with whom they had a nonmarital sexual relationship, compared with fewer than 7 percent of the male victims. Clearly, if a woman has reason to fear being murdered by anybody, it is by a man she has an intimate relationship with. Furthermore, studies of domestic homicides show that the point at which a man most often kills a woman is when it appears that the woman is abandoning him, emotionally or physically.

In a study of spousal homicides in Florida, for example, Dr. George Barnard and his colleagues found that the most frequent type of killing of wives by husbands was what they characterized as "sex-role threat" homicides. These are killings triggered by things that the man perceives as threatening his dominant masculine role. "In some cases, the threat is reported to be a potential or actual desertion. In other cases, the threat is the denial of the right that the eventual killer believed he had to dominate his wife and exercise control over her actions. In other cases the threats are intertwined." The killings were triggered by "a walkout, a demand, a threat of separation [which] were taken by the men to represent intolerable desertion, rejection and abandonment. Thus...the threat of separation is usually the trigger for violence in these cases." Ominously, most of the males in the study were in fact separated from their wives when they killed them. It was precisely the fact that they had left these violent men that put the wive's lives in deadly danger.

Similarly, a Virginia study of male spouse-murderers found that in all but one case, the killing came shortly after the wife had made it clear that she intended to end the marriage. In many of these marriages the wife had left the husband before and then returned, but in the final episode she had served him with divorce papers or flatly rejected his attempts at one more reconciliation. The husbands were men who were extremely dependent emotionally on their wives and were unable to tolerate the sense of rejection and abandonment they felt at their wives' threatened departure. Although every one either knew or believed that his wife was being unfaithful, it was not the real or imagined infidelity that triggered his lethal assault but the leaving.

Dr. Robert Simon, a Washington, D.C., psychiatrist, studied the relationships of a group of murderers in that city to their victims. The second most numerous classification was the one he labelled Type AB: these were all males who had a long-term relationship with their victims which was "characterized by deep dependency with strong sadistic trends toward the victim. The threat of separation by the victim was usually the trigger for violence."

One reason most frequently cited by battered women for staying in violent relationships is fear. As these studies make clear, a battered woman's perception that the only choice she has is between staying and being beaten and leaving and being killed is an utterly realistic one. It should hardly be surprising that many of them decide to stay.

IV

The list of circumstances that weigh against a battered woman's ability to get out of a violent relationship is formidable: fear of death, not just her own but her children's, her relatives' and friends' and her husband's; isolation that deprives her not only of help and support but of other relationships against which to measure the abnormality of her own; psychological battering which undermines her sense of self-worth and causes her to place the blame for the treatment she receives on her own inadequacies; lack of money, job skills, transportation, or any place to go; fear that she is incapable of living and raising her children alone; love for her husband and commitment to her marriage and family. The combined effect of these factors is often absolutely overwhelming. Thwarted in every attempt to get help, despairing of ever being able to leave, many battered women simply seem to give up and resign themselves to their fate, lapsing into a state of depression and utter helplessness.

Emerson and Russell Dobash have described the downward spiral thus:

> Each successive violent episode leaves the woman with less hope, less self-esteem and more fear. The positive aspects of the relationship become weaker and the man becomes accustomed to beating his wife and inured to the sight of her pain. By and large the husband ceases to see himself as engaged in anything wrong or unjust. The woman's struggle to change the pattern of violence through adaptations in her own behavior is almost invariably ineffective because she is engaged in an impossible and false struggle: the problem of wife beating is primarily the husband's problem. When women's efforts fail, as they must, their isolation from outside sources of support or assistance leave them with an overwhelming sense of hopelessness...
>
> It is at this low point that many women entirely cease to struggle to improve the relationship. They cease to argue and to defend themselves from even the most blatantly false accusations or unjust treatments in the hope that they will avoid an escalation of violence.

According to Del Martin,

> If things go wrong, well-trained wives feel ashamed for having failed their husbands in some way. They may even believe they deserve their beatings. Attempting to improve, but failing to end the beatings, they sink further and further into despair and misery. When such women do seek outside help and, as is usually the case, do not receive it, their circumstances begin to seem utterly hopeless. They feel trapped and regard attempts at freeing themselves as futile.

Next to not leaving, this tendency of some battered women to give up and cease trying to do anything at all to remedy their situation appears to be the one that most perplexes and frustrates jurors in women's self-defense cases. They seem to have a hard time perceiving the woman's fear as real and reasonable when she not only did not leave but did not persist in trying to change her situation or get help from anyone. Dr. Lenore Walker has drawn on the psychological theory of "learned helplessness" to explain this phenomenon. Experimental psychologist Marvin Seligman and his colleagues developed the concept of learned helplessness to explain the fact that dogs and other animals subjected to electric shocks that they are powerless to control will soon cease to try to control the shocks; later, if they are placed in a situation where they can control or escape the shock, they do not try to do so. Seligman postulated that they learn (from their earlier experience) that they are helpless; and even when they no longer are in fact helpless, they still perceive themselves to be and act, or decline to act, accordingly. Similar results have been obtained experimentally using human subjects and Seligman has suggested learned helplessness as one source of externally caused depression, anxiety, and loss of the will to live in humans.

Dr. Walker suggests that a battered woman's experiences teach her that nothing that she does will have any effect on her batterer's behavior. No matter how hard she tries to please him or appease him, fight back against him, or apply social sanctions to stop his violence, he will always beat her again when he feels compelled to. A battered woman thus learns that she is helpless and gives up any effort to help herself although her perception may be wrong; there may, in fact, be things, such as going to a shelter, that she might do to alleviate her situation.

> Once we believe we cannot control what happens to us, it is difficult to believe we can ever influence it, even if later we experience a favorable outcome. This concept is important for understanding why battered women do not attempt to free themselves from a battering relationship. Once the women are operating from a belief of helplessness, the perception becomes reality and they become passive, submissive, "helpless." They allow things that appear to them to be out of control actually to get out of control. When one listens to descriptions of battering incidents from battered women, it often seems as if these women were not as helpless as they perceived themselved to be. However, their behavior was determined by their negative cognitive set, or their perceptions of what they could or could not do, not by what actually existed. The battered women's behavior appears similar to Seligman's dogs, rats and people.

Other experts have pointed out that a pervasive sense of helplessness and virtual emotional paralysis is a very common aftermath of experiencing a traumatic, life-threatening event. Angela Browne, in a review of a number of studies, notes that victims of violent crimes, combat veterans, survivors of natural disasters, concentration camp inmates, and people who have been held in hostage situations all seem to go through a similar reaction pattern characterized by fear, anger, denial, disbelief, and acute feelings of powerlessness and helplessness. When life-threatening danger is immediate, they focus entirely on survival and self-preservation rather than flight. They often become depressed and apathetic, withdrawn and passive, so that they are unable to accurately assess their situation or take appropriate measures to escape their peril. Feelings of fear, helplessness, and confusion can linger for months after the traumatic event that precipitated them is over.

These reactions are, in fact, so typical that the American Psychiatric Association, in its current *Diagnostic and Statistical Manual*, has recognized a condition that it labels Post-Traumatic Stress Disorder, which consists of the development of a characteristic set of symptoms following the experience of a psychologically traumatic event. The kind of event that gives rise to the disorder is something that is beyond the ordinary range of unhappy human experiences like divorce or the death of a loved one. These triggering events include natural disasters like floods and earthquakes, accidental man-made disasters like plane crashes and major fires, and deliberate man-made disasters such as rape and assault, torture, death camps, and military bombardment. It makes no difference whether the victim is a single individual or a member of a larger group. Human-generated traumas seem to produce a more severe and long-lasting reaction than natural disasters do.

The primary symptoms of Post-Traumatic Stress Disorder include the constant re-experiencing of the event, through intrusive, vivid recollections as well as in dreams and nightmares, and a kind of "psychic numbing" or "emotional anesthesia" that is characterized by a diminished responsiveness to events in the outside world. In addition, there are apt to be a variety of other symptoms such as hyperalertness, sleep disturbance, nightmares, impaired memory, and difficulty in concentrating or completing tasks. Taken together, the symptoms of post-traumatic stress can seriously impair a sufferer's ability to function normally in everyday life. Anxiety and depression are frequent associated symptoms as well, and are sometimes severe enough to be diagnosed and treated as additional psychiatric disorders.

Dr. Elaine Hilberman has described the effects of what she calls Stress-Response Syndrome in every one of the battered women she studied:

> In contrast to their dreams, in which they actively attempted to protect themselves, the waking lives of these women were characterized by overwhelming passivity and inability to act. They were drained, fatigued, and numb, without the energy to do more than minimal household chores and child care. They had a pervasive sense of

hopelessness and despair about themselves and their lives. They saw themselves as incompetent, unworthy, and unlovable and were ridden with guilt and shame. They thought they deserved the abuse, saw no options, and felt powerless to make changes.

Interest in Post-Traumatic Stress Disorder has intensified in recent years because it has been so commonly associated with Vietnam veterans, but, as the *Diagnostic and Statistical Manual* makes clear, the phenomenon is not limited to combat survivors. Many victims of life-threatening traumas, including battered women and rape victims, suffer the identical severe reaction to their appalling experiences. What jurors and others interpret as a battered woman's helpless, hopeless acquiesence in her situation is often just the "emotional anesthesia" that is characteristic of any human being's attempt to cope with a close brush with violent death.

Psychological concepts like learned helplessness and post-traumatic stress may be helpful in explaining to juries why some battered women seem to accept their fate so passively. Many feminists, however, are troubled by this "clinicalization" of battered women, with its implicit view that their response to violence is negative behavior that stems from weakness or emotional damage and requires explanation in clinical terms. They point out that what may appear to some to be a puzzling passivity on the part of many battered women is often, in fact, an exhibition of quiet strength. Battered women manage to go on functioning in incredibly difficult circumstances. They keep their households running, nurture and protect their children, often hold down jobs, and suffer their pain and injuries in silence. They maintain their sanity and keep themselves alive. The courage and perserverance that many of them display in the face of ongoing danger—and often daunting violence—would surely be considered heroic in any other set of circumstances.

6

Expert Testimony on the Battered Woman Syndrome

When a battered woman kills her batterer and is made to stand trial for homicide, she often faces in court a prosecutor who pounds away at her story using every myth, stereotype, and misconception about battered women and domestic violence to convince the jury that she did not act in self-defense. He, or she, invariably argues that the woman is exaggerating or simply lying about her partner's former violence. If it was as serious as she claims, why didn't she call the police? Why didn't she tell someone? Get help? Why didn't she leave? If she did leave, why did she go back to him again? If the violence was not as bad as she claims, or if she killed him after one beating was over and another one had not yet begun, then she had no real reason to fear him; thus, her belief that he was about to injure or kill her was not reasonable. If she stayed in the relationship because she had some kind of neurotic need to be punished and therefore provoked and welcomed the beatings, her reaction to getting what she asked for could not be said to have been reasonable. If she weren't a masochist, wouldn't she have left? If she was really being beaten and abused, wouldn't she have left? Wouldn't anyone?

As we saw in the last chapter, there are perfectly good answers to those questions. The research of the last decade on wife-battering has revealed that women who have been chronically beaten tend to react to their situation in characteristic ways, ways which often run counter to people's expectations of what the normal human reaction would be. Psychologists have come to call this cluster of typical behaviors and emotional responses to the experience of living with and loving a man who is physically abusive the "battered woman syndrome."

Because a battered woman's perception of her situation is so shaped by her battering experience—and because it is so hard for jurors to understand how a woman could be brutally beaten by a man, fear him profoundly, and yet stay with him and love him and believe he loves her—many defense attorneys feel it is absolutely crucial to get information about the battered woman syndrome before the jury in these cases. The only way to counter the prosecutor's arguments that the woman must be lying (either about the violence or about her fear) is to explain to the jury that the woman's behavior, which seems to defy common sense, was entirely characteristic of women in her situation. The way that this can be done in a criminal trial is by means of an expert witness.

Our legal system has long recognized that some subjects are far enough removed from the everyday knowledge and experience of ordinary jury members that the only was they can understand the issues before them and render a just verdict is if someone with expertise is brought in to explain matters to them. A trial judge has very broad discretion to decide whether a particular subject is sufficiently esoteric to merit elucidation by an expert. If the judge concludes that the subject is not "beyond the ken of the average juror," she or he can refuse to allow expert testimony about it. In many jurisdictions, the judge must also decide whether research in the field is far enough advanced that people with expertise about it can reasonably be said to exist and whether the person who has been put forward as an expert witness does in fact possess such expertise. If all three of these tests are met and, in addition, the judge finds that the testimony is relevant to some question at issue, the expert's testimony will ordinarily be permitted, but not always. The judge can still refuse to allow expert testimony, which meets all of these guidelines, if it appears more likely that it will confuse or prejudice the jurors in their search for truth rather than aid them.

In a woman's self-defense case, the expert offered will be someone with first-hand knowledge of the characteristics of battered women. This is most often a psychologist who has clinical experience with battered women; but it may also be an academician who has done research in the field, a psychiatrist, or someone who has extensive direct experience with such women through, for example, operating a shelter. Ideally, the expert should also have had an opportunity to interview the defendant thoroughly prior to the trial. Then at the trial, the expert is able to describe to the jury the characteristics of the battered woman syndrome and testify, on the basis of her or his examination, that the defendant is a battered woman who exhibits those same characteristics. In some cases, an expert who has not examined the defendant has been permitted to testify about the general characteristics of battered women, leaving it to the jury to determine whether the defendant herself fits the description. In still others, two experts have been used, one to talk about general characteristics derived from research and one who has examined the defendant and can testify about her actual state of mind.

Testimony about the battered woman syndrome can be extremely helpful to the defendant's case in a number of ways. By informing the jury about how widespread domestic violence against women is in our society, it can overcome the jurors' reluctance to believe that men ever treat women that way. It can help the jury understand the otherwise puzzling aspects of the defendant's behavior—especially her failure to leave or get help or tell anyone—by explaining how impossible most of those options are and showing them that her reaction to being beaten by the man she lived with was typical of most battered women. By describing the repetitive and ever-escalating nature of most battering and the paralyzing fear that it often generates in its victims, it can help the jurors to put themselves in the woman's shoes and see the situation in the same way that she saw it.

It is extremely important to understand that battered woman syndrome testimony is offered in a self-defense trial to shed light on the *reasonableness* of the defendant's behavior. In legal terms, that is its relevance. As we have seen, the reasonableness of the woman's perception that she was in serious and possibly lethal danger, which required her to resort to a deadly weapon to defend herself, is the ultimate question in these cases. An expert can help the jury to understand that, given the woman's past experience with her batterer and her knowledge of his behavior patterns, her perception of the danger she was in was in fact perfectly reasonable. The purpose of battered woman syndrome testimony in a homicide trial is *never* to put forward the proposition that the mere fact that the woman was beaten by the man in the past somehow justifies her killing him in cold blood at some later date. It is not a rationalization for vengeance or vigilantism. It is certainly not a claim that battered women have legal rights that others do not. In that sense, there is no such thing as a "battered woman defense" to a homicide charge. The sole purpose of such testimony is to help the jury to understand why the woman reasonably believed she had to act as she did to defend herself.

In addition, it is important to understand that a defense based on the battered woman syndrome is in no way an insanity defense. This is sometimes misunderstood because the experts who are brought in to testify about the characteristics of battered women are often psychologists or psychiatrists, and the term "syndrome" is often used to describe mental illnesses. The purpose is not to argue that the defendant should not be held responsible for her actions because the beatings rendered her temporarily or permanently insane. On the contrary, its purpose is to bolster her argument that her actions were rational and reasonable under the circumstances.

One of the most hotly contested and commented-upon questions in the whole area of self-defense law today is whether a female defendant who has killed her batterer is entitled to present testimony by an expert witness about wife-beating and the battered woman syndrome. Ironically, this has come about because such testimony has proved to be so effective in gaining acquittals from juries. Prosecutors have learned that they must fight hard to exclude such testimony if they are to win convictions in these cases, and they have gotten steadily better at it. It is not unusual, these days, for the battle over whether or not to permit an expert on wife-beating to testify to become the major focus of the entire trial, with prosecutors bringing in experts of their own to attack the credentials and expertise of the experts presented by the defense.

Unless the defense is allowed to educate the jurors and the judge about what has been learned about battered women in recent years, they will have no choice but to fall back on what they "think" they know—all of the myths and stereotypes about wife-battering and its victims. Lenore Walker has identified a number of these misconceptions that are widely held in our society. Among them are the ones that we have seen are frequently played on by prosecutors in self-defense cases: that battered women are masochists, that they provoke the assaults inflicted on them, that they get the treatment they deserve, that battered women are free to leave these violent relationships at any time if they want to. Some of Walker's other myths about battering that prosecutors are not apt to harp on so overtly (but which no doubt also influence jurors' consideration of a defendant's reasonableness in defending herself) are that woman-beating is not at all common, that men who are personable and nonviolent in their dealings with outsiders must be the same in their dealings with their intimates, that middle-class men don't batter and middle-class women don't get beaten, and that battering is a lower-class, ethnic-minority phenomenon and such women don't mind it because it is part of their culture. A battered woman defendant in a self-defense case can hardly be said to have a fair trial if she is denied the opportunity to counter these misconceptions and educate the jurors about the realities of her situation.

  *One of the earliest self-defense cases to make use of expert testimony about the effects of battering provides a good example of how it is used and the enormous difference an expert witness can make, Idalia and Ralph Mejia were married for fourteen years. They met when they were only sixteen years old. Idalia's family were migrant field laborers. She grew up in Brownsville, Texas, the second eldest in a family of eleven children. Her schooling ended after the third grade when she went to join the rest of the family working in the fields and vineyards. She was so strictly raised that Ralph was quite literally only the second boy outside her family that she had ever spoken to. They met in a migrant labor camp in Tulare County, California, where Ralph's family was also working. He proposed marriage to her only three weeks after they met. Since her family was opposed, they ran off together; and since they were too young to marry legally, they lived together in Visalia, California. Eventually they travelled to Texas to ask her family's forgiveness and obtain their permission to marry.

They settled in Tulare County where Ralph managed to get out of the fields and set himself up in an agricultural spraying business. He, too, came from a large migrant family, one of twelve children born to his mother in Mexico; and he had only an eighth-grade education. He was, by all accounts, an extremely hard-working and ambitious man who did a very good job of caring for his family and establishing a successful business against almost overwhelming odds. But he was also a heavy drinker and prone to violence against both his wife and his children when he was drinking. At first, the beatings came mostly on weekends. "When he was drinking," Idalia told an interviewer, "he came in, and if I was standing near the door, he would just hit me or start up cussing me, like saying that my mother was some kind of bad woman or my sisters, and things like that. . . . Sometime when he came, the kids were outside playing and he got mad 'cause they were outside and he start hitting the kids. I tried to stop him and then I got hit." After a beating he would be terribly remorseful and tell her how much he loved her and promise not to do it again.

Idalia never tried to leave or to get help. Ralph was the head of the family, expected absolute obedience, and believed that he had a right to treat them any way he chose. Idalia believed so too. "My father drank a lot and he used to beat up my mother....You get married and you listen to everything they say and if they feel like hitting you, you have to take it. They're the boss of the family."

She did call the police four different times early in the marriage, but each time they came they told her that there was nothing they could do because they had not witnessed any crime. Ralph was charming to them when they were there and then beat her badly after they left. After a while she stopped calling them.

Toward the end, Ralph's drinking and violence began to get worse. He became obsessively jealous and wanted to know her every move. He would come home drunk and angry two or three times a week, threatening to kill her and the children and making ominous promises of horrible punishments to come. No matter how hard she tried to soothe and placate him, something would always trigger an explosion; he would beat her, usually with his hands and fists but sometimes with his belt and its heavy buckle. He developed a habit of lying in bed at night pretending to be asleep and saying ugly things to Idalia as though he were talking in his sleep. He used this way, for example, to accuse her of responsibility for the death of their fifth child, who had died soon after birth.

On the afternoon of December 18, 1977, there was a neighborhood gathering to celebrate the birthday of a friend's little boy. Idalia went and took the children; but when she got there, Ralph flew into a rage because he had not given her permission to come. Furious, he ordered her to take the children and go home at once, which she did. Several hours later, Ralph came home, very drunk. He slapped Idalia and then turned on his thirteen-year-old son, telling him he was never to go anywhere without his father's permission, even if his mother said he could, and threatening to beat him severely if he ever disobeyed again. Ralph then sent the boy to bed and ordered Idalia to go to bed as well. As she was leaving the room, Ralph turned to his brother-in-law (who was also present) and informed him he was planning to buy a bar in the town and that when he was a bar owner, he would surely be able to win a certain woman with big breasts whom he had been pursuing. Idalia knew the comment was meant for her to hear.

Idalia obediently went into the bedroom, took off her shoes and lay down on the bed. A little while later, Ralph came in, undressed and got into the bed with her. He tried to hug Idalia, but she resisted his advances, telling him to go to the woman with the big breasts instead. He grabbed her by the hair and started smashing her face into the wall. Then he seized her and pulled her on top of him, so that the middle of her torso lay across his face. Then he sank his teeth savagely into her flesh. He pretended to go to sleep then, starting his mumbled "sleep-talk." This time he went on about the other woman and the bar, saying how he did not love Idalia or the children and never had. Earlier that night, Ralph had once again threatened to kill her and the children. Fearing for all of their safety, Idalia crept out of bed and went to the closet where she got Ralph's gun out of its box. She later testified that she intended to take the gun, gather up her children and leave the house. Suddenly Ralph saw that she had the gun and sat up in the bed, telling her, "Don't do it." Believing that he was getting up out of the bed to attack her, she fired at him, killing him. Then she stood there crying at the foot of the bed with the gun in her hand until the sheriff's deputies arrived.

Idalia was arrested and charged with first-degree murder. At her trial—the first of three—the prosecutor argued that she had murdered her husband in cold blood as he lay, naked and defenseless, in his own bed. Her attorney, an experienced public defender, decided to depart from the temporary-insanity defense that was, in 1977, still the usual approach to defending women who killed their husbands in such circumstances. He was afraid that the conservative, rural jury he faced would be hostile to psychiatric testimony. Instead, he argued that Idalia had acted in self-defense and that her fear that she and her children were in deadly danger was a reasonable one. The jury hung, split between those who wanted to convict her of second-degree murder and those who believed she was only guilty of manslaughter. The state prepared to try her again.

At her second trial she was represented by another public defender, Joe Altschule. He decided to continue with the self-defense approach. As part of his preparation for the trial, he contacted Dr. Barbara Star, who was a professor at the University of Southern

California's School of Social Work. Dr. Star had done research on battered women and was a recognized expert on the subject. She served as a consultant to the defense in the second trial but was not offered as a witness. Once again, the prosecution argued that Idalia had killed her husband with deliberate malice, motivated by anger and jealousy. Once again there was a hung jury, but this time none of the jurors voted to convict her of either first or second-degree murder. Instead, they split over the manslaughter charge.

The state decided to go for a third trial. "We went with it for the third time, " the prosecutor told the press, "because we needed to make the point that you can't get away with murder in this country....That's just what it was. It's indefensible. Why didn't she leave him? Why didn't she just wound him?"

Altschule set out to answer those very questions for the jury in the third trial. He decided this time to ask the court to allow Barbara Star to testify as an expert witness on wife-battering. After a full morning of courtroom argument—during which the prosecution asserted that research about domestic violence was so new that there was no developed expertise in the field, and the defense argued that Dr. Star's long record of research and clinical experience made her a nationally recognized expert—the judge decided to permit her to testify.

Dr. Star was able to take the stand and tell the jury that she had interviewed the defendant and found her to fit the pattern that the doctor's research had shown was typical of battered women. She explained how Idalia's strict upbringing had trained her to be obedient and passive, never questioning authority or arguing back. She told them Idalia grew up with very little social sophistication and almost no sense of herself as a person with rights of her own. Nothing in her background prepared her to deal with the violence she encountered in her marriage, other than to submit to it. She explained how such a woman's self-esteem is further undermined by her husband's constant criticism of everything she is and does—her intelligence, her housekeeping, her cooking, her mothering of her children—so that she ends up feeling that there is something wrong with her and the violence is somehow deserved. She told the jury that battered women do not leave their husbands because they are afraid, with good reason, that their husbands will hunt them down and kill them and that by seeking help from others, they may be putting those people's lives at risk as well. She testified that, in addition to the fear, battered women stay in their marriages for many other reasons and explained how difficult it is for such women to break the emotional bonds that hold them there and to overcome the physical and financial obstacles to leaving.

She told them that, as a result of all of this, Idalia was virtually helpless before her husband's violence and anger, could see no way to leave, and passively accepted the situation for fourteen years because she did not believe there was any way she could resist him or fight back. Mejia was a huge man and literally twice his wife's weight. It was only when she picked up the gun that the situation was sufficiently equalized that she could even consider defending herself.

Barbara Star's testimony was enormously effective. For the first time, a jury was enabled to see Idalia's situation the way that she saw it. In all three trials the prosecution had argued that the she had no real reason to fear her husband and that Mejia's violence could not have been as bad as she claimed. If it had, she would surely have left him or told someone about it or tried to get help. All of the aspects of her behavior during her marriage that had puzzled the jurors in the two previous trials, and had seemed to cast doubt on her version of what she did and why she did it, at last became clear. The jury deliberated for several hours but finally came back with a verdict of "Not guilty."

The expert testimony of Dr. Star was not, to be sure, the only difference between the first two trials and the last one. By the time the third trial began in September of 1978, Idalia's case had become a popular cause in Tulare County. The courtroom was packed and pickets marched outside the courthouse carrying signs that read, "First her husband, now the courts." The jury could see that this was clearly not just a routine murder case. Far more important, there was other testimony in this trial that had not been heard by either previous jury. Idalia and Ralph's two oldest children testified about their father's mistreatment of them, testimony which moved almost the entire courtroom to tears. And Idalia, for the first time, found the courage to speak publicly in court about Ralph's sexual behavior. She testified that he had sexually assaulted the couple's twelve-year-old daughter and had, on one occasion, tried to force Idalia to have sex with a dog.

For its part, the prosecution presented the same basic case that it had before, but fought hard, even taking the trouble to build a full-scale mock-up of the Mejias' bedroom right in the courtroom. The prosecutor, too, brought in a novel expert witness. A forensic odontologist was produced to analyze the bite marks that Ralph had left on Idalia's body shortly before the shooting. The expert concluded that there was no sign in the skin that she had pulled away from Ralph when he bit her so that it might be safely assumed that her lacerations were "love bites."

A number of things contributed to Idalia Mejia's ultimate vindication in the courts, not the least of which were her own incredible courage and tenacity in going through trial after trial insisting on her innocence rather than bargaining a guilty plea, and an imaginative and equally tenacious defense attorney. I believe that it is safe to say, however, that what really made the difference in the last trial was Barbara Star's expert testimony.

Although trial judges ordinarily have wide discretion to decide whether to admit or reject expert testimony, once a state appellate court has decided the question, its ruling will generally be binding on all of that state's trial courts. Consequently, the legal battle over the admissibility of battered woman syndrome testimony has been moving into the state courts of appeals. Where the question has reached state appellate courts, decisions have gone both ways. All three of the tests that expert testimony must meet in order to be admissible have caused problems for battered women defendants who seek to get testimony about the psychological effects of battering before trial juries.

The first is whether the information that the expert is prepared to impart is "beyond the ken of the average layman." This is usually interpreted to mean that it is so distinctly related to some science, profession, business, or occupation that an ordinary person would not be able to understand it without help. Some judges, viewing the issue very narrowly in women's self-defense cases, have held that the subject the expert is proposing to testify about is just ordinary fear—specifically the reasonableness of the woman's fear—and fear is a common human emotion that any juror is familiar with and can understand without help from an expert. Other judges, and fortunately they seem to be an increasing majority, have taken a broader view. They have understood that the reason that testimony about battering and battered women's typical response to it is helpful to a jury precisely because it runs so counter to most people's expectations of human behavior. Without information about why battered women seem so passive, why they don't leave or try to get help, why they reconcile with their batterers again and again, as well as the cyclical, escalating nature of most wife-beating and battered women's highly developed sensitivity to cues about their batterers' impending behavior, the jurors cannot fairly evaluate the reasonableness of the defendant's fear that she was about to be seriously injured or killed.

The clearest rejection to date of expert testimony on the ground that the battered woman syndrome is not outside the understanding of the average juror was a ruling by the Ohio Supreme Court in 1981. This was the case of Kathy Thomas, a young, black Cleveland woman who shot her common-law husband, Reuben Daniels, in January 1978. She testified at her trial that during the three years she and Daniels lived together, he had repeatedly beaten and abused her. When she tried to leave him, he forced her to return at gunpoint. Four days before she shot him he had brutally pistol-whipped her. The night he was killed, Daniels became angry at her because he claimed she had burned the fish she was cooking him for dinner. He slapped her and shoved her into the living room and down onto the couch. Then he went and sat down on a chair in the same room. There was a loaded pistol on the couch and Kathy picked it up. She testified that Reuben was getting up from the chair and was about to attack her when she fired, fearing that he would take the gun away from her and kill her with it for having had the gall to pick it up. The prosecution's version of the facts was that Daniels did not get up from the chair and that Kathy walked over to him and shot him in cold blood as he sat there.

At her trial, Kathy's attorney tried to present expert testimony about the battered woman syndrome, but the trial judge refused to permit it. Kathy Thomas was convicted of murder and was sentenced to a term of fifteen years to life. Her case was appealed to the Ohio Court of Appeals which overturned her conviction and granted her a new trial solely on the ground that the trial judge should have allowed the testimony. In its unpublished opinion, that court said that, without the testimony, the jurors could not comprehend the "unique psychological characteristics and differences in reaction and perception" of a battered woman and thus would be unable to properly evaluate her state of mind when she acted and the reasonableness of her act.

Kathy's victory was short-lived, however, because the state appealed this ruling to the Ohio Supreme Court, which overruled the

Court of Appeals and reinstated her murder conviction. The state's highest court held that the trial court was correct in refusing to allow the expert testimony. It said that the jury was perfectly capable of deciding, on the basis of the defendant's story and other direct evidence, whether or not she acted in self-defense and that the subject of the expert testimony (the psychological characteristics of battered women) was "not distinctly related to some science, profession or occupation so as to be beyond the ken of the average person."

It is important to note that the Ohio Supreme Court was not ruling on whether or not Kathy Thomas was acting in self-defense when she shot Reuben Daniels. What is did was drastically limit what she, and presumably other similar Ohio defendants, could do to try to convince a jury that she was indeed acting in self-defense. The expert testimony might well have helped the jury to see the reasonableness of Kathy Thomas' perception that, by picking up the gun, she had crossed a line that placed her in inescapable and extremely serious danger, whether or not Daniels had begun to get up out of the chair when she fired.

Just how effective such testimony might have been is illustrated by another Cleveland case that had the good fortune to come to trial during the period between the two appeals courts' rulings in Kathy Thomas' case, when the Court of Appeals' decision that expert testimony was admissible had not yet been overturned. JoAnne Burns was charged with the murder of her husband when she shot and killed him as he lay asleep in his bed. There was testimony at her trial, confirmed by neighbors, friends, and the couple's children, that Willie Burns had been in the habit of assaulting his wife with a six-foot-long bullwhip. At least fifteen of these whippings had been witnessed by others, as well as pistol-whippings and at least one incident in which he had shot at her. Over the years, Mrs. Burns had filed criminal assault charges against her husband eleven times, but the cases were always continued by the judge; not one ever came to trial. During the two months previous to the killing, in addition to Willie's violence against JoAnne, he had sexually assaulted the couple's fourteen-year-old daughter four times and attempted to rape another young girl.

A psychologist who had extensive experience working with battered women, Lee B. Rosewater, was permitted to testify at the trial. She addressed, in particular, the desperation that is engendered by society's failure to provide protection when a woman seeks it, the constant terror battered women feel when they can see no way out and no way to protect themselves and their children, and the tendency of such women not to react decisively to violence as it is happening or immediately afterward but to react instead during a quieter, safer phase of the cycle. The jury was enabled to understand that JoAnne Burns' perception that she and her children were in serious, ongoing danger was a reasonable one and that, from her point of view, the only way she could realistically defend them and herself against further harm was to seize an opportunity when her husband was off guard. JoAnne was found not guilty. If her case had arisen six months later, after the Ohio Supreme Court's ruling in *Thomas*, the psychologist would not have been permitted to testify, and there is every likelihood that JoAnne Burns would be in prison today.

Most of the other state appellate courts that have considered the question of whether expert testimony about the battered woman syndrome deals with subject matter outside the understanding of the average juror have ruled, or strongly implied, that it does. In 1981, for example, the Georgia Supreme Court overturned Josephine Smith's manslaughter conviction because the trial judge had refused to allow expert testimony by a psychologist about the effects of battering. According to Ms. Smith's testimony, she had met her boyfriend at seventeen, when she was a junior in high school. She became pregnant with his child and later had a second child by him but, although she lived with him off and on, she never married him. She testified that he had first beaten her about a month after they met, punching her in the eye with his fist. The beatings continued, often triggered by his jealousy of other men, and became more frequent after she moved out of her mother's house into an apartment of her own. After every beating he would apologize, telling her that he loved her and promising never to do it again. Ever hopeful, she believed him every time and never called the police or sought help from her family or friends. She was afraid to stop seeing him because he threatened awful consequences if she ever tried to leave him.

The night of the shooting, Josephine came back into her apartment at about eleven in the evening and found him waiting there for her. She did some laundry, and they went up to bed. Her boyfriend started making sexual overtures to her, which she rejected, explaining that she was too tired. He shook her and said, "You don't tell me when to touch you."

According to the Georgia Supreme Court report,

> The defendant [Josephine] got out of bed, put on some pants and started to go back downstairs when the boyfriend balled his fist and told her she was not going anywhere. She then sat on the foot of the bed and started to roll her hair. The boyfriend kicked her in the back. When he started to kick her again the defendant put her hair pick behind her and the boyfriend kicked it. As the defendant stood up, the boyfriend hit her in the head with his fist. He then grabbed her by the throat, choked her and threw her against a door.
>
> When the defendant got loose, she ran to the chest of drawers, grabbed her gun and ran downstairs to call her mother. She was unable to use the telephone because the boyfriend had taken the phone off the hook upstairs and ran downstairs and took the phone away from her. The defendant tried to go back upstairs but the boyfriend grabbed her. The defendant then ran to get out of the apartment. As she was running out, the boyfriend slammed the door on her foot. The defendant then fired the gun three times with her eyes closed. She went to a neighbor's house and called the police.

Had she been allowed to testify, the expert witness, who was a clinical psychologist with extensive experience working with battered women, was prepared to tell the jurors that in her professional opinion, Josephine was a battered woman and exhibited the characteristics of battered woman syndrome. It was a violent four-year relationship in which abuse began very early and escalated over time. Ms. Smith stayed with the man because she loved him, because she believed his protestations of love and promises to reform, and because she was afraid that he would kill her if she tried to leave him.

The judge, however, permitted the jury to hear none of this. Charged with murder, Josephine was convicted of voluntary manslaughter and sentenced to fifteen years in prison. Arguing that the expert testimony was improperly excluded, she appealed her conviction to the Georgia Court of Appeals, which upheld it, but a further appeal, to the state Supreme Court, was successful. That court held that the conclusions that would have been drawn by the psychologist, about why a battered woman would not leave the violent relationship, why she would not call police or tell her friends, why she would have reason to fear an increase in the violence, were not conclusions that the jurors could ordinarily draw for themselves. In other words, the expert's knowledge was beyond the ken of the average juror.

Since 1979, courts in the District of Columbia, Maine, Florida, Wyoming, New Jersey, New York, Illinois, Kansas, Kentucky, and Washington have also held that expert testimony about the battered woman syndrome deals with a subject that is outside the knowledge of ordinary jurors and that it cannot be excluded on that ground by a trial judge in a self-defense case involving a battered woman. The trend is clearly in that direction. However, that is only one of the three tests that such testimony has to meet in order to be admissible. In a number of cases, the battered woman defendant has managed to get over this first hurdle only to be tripped by the second or third: that the state of the art in the field be sufficiently advanced that expertise is possible and that the proposed expert be possessed of that expertise.

Generally speaking, trial courts tend to be cautious about permitting expert testimony, in large part because jurors are apt to give great, perhaps undue, weight to the opinions of someone who comes before them wearing the official label of "expert." So it is important that the expert's credentials be beyond dispute and that her or his opinions reflect an accepted body of knowledge that has been derived from valid methods of research. This is not always easy to establish when the field at issue is quite new. Although women have been victims of male violence throughout human history, our society has only recently begun to recognize the problem. The social sciences did not find domestic violence even worth studying until the seventies. Most of the battered woman syndrome research has been done in the past ten years, and many of the studies have been done, of necessity, on self-selected samples. The courts have been troubled by whether enough methodologically sound research work has been done to give rise to a field of knowledge about which there can be said to be expertise and how one can determine who is a *bona fide* expert. The first battered woman self-defense case revolving around expert testimony to reach an appellate court illustrates this unease very well.

Beverly Ibn-Tamas shot and killed her husband, Washington, D.C., neurosurgeon Yusef Ibn-Tamas, in February of 1976. At her trial for murder, she testified that there had been recurring episodes of violence by Dr. Ibn-Tamas during the three and one-half years they were married. Among other assaults, she testified that he had knocked her to the ground and pressed his knee to her neck until she lost consciousness, threatened her with a loaded pistol when she hesitated to sign some financial documents, and threw her out of a car along an interstate highway to end an argument with her. He had threatened to kill her if she ever called the police and told her he would fracture her skull if she ever tried to leave him. He kept a number of guns in the house along with several hundred rounds of ammunition. In addition to her husband's violence toward her, Beverly became aware that in his first marriage he had committed similar assaults—sometimes involving loaded guns—against his former wife, a woman friend of hers, and some of her relatives. Two criminal complaints had been lodged against him by victims of these assaults.

In February of 1976, Yusef had completed his medical residency in Florida, and the couple had recently moved to the District of Columbia where he had set up a practice in an office adjacent to their home. They had a daughter and Beverly was pregnant again. Although there had been a period of relative harmony following the move, the violence had resumed and had become more frequent during the first two months of that year.

The morning of the killing, there had been an argument at the breakfast table. Dr. Ibn-Tamas set upon his wife, beating her first with a magazine and then with his fists. He dragged her physically up the stairs to the bedroom where he handed her a suitcase and told her to pack and be out of the house by ten that morning. When she told him that she could not, he attacked her again, beating her on the head, under her arms and on her thighs with his fists and later with a wooden hairbrush. Despite her pregnancy, he kicked her in the stomach, and she did her best to curl up so that most of the blows fell on her back and legs. He then picked up a loaded .38 caliber revolver that was lying on the dresser and, pointing it at her face, said, "You are going out of here this morning one way or the other."

Yusef then put the gun back on the dresser and went downstairs to his office, leaving Beverly and her young daughter in the bedroom. She picked up the phone and called him, pleading with him to be reasonable, but he repeated his order that she pack and leave.

A few minutes later the doctor came upstairs to the bedroom and began beating her again. She was pushed over near the dresser where the gun was lying. She saw him looking toward it and, thinking he was about to grab it, she seized it and fired a warning shot toward the bottom of the bedroom door, begging him to go out and leave her alone. Ibn-Tamas backed out of the room saying, "You are going now." She testified:

> And I heard him go down the steps, and so I had my little girl's hand. I knew after I shot that shot I had to get out of the house. I just knew he was going to kill me.

Believing that her husband had gone all the way down, she took her daughter by the hand and started to walk down the stairs. Suddenly, Yusef jumped at them from the corner landing. She pulled her daughter back around the corner and fired the gun toward her husband. She testified:

> He backed up against the wall, went back to the wall, and he kept down at the steps with his eyes still on my face, and he went down the stairs, jumping two at a time, doing like that, and he kept looking back with his back to the wall, and on the way down the steps he said, "I am going to kill you, you dirty bitch."
>
> He got at the bottom of the steps and he looked at me and he just went in the office, and I knew I had to get out of that door.
>
> I knew it. And I had my little girl by the hand. She seemed like—when he got to the bottom of the steps, she thought we were supposed to follow him. She jumped like she was going in front, and she looks and she says, "Daddy." And I looked in there and he was, he was just like he was waiting for me. He was standing over just like that—something like that. (Indicating.) And I just knew he had a gun. I shot in the room, and I turned to go out the front door, and after I turned my head I heard him fall. I heard him fall and I knew I had shot him.

Beverly was charged with second-degree murder. Throughout its case, the prosecution argued to the jury that she had lured her husband back into the house with her phone call and then shot him in cold blood on the landing, followed him down the stairs and shot him again as he lay wounded and helpless on the office floor. Her motive was variously said to be anger at his threat to throw her out of her house, jealousy about his affairs with other women, and greed, in that she was the beneficiary of his life insurance policies. The prosecution tried to counter her claim that she believed herself to be in life-threatening danger by questioning whether her marriage had been as violent as she said and therefore whether she really had reason to fear her husband. In cross examination and in its closing argument to the jury, the government implied that if she had really been a battered woman, she would have called the police or left her husband.

The defense sought to present testimony by an expert, Dr. Lenore Walker, to counter these arguments by explaining to the jury that Beverly's reaction to the violence she encountered in her marriage was typical of a battered woman. The trial judge refused to let Dr. Walker testify. Beverly Ibn-Tamas was convicted of second-degree murder.

On appeal she challenged the trial court's exclusion of Dr. Walker's testimony. The District of Columbia Court of Appeals ruled that such testimony, in a case in which a battered woman claims self-defense, is admissible in that it addresses matters that are beyond the ken of the average juror. This was a landmark decision because it was the first time that an appellate court had made such a finding. However, it also found that the trial judge had not made it clear whether his exclusion of the testimony was also based on a ruling that it did not meet the other two tests of admissibility. It returned the case to the trial court for clarification of this question. The trial judge said that he had indeed excluded the testimony in part because the defense had not demonstrated that Dr. Walker's methodology in studying battered women had obtained general acceptance among her colleagues. It therefore failed to meet the second test and was properly kept out. The Court of Appeals subsequently deferred to the trial judge's ruling on this point and affirmed Beverly's murder conviction.

Other appellate courts have proved to be equally reluctant to overrule or second guess a trial judge's findings on the qualifications of a particular expert or the adequacy of the research on which an expert's conclusions about the battered woman syndrome are based. In a number of recent cases, courts of appeal have either let stand a trial court's exclusion of expert testimony on the ground that the research is not sufficiently advanced, or have returned the issue to the lower court to be settled in a new trial. In a breakthrough case from Washington State (in 1984), however, the state's highest court ruled that scientific understanding of the battered woman syndrome has indeed now developed to the point that it is admissible without further argument on the point in any self-defense case in that state in which the defendant establishes her identity as a battered woman.

The Supreme Court of Kansas has subsequently made a similar ruling, as has an intermediate appellate court in New York state.

Even where expert testimony, when it is offered, meets the three-part test of admissibility, a trial judge may still refuse to allow it because it is not relevant. Relevant evidence is evidence that has probative value relative to some fact or question that is at issue and, if believed, would render a desired inference more probable than it would be without the evidence. In a number of trials of women who claimed to have acted in self-defense, judges have declined to admit expert testimony about battered woman syndrome because they have felt that testimony about the effect of the woman's past experience with being battered, or testimony about the experiences of other battered women, has nothing to do with the question of whether, at the moment she struck, she reasonably believed she was about to be seriously injured or killed. Fortunately, most of the appellate courts that have addressed this question have had no trouble seeing that such testimony is indeed relevant to the question of reasonableness because it can help the jurors to understand why the defendant perceived herself to be in imminent danger in circumstances where another person might not. Appellate courts have also found that such testimony is relevant to the question of her credibility, both about the genuineness of her belief in the need to defend herself and about the truth of her story about past abuse although she didn't leave, or tell anyone or seek help.

Battered woman syndrome testimony has also been found relevant to issues other than whether or not the woman was acting in self-defense. Psychologist Lenore Walker reports, for example, that she has been called upon to present expert testimony at the sentencing phase of the trials of thirty-two battered women who have been convicted of homicide in the killing of their husbands, and she has been very successful in convincing judges to grant probation or much lighter prison sentences than the prosecution was asking for. Such testimony has also been used effectively in pre-trial maneuvering to get charges against battered women dismissed.

Battered woman syndrome testimony has also been found to be relevant to issues at trial other than the woman's perception of danger at the immediate time of the killing. Jeanette Minnis sought to produce such testimony at her trial for the murder of her husband to explain why she hacked his body up after she killed him and deposited parts of it, wrapped in plastic bags, in various dumpsters around the city of Decatur, Illinois. She testified that her husband, Movina, forced her to go out and pick up women to bring home for him to have sex with because he claimed that she did not satisfy him sexually. From his activities with these women, in which she was apparently expected to participate, she was supposed to learn how to please him better. If she was unable to obtain enough women for his purposes, he would beat her. She testified that these beatings came as often as once a week; at least twice she required hospital treatment.

Late one Friday night, Movina came home, woke her up, and told her that he had brought some company home. He introduced her to a man named Duane who Movina said was a male prostitute. Movina was a weight lifter. He and Duane spent some time in Movina's weight room and then came back to the living room carrying a heavy pair of barbells. Jeanette was sitting on the floor watching television and they placed the barbells across her outstretched legs, pinning her under them. Movina and Duane then had intercourse with each other in front of her and Movina told her, "If you would just do what you are supposed to do, I wouldn't have to do this." When they were finished, Movina removed the barbells and Jeanette ran to the bathroom where she was sick to her stomach. After that she tried to leave the house but Movina grabbed her and both he and Duane forcibly raped her. Movina then gave her a beating and raped her again. Afterwards, he tied her to a doorknob in the bedroom, telling her he was afraid she would go out and tell people he had had sex with a man, and left.

She was not sure how long she was tied up but it appeared to have been at least one day and maybe two. When Movina came back he was still carrying on about the possibility she might tell someone about Duane. When he untied her she went into the bathroom to take a bath but Movina followed her in and shoved her head into the toilet bowl, threatening over and over to kill her. He forced her to perform oral sex on him on the floor of the bathroom and then he dragged her to the waterbed where he raped her. When he was finished he began to strangle her. She testified that she prayed for the strength to get him off her and then heaved as hard as she could with her knees which were bent up against her chest. His body rolled away and did not move. She lay there terrified that he would get up and kill her. She reported:

I gave it all I had. If he comes back, I'm just dead. But he didn't get up. And I got up, I went to the corner and I sat in it. That's where I was always supposed to sit when...when I was on punishment or didn't do anything he thought I was supposed to do. I was made to sit in that corner, to sleep in that corner.

Believing that Movina was alive and watching her, she stayed in the corner for a long time before she crept over to his body and discovered he was dead. She dragged his body into the bathtub and went to the garage for plastic garbage bags and a saw. Realizing it was Monday morning, she went to the house of the man Movina usually rode to work with to tell him her husband would not be going that morning. Then she went home, cut up the body, loaded the bags into her van and headed into the city. She put some of the bags in dumpsters and threw the rest in the river. The latter, containing the head, neck and upper torso, were never found.

Several weeks later, Jeanette was arrested and charged with murder. At her trial, the prosecutor argued that she had strangled her husband in his sleep, although his case was completely circumstantial since the relevant body parts were missing. Consequently, he relied very heavily on the argument that her action in disposing of the body was evidence of her consciousness of guilt. The defense proposed to offer two expert witnesses on battered woman syndrome, a clinical psychologist and a psychiatrist, both to bolster her claim that she was acting in self-defense and to explain her conduct after the killing occurred. The judge refused to allow it for either purpose. He was of the opinion that battered woman syndrome testimony is only relevant in the kind of self-defense case in which a woman kills a sleeping husband, not the kind where there is an actual confrontation, which the jury can understand perfectly well without help. Since her story was that she had pushed him away when he was awake and choking her, expert testimony was not relevant to her claim of self-defense. (It never was learned how he died; her theory was that he struck his head on the side rail of the waterbed when she shoved him.) The trial judge also ruled that she could not call experts to address her behavior in cutting up and concealing the body because he believed that battered woman syndrome testimony was only relevant to the woman's actions at the actual killing and not to what happened afterward.

Jeanette was convicted of murder and sentenced to twenty-five years in prison. On appeal, she argued that the expert testimony should have been admitted. The Appellate Court of Illinois, Fourth District, let stand the judge's ruling on the self-defense issue but agreed with her that the testimony would have been relevant to her later behavior because the experts were prepared to testify that her conduct after her husband's death was influenced by the fact that she was a battered woman. Her conviction was reversed and she was granted a new trial.

Although Jeanette Minnis' case broke new ground on one aspect of the relevance of battered woman syndrome testimony, it also points up a problem with another. This is not the only court that has proceeded on the assumption that expert testimony about battering is only relevant in so-called "nonconfrontation" cases. It reflects a belief that when the woman and her attacker are in an actual struggle, the situation is no different from an ordinary self-defense case between two men. The jury is presumably able to decide simply from the facts whether or not the woman was acting in self-defense. It is only in those cases where the woman kills a man when he is not actually assaulting her, according to this view, that the jury will be aided in understanding her actions by expert testimony. This is a disturbing development because, as we have seen in case after case in which women were convicted for killing men who were actually beating or choking them or were threatening them with weapons or lunging toward them with obviously hostile intent, jurors have a great deal of difficulty in recognizing self-defense in traditional confrontation cases when the defendant is a woman who kills her mate. Testimony about battering is every bit as helpful to them in those cases as it is in the nonconfrontation ones.

On the other hand, a number of trial courts have excluded expert testimony on battered woman syndrome precisely because the situation did *not* involve an immediate confrontation of the traditional self-defense sort. Eleanor Fultz, for example, attempted to use such testimony to explain why she believed she was in imminent danger of a serious beating although her husband, seated on a couch a few feet away, had merely pointed his finger at her and whispered a threat to kill her. The trial court, upheld on appeal, ruled that the testimony was not relevant because Mr. Fultz had not yet committed any overt aggressive act on that occasion that would have caused her to believe that she was in danger, the very belief which the testimony was offered to show. In effect, the court ruled that because her belief was not reasonable, she had no right to produce evidence that it *was* reasonable.

Despite these problems, many trial judges, in cases that have never reached the appellate courts, have permitted expert testimony for years without a quibble, because they have understood its relevance and importance to a claim of self-defense by a woman who has been chronically beaten by the man she ultimately kills. There is reason to hope that as research into domestic violence continues to develop and as appellate courts continue to view its appropriateness receptively, the admissibility of expert testimony will cease to be the battleground on which the question of whether a battered woman who kills her batterer acted in self-defense will have to be fought.

As the use of battered woman syndrome testimony in women's self-defense trials has become more widespread, some feminist commentators have begun to express uneasiness with the direction that it is taking. Their concern is with both the content of the testimony and the way that some appellate courts seem to be interpreting what the experts say. Professor Elizabeth Schneider argues that testimony that focuses on the helplessness and passivity of battered women tends to reinforce some of the very stereotypes about women that expert testimony about the battered woman syndrome was originally intended to counter. The legal system's traditional expectation that a woman who kills a man will rely on an insanity or impaired mental capacity defense (if she does not simply plead guilty to murder or manslaughter), reflects a stereotype of women as irrational and emotional—incapable of behaving as reasonable men would. This stereotype is perpetuated in another form when attorneys and their experts frame battered woman syndrome testimony primarily or exclusively to explain why a battered woman did not leave or seek help. Rather than underscoring the reasonableness and need for her violent act, such testimony instead sometimes paints the battered woman as so damaged or emotionally disabled by the violence that her perception of reality is distorted; thus, her ability to act reasonably, or to act at all, is impaired. While it is important to explain to the jury why the woman stayed and tolerated the violence, testimony that overemphasizes that issue and neglects the far more essential one of reasonableness may well leave the jury without an explanation of how a woman who was rendered so helpless by her situation could ever have committed an act as aggressive as killing.

Even where expert testimony is not framed solely in terms of passivity and helplessness, judges and appellate courts frequently seem to hear it that way anyway. The language that a number of appellate courts have used in permitting the testimony suggests that battered woman syndrome is being understood not as probative of the woman's reasonableness but, quite the opposite, as a new and excusable form of female irrationality, not quite insanity but something close to it. As Professor Schneider has observed:

> . . . "[B]attered woman syndrome" carries with it stereotypes of individual incapacity and inferiority which lawyers and judges may respond to precisely because they correspond to stereotypes of women which the lawyers and judges already hold. Battered woman syndrome does not mean, but can be heard as reinforcing stereotypes of women as passive, sick, powerless and victimized. Although it was developed to merely *describe* the common psychological characteristics which battered women share, and it is undoubtedly an accurate description of these characteristics, battered woman syndrome can be misused and misheard to enshrine the old stereotypes in a new form. This repeats an historic theme of treatment of women by the criminal law—women who are criminals are viewed as crazy or helpless or both.

Phyllis Crocker has pointed out that the courts are allowing battered woman syndrome testimony to establish a new stereotype, that of the *bona fide* battered woman. Some expert testimony appears to have given the courts the impression that all battered women are exactly the same and react to their situation in identical ways. If a woman does not fit this preconceived pattern she may not be regarded as a battered woman, whatever the reality of her experience. There have already been a number of court opinions that have relied on deviations from this battered-woman stereotype—that a woman was not absolutely passive but fought back in the past, that she was not economically dependent but held a good job, that she owned or knew how to use a pistol, that her husband left her rather than her being unable to leave her husband, or that she was hit only once before the final assault—to uphold trial judges' exclusion of expert testimony about battering. Crocker points out that women defendants are getting caught between two sets of stereotypes. Prosecutors argue that because she didn't leave or get help or fight back, the violence a woman experienced must not have been so bad; therefore, her fear was unreasonable. Appellate courts, on the other hand, rule that if she did leave, get help or fight back, she wasn't really a battered woman.

In this connection, Professor Schneider has also raised the difficult question of whether the current battered woman syndrome model may be based too much on the experiences of middle- and upper-income white women whose passive responses to spousal violence may be different from those of women from other economic or ethnic backgrounds. Some battered woman defendants may not only be penalized for not acting like reasonable men, they may be penalized for not acting like middle-class white women as well.

Phyllis Crocker also expresses concern that a "reasonable battered woman" standard is developing to replace the reasonable-man standard in battered women cases, leaving the reasonable-man standard untouched in all other kinds of self-defense cases. A woman defendant's conviction or acquittal consequently may turn on whether she can prove she was a genuine battered woman rather than whether she acted in reasonable and necessary self-defense. In addition, Crocker sees an assumption developing that a woman's right to defend herself, and to present evidence supporting the reasonableness of her action, only applies to battered women and not women who defend themselves against rapists and other attackers who are not their domestic partners. She asks, with good reason, what would happen in court today to Yvonne Wanrow and Inez Garcia, neither of them battered women but the two women whose cases set in motion the entire recent rethinking of women's right to self-defense.

These are all legitimate concerns. It would be tragic if the one most promising approach to achieving justice for women who are defendants in self-defense cases should develop into yet another set of assumptions to be used against them. It is certainly essential that defense attorneys and mental health professionals who testify in women's self-defense trials be sensitive to the implications of what they say in court and how that might be interpreted. This is a very different question, however, from whether the courts should permit such testimony. When a battered woman defendant believes that testimony on the battered woman syndrome will be useful to her case, simple justice requires that she be allowed to present it. Under our system, every criminal defendant is guaranteed the right to put on the most effective possible defense. A battered woman defendant is asking for no special favors from the courts in this regard. All she is asking is the opportunity to help the jury understand the reality of the danger she faced and to try to convince them of the reasonableness of her response.

7

Summing Up

The law of self-defense discriminates against women. The right to take an aggressor's life to save one's own is one of the oldest recognized by Anglo-American criminal law; and it is a right that must, of course, be carefully limited. It is not in any civilized society's interest to encourage people to take the law into their own hands or to sanction unnecessary killings. Over the centuries a number of rules limiting the right to self-defense have been developed which seek to balance the private right against the public order. These rules, for the most part, have been written not by legislatures but by judges, virtually all of them male, in cases predominantly involving male defendants. The result has been a law that permits men to exercise their right to defend themselves in the situations in which men have customarily felt the need to do so, but it does not permit women to exercise their right to self-defense in the situations in which they believe they must do so.

That is sex discrimination, and the solution is obvious: we must fashion a law of self-defense that allows both men and women to defend themselves in all of the threatening situations that they are likely to face, but that still protects society's interest in preventing the wanton or unnecessary taking of life. We do not need a different law for men and women; still less do we need separate laws for battered women and everybody else. Women are not special victims who need special treatment from the law. Women are equal citizens who need and expect the same right to defend themselves that men have, in the circumstances in which women need to exercise that right. It is not equal treatment to tell women that they may defend themselves if they should stumble into the male scenario that the law contemplates—a one-time confrontation with an armed stranger of the same gender in a public place—but that they may not defend themselves in any of the situations where they are most apt to be threatened with serious injury or death. Women need and expect the same right to self-defense that men have, not just on paper but in fact.

This does not mean that we must throw out the present law in its entirety and start over. Nor does it mean making radical changes in long-established legal principles. What is needed is some adjusting of the present rules so that the law can more fairly protect the right to self-defense of everybody who needs to use it. This would not be a novel undertaking. Although the general principle of self-defense has remained the same for many centuries, the law has shown itself to be remarkably flexible. As we have seen, it has changed a great deal in its details in response to society's needs at different times and places. In the middle ages it was quite unfettered, reflecting the dangerousness of the times and the wide availability of personal weapons. As England became more urban and orderly, the right to self-defense was gradually narrowed but did recognize that it was sensible to apply different rules to different self-defense situations (the brawl that turns deadly and the sudden assault by a homicidal stranger). The American frontier, facing conditions not unlike those of Medieval England, required a swing back again to a much broader right of self-defense. Since then, the settling of the country, the growth of urbanization, and effective law enforcement have caused an understandable narrowing of self-defense once again. It is my argument that justice requires a slight easing of the rules once more to accommodate not new but newly acknowledged conditions.

As long ago as 1921 Justice Oliver Wendell Holmes observed, in a self-defense case involving the obligation to retreat, that ''concrete cases or illustrations stated in the early law in conditions very different from the present...have had the tendency to ossify into specific rules without much regard for reason.'' When that happens, it is time to do what Justice Holmes did in that opinion, which found the retreat requirement to be an archaic relic that did not belong in federal self-defense law: change the rules.

Two aspects of the law of self-defense limit how this can be done. The first is that self-defense law, like all criminal law, is a state matter. Every state's law is a little different from the others' and is based primarily on cases decided within that state. Consequently, there is no single, simple remedy that can be sought at the federal level nor is there any generic solution that will be applicable to all the states interchangably. The law must be changed state by state, much as rape laws and domestic violence laws have had to be changed, and that is difficult.

The second aspect of self-defense law that affects what can be done and how to do it is the fact that it is almost entirely judge-made. This surprises many people, who assume that all of our criminal law is made by legislatures and embodied in statutes. But self-defense is a common law defense, one of a number that a person accused of a crime can present at trial. It was created by judges and has always been interpreted by judges. Many states, although by no means all, now have statutes that acknowledge the right to self-defense; but they tend to be very general in their terms. Most commonly, they state that one who is not the aggressor has the right to use deadly force against an assault, provided that he reasonably believes he must do so to prevent imminent death or serious bodily harm. The legal rules that define those general terms—imminent, reasonable, and so forth—are developed, case by case, by trial court and appellate judges, as are additional requirements such as whether and from where one must retreat before defending oneself.

This aspect of the law is a problem because judges are not accountable to an electorate the way legislators are. They cannot be lobbied or subjected to public pressure as they carry out their lawmaking function. Indeed, almost no one (except the parties to particular cases) is aware of it when judges make law and no one, except the lawyers making arguments, has any right to address them on the subject of what the law should be. In self-defense law, this process of developing legal rules takes place at the trial court level in the instructions about the law that judges give to juries before they begin their deliberations. At the appellate level, it takes the form of opinions about the correctness of trial instructions as well as the propriety of other trial court decisions, such as whether to permit expert testimony. We are quite accustomed to attacking sex-descriminatory statutes and using the courts to challenge sex discrimination imposed by private parties such as employers. This kind of sex discrimination, which is imposed by judges in seemingly sex-neutral legal rules and developed in cases that had nothing to do with women defendants, is much less familiar territory and much less amenable to traditional techniques of legal reform.

Although the judge-made nature of self-defense law presents

problems, it also presents opportunities by allowing changes to be pursued at two levels, through the courts and through the legislatures. Some of the best changes for women involving self-defense have come through the courts where lawyers have been able to convince judges that justice requires a new look at old rules. The recent trend toward admitting expert testimony is an example; the Wanrow decision is another. On the other hand, where state appellate courts are not amenable to making the laws more sensitive to women, or where a state's supreme court has made a final ruling on an issue that establishes especially bad law, it may be possible to look to state legislatures to make changes. Legislatures can overrule judges. Except on constitutional issues, judges cannot overrule legislatures. For example, after the Supreme Judicial Court of Massachusetts issued its ruling in Roberta Shaffer's case, holding that in Massachusetts there is a duty to retreat even from one's home, the state legislature amended the law to make the castle doctrine applicable there after all.

The following suggestions for changes in the law of self-defense to make it more fair for women can be pursued through both avenues. This is not intended to be an exhaustive proposal but merely an indication of the direction change should take.

1. *Equal Force.* The equal force rule, which holds that a person cannot use a deadly weapon in self-defense unless one is being used against him or her, should be abandoned. It is, in fact, already on the way out. It has never made much sense even for men, because its two underlying assumptions—that every man can defend himself with his fists against the assault of any other man and that an unarmed assailant is incapable of killing or seriously injuring his victim—are patently untrue. The courts of many states have been backing away from this requirement for a number of years; but it still comes up, as we have seen, in battered woman cases, and ought to be laid to rest. The amount of force one chooses to use in defense against an assault is properly a question of the reasonableness of one's action.

2. *Imminence.* The imminence requirement needs to be eased a bit from its present interpretation by most courts as meaning "immediate." The rule was developed to apply to the traditional male situation of a one-time confrontation between two strangers in a public place. The two-pronged rationale was, first, that self-defense should only be permitted when there is no possibility of resorting

to law enforcement for protection and, second, that self-defense should only be permitted when there is no possibility the assailant will change his mind and back off of his own accord. One never knows when a menacing stranger may be bluffing, so one is obligated to wait until he begins to carry out his lethal threat. When a confrontation in a bar turns ugly and someone calls the cops, they can come and simply break it up. Even if they don't arrest anyone, the threat is over, and the intended victim can go safely on his separate way. Certainly no one should be able to take another's life if waiting a few minutes may eliminate the need to do so.

Neither rationale supports applying a strict immediacy standard to the very different situation faced by a woman being threatened in her home by a mate who has carried out his past threats to harm her. Calling the police accomplishes nothing, because they cannot arrest her husband for merely threatening to hurt her. Breaking up the confrontation will not end the episode, as it does between strangers in a bar, because the two parties to it live together. As soon as the police leave, the threatening situation can resume and may well have been made more serious, not less, by the police being called. Likewise, the argument that one ought to wait to see if an assailant is merely bluffing makes little sense in the context of an assault by someone whose behavior patterns are known and whose threats are customarily carried out.

Rather than avoiding unnecessary violence, requiring a woman in those circumstances to wait until an assault has begun is likely to place her in greater danger because once her assailant gets his hands on her, she will no longer be in a position to defend herself. For the battered woman, and, as we have seen, for the rape victim as well, the imminence rule often has the effect of depriving her of her right to self-defense altogether.

One remedy for this is suggested by the American Law Institute's Model Penal Code. It has dispensed with any reference to imminence and instead would permit a person to use a deadly weapon against the use of unlawful force by another person "on the present occasion." This revision would open up the time frame enough so that women, or men—who have good reason to believe that an assailant is about to launch an attack or will, with certainty, carry out a clear threat to do so—can act before it is too late. It appears to work quite well in the states that have adopted this provision of the Code.

Even without such legislative change, courts can define the statutory term "imminent" for juries in a way that distinguishes it from "immediate" and allows a broader time frame than the usual strict definition. The terms are not necessarily synonymous. Imminent, according to the *Random House Second Unabridged Dictionary*, means "likely to occur at any moment; impending...about to happen," as in an imminent catastrophe or an imminent merger. The term is perfectly consistent with a gap in time between when an imminent event is perceived and when it happens. A few courts over the years have recognized this and opted for a definition that looks beyond immediacy. One state supreme court, in Kansas, has recently made the same distinction in a series of women's self-defense cases, and it is a development that should be pursued elsewhere.

Courts can also permit juries to distinguish "stranger" cases from "known-assailant" cases and apply appropriate standards to each. In Una Bush's case, for example, a California appellate court held that the trial judge should have used a jury instruction proposed by the defense that told the jurors that a person who has been threatened by someone in the past is justified in acting more quickly and taking harsher measures to defend herself against a renewed threat than someone who has not been threatened before.

3. *Retreat.* As we have seen, about half of the states require a person to retreat, if possible, from an attacker before standing ground and fighting back. Originally the requirement only applied to mutual combat situations and was intended to prevent fist fights and brawls from turning lethal, even if that required the sacrifice of a little masculine pride. In American law this limitation has withered away and now, in most states where the rule exists, one must retreat in all circumstances if one can do so safely. The rule has also come to require much more than backing away from a fight. It has evolved into an affirmative requirement to run away or escape from a potential assailant.

The law of every retreat state recognizes an exception to the requirement if one is in one's own home. The modern rationale for this "castle doctrine" is that one's home is one's place of ultimate safety. There is no safer place to which a person can be expected to flee when threatened there.

The aspect of the retreat requirement that has caused the most problems for women defendants has been the series of exceptions that has grown up here and there to the castle doctrine, holding that one must retreat from one's home in the face of an assault by a co-tenant or someone who is there by invitation. Most appellate courts that have considered it (usually but not always in cases involving male defendants) have concluded that the rule makes no sense and have abandoned it or refused to adopt it. Still, it has been accepted by the appellate courts in a few states and keeps coming up in trial court instructions to juries.

Since most women defend themselves in their homes from men who are spouses or lovers, this exception is particularly unfair to women defendants. The rationale for the castle doctrine applies, if anything, more cogently to women than to men. A woman forced to flee her home is apt to be in far greater danger at night on the street with no place to go than a man would be. There is really no good argument in favor of having such an exception, and it should be eliminated.

The other aspect of the retreat doctrine that I suspect causes problems for women is the confusion, by juries and sometimes by courts, between the concept of retreat and the question of why the woman stayed in the relationship. As we have seen, there is nothing in the law of self-defense that in any way obligates a woman to leave a violent mate or presumes that she waives her right to self-defense if she fails to do so. But this is a question that troubles many jurors, and the difference between leaving and retreating is not apt to be obvious to them. I believe a battered woman defendant is entitled to a jury instruction that explains the distinction and informs the jury that she was not obligated to leave her marriage. For the same reason, in states that do not require retreat, a defendant should be entitled to a jury instruction to that effect. Silence on the issue allows the jury members to impose their own informal retreat requirement, something they may be especially apt to do in a battered-woman case if they are troubled about why she didn't just leave the man before she had to kill him.

4. *Rape.* A person's right to use deadly force in defense against a rape ought to be clearly recognized by state statutes. Under the common law it was always a woman's right, and it ought to be a right of men as well. Rape itself involves such an overwhelming invasion of personal bodily integrity that it constitutes, by itself, the serious injury contemplated by self-defense law. There should be no requirement that there be additional physical injury or attempted homicide before a rape victim can use any means available to fight back.

5. *Reasonableness.* The use of an objective standard of reasonableness—the reasonable man/reasonable person test—works against women defendants in two ways. As we have seen, it causes women's actions to be judged by an inappropriate masculine yardstick. In addition, it is often the basis of trial courts' refusing to admit expert testimony in cases involving battered women on the ground that testimony about the defendant's subjective perceptions is irrelevant to the question of whether a theoretical reasonable person would have acted as she did.

For both of these reasons, I believe that a subjective standard of reasonableness or a purely subjective standard of *bona fide* belief in the need for acting in self-defense is much more fair to women defendants. Because most states that require defensive acts to be reasonable do so by statute, a purely subjective standard (which eliminates reasonableness altogether) would generally require legislative action. This has happened in a few states that have adopted the Model Penal Code without change, as we have seen. However, many state legislators appear to have a real problem with the idea of abandoning the notion of reasonableness, perhaps because doing so appears to be sanctioning unreasonable behavior, and most states that have codified their criminal laws in the last quarter century have declined to follow the Model Code on this issue.

Where reasonableness is required by statute it is usually the appellate courts that decide whether an objective or subjective standard is applicable. Consequently, this is a change that can be pursued through the courts rather than the legislatures, although presumably it could be the subject of legislation as well.

Whatever standard of reasonableness or genuineness of belief a state has adopted, a trial court should always admit testimony about all of the deceased's past assaults and threats against the defendant and other violent acts of his that were known to her at the time of the killing, no matter how far back in time they occurred. A battered woman's entire experience with her batterer is relevant to the reasonableness and genuineness of her belief that she had to defend herself. No such testimony is too remote in time or too cumulative to have no probative value. Indeed, the longer the abuse went on and the more of it there was, the more bearing it was apt to have had on her perception of danger.

No matter whether a state has a subjective or an objective standard of reasonableness, a trial court should never give jury instructions that employ only the masculine pronoun in a case involving a woman defendant. Telling jurors in such a case that a *man* has a right to use deadly force if *he* reasonably believes that *his* life is in danger inevitably invites the jury to judge the reasonableness of the woman's actions by an inappropriate masculine standard.

6. *Expert Testimony*. The usefulness to juries of expert testimony about the battering experience in women's self-defense trials is clear. If it meets the established standards, it should always be admitted. This is not an argument for the establishment of a separate battered-woman defense or for special legal rights for battered women that other defendants don't have. Expert testimony that meets the established criteria for admissibility and relevance can be helpful to juries in other self-defense situations and can benefit men as well as women. There has already been at least one case in which a gay man has successfully used battered woman/spouse syndrome testimony in his trial for the killing of his partner. Rape Trauma Syndrome testimony could be helpful to a defendant of either sex who has fought back against a rapist and testimony about Post-Traumatic Stress Syndrome might well be useful in cases involving war veterans and others of both sexes whose past experiences have a bearing on the reasonableness of their response to a perceived threat.

While expert testimony is often an essential element of the legal strategy in women's self-defense cases, it is important to resist the temptation to see it as the only solution or the whole solution. Elaborate trials involving expert witnesses are extremely expensive and not inevitably effective. A recent analysis pointed out that of 26 reported cases in which battered woman syndrome testimony was used at trial, only 9 resulted in acquittals. Although the effort to get such testimony admitted in all of the states must go on, I believe that reforming the law, in the long run, holds a better promise of obtaining justice for women in self-defense cases.

These are all modest proposals. Their aim is not to revolutionize the law of self-defense but merely to nudge it gently toward sufficient flexibility to meet the needs of women who must defend themselves. Every single one has been adopted by some jurisdiction with no adverse consequences. None of these proposed changes applies only to women or sets up a separate defense for women. On the other hand, I believe that none stretches the traditional law so far that the people whose activities it has always primarily applied to—violent males in conflict with each other—are given any new license to kill.

While revising the law is essential if women are to have an equal right to self-defense, it is important to recognize that the law is only part of the problem. The other part, equally telling, is the way that our society's attitudes about women and violence against women influence the way that women defendants in self-defense cases are perceived by judges, prosecutors, juries, and sometimes their own lawyers. We have looked at a number of cases in which the elements of self-defense law probably prevented juries from acquitting women who clearly believed they were acting in necessary self-defense. But we have also seen case after case in which the jury could have acquitted if it wanted to; cases where there was an actual assault taking place; where serious injury had been done before and was clearly going to be done again; where death threats had been made; and where escape, if required, was impossible. These are cases that fit easily within the limits of present self-defense law, and still the defendants were convicted. We must look beyond the terms of the law to explain why prosecutors, judges, and juries are so ready to disbelieve women's stories of what happened, to distrust their perception of the need to defend themselves, to assume the worst about their motives, and to find their actions unreasonable.

Every time a woman walks into a courtroom in this country, as a defendant, as a witness, as a party to a lawsuit, even as a lawyer, she faces a stacked deck. Two states, New York and New Jersey, have recently undertaken studies of gender bias in their court systems. Both have concluded unequivocally that women are systematically discriminated against in the courts. Both studies found that myths, biases, and stereotypes about women pervade the judicial decision-making process and often affect the outcome of cases. Women are apt to be regarded as inherently less credible than men and, when they appear in court seeking justice as victims of violence, they are frequently the targets of the most callous sort of victim blaming. The New York Task Force concluded: "Decision making is marred when the results reached in cases consciously or unconsciously reflect not the merits of the case or the spirit of the law to be applied, but instead prejudiced views of sex roles and characteristics—that women's claims are not to be believed and that women are subordinate to men in the marital relationship."

We have seen this pervasive sexism at work throughout our exploration of women's self-defense cases. We have seen it in the arguments prosecutors make to juries. Prosecutors would not make the sexist, victim-blaming arguments they do if those arguments were not persuasive to their audience. It is hard to imagine a prosecutor standing before a jury and making the patently absurd argument that battered women stay with their husbands because they enjoy being beaten if he or she did not know perfectly well that the jury would find the argument not ludicrous but convincing.

We have seen sexism reflected in the rulings that judges make, excluding testimony about past beatings, framing instructions so narrowly that juries are forced to convict, and refusing to allow the expert testimony that is designed to overcome just such biased attitudes in the jurors. It is sexism that causes the sort of myopia that allows a judge—who has heard a woman describe a scene in which her partner, after he pistol-whipped her, sat pointing a loaded gun at her, made what she heard as a threat to kill her and then told her to go and get the handcuffs so that he could shackle and beat her—to rule that she has not even made enough of a case for self-defense to send the question to the jury.

We have seen sexism in the preoccupation of juries with the question of why the woman didn't leave. The question assumes that controlling male violence or putting an end to it is the woman victim's responsibility, not the man's. If she fails to do so, she must leave, not he; and if she stays, she deserves—or must want—whatever she gets. The question assumes as well that the family home is not her home but his, and he has the right to drive her out of it. She is the one who must abandon her home, her treasured possessions, possibly her children, and often her personal freedom to hide behind locked doors in some miserable, overcrowded shelter. It is a measure of how far we have yet to go that "why didn't she leave?" is so seldom recognized as the outrageous question that it is.

These same sexist attitudes contribute to the persistent unwillingness of juries to believe women's versions of events and their inability to recognize even the most obvious acts of self-defense unless an "expert" is brought in to provide the credibility that women's own testimony is not deemed entitled to. They are reflected as well in the fact that a woman's reasonableness is so suspect that she must provide an expert witness to explain to a jury that a woman who has been repeatedly beaten and threatened with death has good reason to fear her tormentor when he attacks her again. How else can one account for the fact that a jury that has heard testimony that a man once plunged his hand up to the elbow into his wife's rectum and tore out a fistful of her intestines should need an *expert* to explain that when the man grabbed her and choked her and threatened to rip out her windpipe her fear that he might do it was reasonable?

Clearly the work of educating the public and the courts about the realities of wife abuse must continue, and we must go on searching for better ways of protecting women and placing the blame for male violence where it belongs. More than that, however, a women's right to self-defense must become a more visible part of the woman's rights agenda. In addition to working to change the law, through legislation and litigation, we can make an effort to educate judges and prosecutors and the defense bar about the women's rights issue involved here, as we have done about rape and wife abuse. We can form support groups for women imprisoned for defending themselves and work to get them paroled, resentenced, or pardoned. Above all, we can give women who must defend themselves against male violence the public support they need and deserve. The rising visibility of the issue of a woman's right to self-defense has shown that public attention and media coverage can make a great deal of difference in these cases. Prosecutors, judges, and juries are far more conscious of the possibility that they may work an injustice and are far more likely to take care that justice is done when they know that the world outside the courtroom is watching what they do.

Appendix

TABLE OF CASES

The foregoing discussion was based on the following appellate court opinions. Those discussed or cited in the text appear in boldface. In addition, I have drawn on over 100 press and other published reports and private communications about women's self-defense cases that were not appealed and therefore do not appear in published court reports.

195

Notes

Notes are keyed by page number and catchphrases from the text. Cross-references to notes give page number and catchphrase.

PREFACE

viii. ARTICLES IN LAW JOURNALS: Among the best of these early articles, which essentially laid the groundwork for a feminist analysis of self-defense law, were Elizabeth M. Schneider and Susan B. Jordan, "Representation of Women Who Defend Themselves in Response to Physical or Sexual Assault," 4 *Women's Rights Law Reporter* 149 (Spring 1978); and Comment, "Battered Wives Who Kill: Double Standard Out of Court, Single Standard In?" 2 *Law and Human Behavior* 133 (1978) by Nancy Fiora-Gormelly. An early article that took quite a different view was Note, "Does Wife Abuse Justify Homicide?" 24 *Wayne Law Review* 1705 (1978), by Marilyn Hall Mitchell.

viii. FOR A GENERAL AUDIENCE: Ann Jones, *Women Who Kill* (New York: Holt, Rinehart and Winston, 1980).

viii. FRACTION OF THE TOTAL: The handful of writers who have published anecdotal accounts of such cases have gathered their material in a variety of ways. Ann Jones (*Women Who Kill*) relied primarily on newspaper accounts. Lenore Walker (*The Battered Woman Syndrome*) and Angela Browne (*When Battered Women Kill*) have reported on women whose cases they worked on as expert witnesses in court. The cases collected in Elizabeth Bochnak's *Women's Self-Defense Cases* were gathered by the Women's Self-Defense Law Project in New York during its two year existence as a resource center for lawyers representing women in self-defense cases. Jane Totman *(The Murderess)* interviewed women incarcerated in a California prison for murder or manslaughter. Professor Charles Ewing, in his recent book, *Battered Women Who Kill*, used a computer data base to find wire service stories about such cases. I gathered many of my unpublished stories by writing to battered women's shelters and victim advocacy gorups around the country asking them to tell me about cases in their areas.

None of these serendipitous methods, of course, can claim to produce anything like a full picture or even a representative sample. It is interesting, though, that each of these efforts has turned up entirely different stories; we are not all just independently discovering the same small handful of incidents.

xi. HANDS OF THE OTHER: The interchangeable terms "serious bodily harm," "great bodily harm," "grievous bodily injury," and the like, have no special, technical meaning in the self-defense context. They are used in their ordinary sense, and it is generally up to the jury to decide whether the harm threatened on a given occasion was serious enough to justify using deadly force in response. For the problems this can cause women defendants see Chapter Three, below.

xii.　(4.2 PERCENT FOR WOMEN): *Crime in the United States–1986* (Uniform Crime Reports; Washington, D.C.: U.S. Government Printing Office, 1987). In 1986, in 4.8 percent of all the homicides committed in the United States the victim was the wife of the offender and in 2.6 she was his girlfriend, a total of 1525 victims. In 2.7 percent of the total homicides the victim was the husband of the offender and in 1.5 percent he was her boyfriend, a total of 865 victims. Intimate relationships are almot twice as lethal for women as for men.

It used to be that men and women killed their mates at roughly equal rates. In the 1973 figures cited by Del Martin (*Battered Wives* [New York: Pocket Books, 1976], 15), for example, 48 percent of spouse-victims were husbands and 52 percent were wives. In the last few years these proportions have begun to change. In 1980, 56 percent were wives, in 1983, 58 percent were wives and in 1986 fully 64 percent of the spouse-victims were wives. (Uniform Crime Reports statistics).

xii.　NO HARD STATISTICS: See William Wilbanks, "Murdered Women and Women Who Murder," in N.H. Rafter and E.A. Stanko, eds., *Judge, Lawyer, Victim, Thief: Women, Gender Roles and Criminal Justice* (Boston: Northeastern University Press, 1982) for an analysis of the surprising lack of hard data on women homicide offenders or victims. A large part of the problem is that the primary source of crime statistics, the F.B.I.'s annual Uniform Crime Reports, does not break its figures down by sex in all instances and does not report justifiable homicides at all.

xii.　RESPONDED BY KILLING THEM: Marvin E. Wolfgang, *Patterns in Criminal Homicide* (Philadelphia: University of Pennsylvania Press, 1958), 212–13; 260.

xii.　IN SELF-DEFENSE THAN ARE MEN: *Crimes of Violence*, Staff Report to the National Commission of the Causes and Prevention of Violence (Washington, D.C.: U.S. Government Printing Office, 1969), 360.

xii.　WHEN THEY KILLED: "Study of Female Killers Finds 40% Were Abused," *New York Times*, 20 December 1977, p. 20; "Right of Women to Self-Defense Gains in Battered Women Cases," *New York Times*, 7 May 1979, p. A18; Elizabeth M. Schneider, Susan B. Jordan, and Cristina C. Arguedas, "Representation of Women Who Defend Themselves In Response to Physical or Sexual Assault," in *Women's Self-Defense Cases*, Elizabeth Bochnak, ed. (Charlottesville, VA: Michie, 1981), 7.

xii.　ASSAULT BY THEIR MATES: George W. Bernard, Hernan Vera, Maria I. Vera, and Gustave Newman, "Till Death Do Us Part: A Study of Spouse Murder," *Bulletin of the American Association of Psychiatry and Law* 10 (1982) 271 at 274, 278.

xii.　WHEN THEY STRUCK BACK: Peter D. Chimbos, *Marital Violence: A Study of Interspousal Homicide* (San Francisco: R. and E. Research Associates, 1978), 55.

xiii.　DURING THEIR MARRIAGES: Jane Totman, *The Murderess: A Psychosocial Study of Criminal Homicide* (San Francisco: R. & E. Research Associates, 1978).

Chapter 1. OVERVIEW: WHEN WOMEN FIGHT BACK

3. ARTHUR LEE DIED INSTANTLY: *People v. Scott,* 424 N.E.2d 70 (Ill. App. 1981); Lee Strobel, "Murderers or Battered Women?" *Chicago Tribune,* 20 September 1981.

4. ASSAULTS OF VIOLENT MEN: Unfortunately, there are no statistics available on how often this happens or has happened in the past. See xii "NO HARD STATISTICS" above. It is the impression, however, of most writers who have examined the question of women and self-defense that, until the last few years, when the development of a coherent feminist legal defense strategy has begun to make a difference, acquittals in these cases were quite rare. When women have been acquitted, it has more often been on the grounds of insanity than self-defense. See, for example, Schneider and Jordan, "Representation of Women Who Defend Themselves in Response To Physical or Sexual Assault"; Loraine P. Eber, "The Battered Wife's Dilemma: To Kill or Be Killed," 32 *Hastings Law Journal* 895 (1981) at 917–18; Alan D. Eisenberg and Earl J. Seymour, "The Self-Defense Plea and Battered Women," *Trial,* July 1978, 35; Ann Jones, *Women Who Kill,* 292ff; Lenore E. Walker, "A Response to Elizabeth M. Schneider's 'Describing and Changing: Women's Self-Defense Work and the Problem of Expert Testimony on Battering,'" 9 *Women's Rights Law Reporter* 223 (1986) at 224.

9. THEIR ACTIONS WERE JUSTIFIED: For an excellent analysis of the press's response to women's new self-defense claims, see Ann Jones, *Women Who Kill,* 290ff.

10. "A LOT OF KILLINGS": *Time,* 28 November 1977, 108.

10. "AN OPEN SEASON ON MEN": Kathleen Begley, "Are Women Getting Away With Murder?" *Chicago Daily News,* 29 November 1977.

10. "SMACKS UNCOMFORTABLY OF FRONTIER JUSTICE": *Newsweek,* 30 January 1978, 54.

10. "IT'S OPEN SEASON ON HUSBANDS": John Switzer, "Self-Defense Decision Causing Double Standard: Women Get More Than Equal Rights After Killing Spouse," *Columbus Dispatch,* n.d. 1978, p. A1.

11. SHARED IN OUR SOCIETY: See, for example, Susan Brownmiller, *Against our Will: Men, Women and Rape* (New York: Simon and Schuster, 1975); R. Emerson Dobash and Russell Dobash, *Violence Against Wives* (New York: The Free Press, 1979); Del Martin, *Battered Wives* (New York: Pocket Books, 1976); Florence Rush, *The Best Kept Secret: Sexual Abuse of Children* (New York: McGraw-Hill, 1980); Diana E. Russell, *Rape in Marriage* (New York: MacMillan, 1982); Susan Schecter, *Women and Male Violence* (Boston: South End Press, 1982); Elizabeth Stanko, *Intimate Intrusions: Women's Experience of Male Violence* (London: Routledge & Kegan Paul, 1985); Murray A. Straus, Richard J. Gelles, and Suzanne K. Steinmetz, *Behind Closed Doors: Violence in the American Family* (New York: Anchor/Doubleday, 1980).

11. SUBSEQUENTLY REGRET IT: Brownmiller, *Against Our Will,* 311ff; Herbert S. Feild and Leigh B. Beinen, *Jurors and Rape: A Study in Psychology and Law* (Lexington, MA: Lexington, 1980), 95ff.

11. MOLESTED BY THE AGE OF THIRTEEN: Florence Rush, *The Best Kept Secret: Sexual Abuse of Children* (New York: McGraw-Hill, 1980), 4–5.

11. THOSE WHO RAPE ADULT WOMEN: See, for example, the study of the outcome of 256 known cases of sexual abuse in Brooklyn, N.Y., reported by Florence Rush, *The Best Kept Secret,* 156–57. Only four cases actually went through to trial and conviction.

11. SOCIETY PREFER TO BELIEVE: Elizabeth Stanko, *Intimate Intrusions: Women's Experience of Male Violence* (London: Routledge & Kegan Paul, 1985), 95; *National NOW Times,* January/February, 1982.

11. ONE AUTHORITATIVE STUDY: Murray A. Straus, Richard J. Gelles, and Suzanne K. Steinmetz, *Behind Closed Doors: Violence and the American Family* (New York: Anchor Press/Doubleday, 1980), 40.

12. DESERVE EXACTLY WHAT THEY GET: Mildred D. Pagelow, *Woman Battering: Victims and Their Experiences* (Beverly Hills: Sage, 1981), 53ff; Lenore E. Walker, *The Battered Woman* (New York: Harper and Row, 1979), 18ff.

12. FROM MEN WHOM THEY KNOW: Angela Browne, *When Battered Women Kill* (New York: Free Press, 1987), 5–6.

13. EITHER A CRIMINAL OR CRAZY: Schneider and Jordan, "Representation of Women Who Defend Themselves in Response to Physical or Sexual Assault," 150.

13. STABBED HIM TO DEATH: "Wives Who Batter Back," *Newsweek,* 30 January 1978, 54.

13. LAUGHED AT HER AND LEFT: *People v. Miles,* 403 N.E.2d 587 (Ill. App. 1980).

14. CONVICTED HER OF MANSLAUGHTER: *People v. Lucas,* 324 P.2d 933 (Cal. App. 1958).

15. ACQUITTED BY A JURY: Bill Mandel, "His Gun Was Her Escape From A Private Kind of Hell," *San Francisco Chronicle,* 7 June 1981; William Carlson, "Battered Wife Cleared In Shooting of Husband," *San Francisco Chronicle,* 10 June 1981. Another self-defense case involving a police officer's wife is *People v. Goodman,* 396 N.E.2d 274 (Ill. 1979). See also *Commonwealth v. Stonehouse,* 517 A.2d 540 (Pa. Super. 1986), for a case in which both parties were police officers. Carol Stonehouse's conviction for third degree murder was upheld, in part because the appellate court said that, as a police officer, she should have been better able to cope with her violent boyfriend's behavior.

16. JEALOUSY OR REVENGE: The police may sometimes believe that the woman's story about her husband's violence is so irrelevant to their investigation that they do not even bother to write it down. See *Fultz v. State,* 439 N.E.2d 659, at 662.

16. SHOTS WERE FIRED: Appellant's Supplemental Brief Appealing Conviction And Opening Brief Appealing Denial of New Trial Motion, *State v. Painter,* Case #5678-6-I, Court of Appeals, Division I, State of Washington, 1979, pp. 61ff.

16. KILLED HER HUSBAND: *State v. Freeman,* 244 S.E.2d 680 (N.C. 1978).

17. WOULD NOT BE ADMISSIBLE: *Hawthorne v. State,* 377 So.2d 780 (Fla. 1979); see also *Hawthorne v. State,* 408 So.2d 801 (Fla. App. 1982) and 470 So.2d 770 (Fla. App. 1985).

18. INVESTIGATE ANOTHER SHOOTING: *State v. Griffiths,* 610 P.2d 522 (Idaho 1980) at 542. Additions and elisions in the original.

19. "WHICH *THEY* FEEL IS WARRANTED": Ibid. at 543.

19. (RACIAL OR SEXUAL PREJUDICE): See Elizabeth Anne Stanko, "Would You Believe This Woman? Prosecutorial Screening for 'Credible' Witnesses And a Problem of Justice," in N.H. Rafter and E.A. Stanko, eds., *Judge, Lawyer, Victim, Thief: Women, Gender Roles and Criminal Justice* (Boston: Northeastern University Press, 1982), 63–82, for a study of sex-bias in prosecutorial decision-making.

19. CASES MUST BE MADE: Studies of prosecutors' decisions about whether or not to bring charges indicate that the overriding consideration is that the case be winnable. Usually, that means that the alleged activity falls within the criminal code and there are witnesses or evidence to prove the accusation. See, for example, Frank Miller, *Prosecution: The Decision to Charge a Suspect with a Crime* (Boston: Little, Brown, 1970), and the materials collected in Burton Atkins and Mark Pogrebin, eds., *The Invisible Justice System: Discretion and the Law* (Cincinnati: Anderson, 1978), 137ff. However, when cases are purely circumstantial, as these domestic self-defense cases so often are, the decision must revolve much more around whether the prosecutor believes he or she can convince a jury to convict without such corroborating evidence but simply on the basis of inferences about the defendant's motives. One indication that prosecutors see these as winnable cases is the fact that they tend to charge women defendants with extremely serious crimes. Psychologist Lenore Walker reports that, in the 96 cases that she has consulted on, all but one of the women was charged with first-degree murder. Lenore Walker, "A Response to Elizabeth M. Schneider's 'Describing and Changing: Women's Self-Defense Work and the Problem of Expert Testimony on Battering'" 9 *Women's Rights Law Reporter* 223 (1986) at 224. It is improper for a prosecutor to charge a higher degree of crime than he or she believes is supported by the facts. *National Prosecutor Standards* (Chicago: National District Attorneys Association, 1977), 131.

19. THAN MEN WOULD BE: Angela Browne cites statistics that fewer men are charged with first or second degree murder for killing women they have known than are women who kill men they have known. *When Battered Women Kill*, p. 11.

21. TO PRISON FOR HER CRIME: *Collier v. State*, 275 So.2d 364 (Ala. App. 1973).

22. GUN WENT OFF, KILLING HIM: *People v. Powell*, 442 N.Y.S.2d 645 (N.Y. App. 1981).

22. WOMEN IN THESE CIRCUMSTANCES: See p. 19n, "cases must be made," above.

23. IN THE TRUNK OF A CAR: Ann Jones, "Can A Wife Beater Prosecute A Beaten Wife For Killing A Wife Beater?" *The Soho News*, 20 October 1981, p. 12.

23. GUILTY OF MANSLAUGHTER: *State v. Anaya*, 438 A.2d 892 (Maine 1981). Linda Anaya's conviction was overturned on appeal. At her second trial she was found guilty again, and that conviction was upheld on appeal. *State v. Anaya*, 456 A.2d 1255 (Maine 1983).

24. PROBLEMS THEY FACE: See Chapter Five, below.

24. INJURIES WITH MAKEUP: Report of Proceedings, *State v. Kelly*, Case No. 10452-7-I, Court of Appeals, Division I, State of Washington, 1982, 333; *Seattle Post-Intelligencer*, 14 November 1982, p. B2.

24. "INJURY AT HIS HANDS": Jones, "Can A Wife Beater Prosecute A Beaten Wife For Killing A Wife Beater?" *The Soho News*, 20 October 1981, p. 12.
25. ACT AS SELF-DEFENSE: See Ann Jones, "When Battered Women Fight Back," 9 *Barrister* 12 (Fall, 1983) at p. 49.
26. FOR THE DEATH PENALTY: Jane Cartwright, "Justice Tempered: Woman Freed Early on 1977 Slaying Charge," *The Seattle Times*, 7 May 1983, A14.
26. WAS FINALLY RELEASED: Maggie Broom, "Second Thoughts From Judge Who Sent Her to Jail," *Seattle Times*, 14 November 1982; Jack Hopkins and Lansing Jones, "If There's Any Justice...I Do Deserve A Fair Trial," *Seattle Post-Intelligencer*, 22 December 1982; Jane Cartwright, "Justice Tempered," *The Seattle Times*, 7 May 1983.
27. RUN OUT WERE UNSUCCESSFUL: "Elizabeth Knott: The Struggle Goes On," *The Northwest Passage*, 1 June 1981.
27. SELF-DEFENSE TRIALS DEMONSTRATES: See Chapter Six, below.
29. TOOK PLACE IN 1977: See p. 16n, "shots were fired," above.

Chapter 2. A LAW FOR MEN

32. IRRELEVANT TO THE WHOLE PROCEEDING: Radcliffe and Cross, *The English Legal System*, 6th ed., G.J. Hand and D.J. Bently, eds. (London: Butterworths, 1977), 9–10; Sir Frederick Pollock and Frederick W. Maitland, 1 *The History of English Law* (2nd ed., 1895; Cambridge: Cambridge University Press, 1968), 38–40, 55.
32. BLOOD-FEUDS WERE COMMON: Radcliffe and Cross, *The English Legal System*, 6–7; Pollock and Maitland, 1 *The History of English Law*, 46–50.
32. PROPERTY TO THE CROWN: Radcliffe and Cross, *The English Legal System*, 8; (a) Pollock and Maitland, 1 *The History of English Law*, 44–45; 74.
33. BY THE SAME COURT: Page, *Northumberland Assize Rolls*, The Surtees Society, vol. 88, 1891, 85, 94. See also Bernard Brown, "Self-Defense in Homicide from Strict Liability to Complete Exculpation," 1958 *Criminal Law Journal* 583, at 585.
33. FORFEITURES IN SUCH CASES: State 24 Hen. VIII c5.
33. STAND TRIAL IN THE FIRST PLACE: For the history of the law of self-defense, a subject that has been of very little interest to legal historians, see Brown, "Self-Defence in Homicide from Strict Liability to Complete Exculpation"; Thomas A. Green, "The Jury and the English Law of Homicide, 1200–1600," 74 *Michigan Law Review* 413 (1976); Rollin M. Perkins, "Self-Defense Reexamined," 1 *U.C.L.A. Law Review* 133 (1953); Joseph H. Beale, "Retreat from a Murderous Assault," 16 *Harvard Law Review* 577 (1903); Pollock and Maitland, 2 *The History of English Law*, 478ff.
35. 90 PERCENT OF THE POPULATION LIVED: George M. Trevelyan, *Illustrated English Social History* (London: Longmans, Green, 1949), 55.
35. "MAJOR SOCIAL PHENOMENON": James B. Givens, *Society and Homicide in Thirteenth Century England* (Stanford: Stanford University Press, 1977), 106ff. Givens estimates that the homicide rate in the towns and villages he studied was about 12 per 100,000 of population, compared with .04 per 100,000 in England in 1977. Table 2, p. 36.

35. "THAN FROM AN ACCIDENT": Barbara Hanawalt, *Crime and Conflict in English Communities, 1300-1348* (Cambridge, Harvard University Press, 1979), 99.
35. AN ALARM WAS RAISED: T.A. Critchley, *The Conquest of Violence: Order and Liberty in Britain* (New York: Schocken, 1970), 28. In the towns there was a watch and ward system under which all adult males were placed on a rotating roster to serve on guard duty at night. Ibid. at p. 35. See also Hanawalt, *Crime and Conflict in English Communities, 1300-1348*, 33-34.
35. FOR HIMSELF AND HIS FAMILY: G.M. Trevelyan, speaking of the late fourteenth century, "when every man was expected to 'take his own part' with stick or fist, with arrow or knife," emphasizes "how ill-policed was England of that day and how weak the arm of the law. Murder, rape, beating and robbery by violence were everyday incidents. Lord, miller and peasant must each guard his own family, property and life." *Illustrated English Social History*, 15-16.
35. ORGANIZED FOR WARFARE: Frances Geis and Joseph Geis, *Women in the Middle Ages* (New York: Barnes and Noble, 1980), 27.
35. THEY WERE CALLED OUT: Critchley, *The Conquest of Violence*, 33ff. Critchley observes, "Thus the whole people were obliged to keep dangerous weapons for the public good; not, as now, forbidden to do so lest they misuse them for private harm," 33. Edward I's Statute of Winchester, in 1285, reaffirmed the "assize of arms," updating the list of weapons required, and reaffirmed the male citizens' "hue and cry" obligation as well.
36. VIOLENT FELONY AGAINST HIM: Brown, "Self-Defense in Homicide from Strict Liability to Complete Exculpation," 584ff; Pollock and Maitland, 2 *History of English Law*, 479. This was most likely the basis of the court's forgiveness of Alice's and Matilda's slaying of their rapists.
36. SOMEONE'S BEING KILLED: Givens, *Society and Homicide in Thirteenth Century England*, 42ff.
36. THEIR BROTHERS OR THE CHURCH: Geis and Geis, *Women in the Middle Ages*, 27; Christine Fell, *Women in Anglo-Saxon England and the Impact of 1066* (Bloomington: Indiana University Press, 1984), 149-57.
36. LESS VIOLENCE THAN MEN WERE: Givens, *Society and Homicide in Thirteenth Century England*, 134ff; Hanawalt, *Crime and Conflict in English Communities, 1300-1348*, 115, 123. Historian Christine Fell notes that in the thirteenth and fourteenth centuries, women's rates of crime were similar to those of today. Christine Fell, *Women in Anglo-Saxon England and the Impact of 1066*, 169-70.
36. "VIOLENT ATTACKS THAN MODERN WOMEN": Hanawalt, *Crime and Conflict in English Communities, 1300-1348*, 123.
36. "RARE VICTIMS OF ROBBERIES": Ibid., 153.
36. KILLED IN THEIR OWN HOMES: Givens, *Society and Homicide in Thirteenth Century England*, 148; male victims outnumbered female victims in Givens's study by about five to one.
37. BEING CONSIDERED AS SUCH: Hanawalt, *Crime and Conflict in English Communities, 1300-1348*, 166.
37. "FALLING INTO ERROR": See below, 173ff.
37. WOMAN HAD DIED OF PLAGUE: Margaret W. Labarge, *A Small Sound of the Trumpet: Women in Medieval Life* (Boston: Beacon Press, 1986), 204.

37. MANNER AT IPSWITCH: J.L. Rayner and G.T. Cook, eds., *The Complete Newgate Calendar*, vol. 4 (London: The Navarre Society, 1926), 8.

37. WOMAN CHARGED WITH TREASON: Hanawalt, *Crime and Conflict in English Communities, 1300—1348*, 166.

38. ESCALATE INTO A DEADLY COMBAT: Givens observes that everyone in those days carried a knife for cutting bread, a fact that he believes accounts for the tendency of fights to escalate into lethal confrontations. *Society and Homicide in Thirteenth Century England*, 188–89. Barbara Hanawalt notes that medieval men routinely carried a knife or a dagger and observes that the ready availability of such weapons is especially obvious in self-defense cases. *Crime and Conflict in English Communities, 1300-1348*, 100.

38. STAND AND FIGHT BACK: The case that originally established the requirement of "retreat to the wall" was decided in 1328. Two men were on their way to a tavern when a "quarrel and a contest against each other" arose. The deceased apparently drew a weapon and his adversary backed away until he came to a wall that ran between two houses and entirely blocked his way. At that point he drew his own weapon and killed his pursuer in his own defense. The court ruled he was entitled to a pardon. Perkins, *Self-Defense Re-Examined*, 141.

40. EVER LAID EYES ON: Lawrence M. Friedman, *A History of American Law* (New York: Simon and Schuster, 1973), 88–89, 98, 145.

41. KILL HIS ATTACKER: Sir William Blackstone, IV *Commentaries on the Laws of England* (London, 1769), 176–88.

42. JUDGES HAD DONE BEFORE THEM: Friedman, *A History of American Law*, 141–46.

43. "OUTLAWRY HAD EVER DONE": Harry S. Drago, *Outlaws On Horseback* (New York: Dodd, Mead), 1964, 82–84.

44. DUTY AS A LAWMAN: James D. Horan, *The Authentic Wild West: The Gunfighter* (New York: Crown, 1976), 81ff.; Joseph G. Rosa, *The Gunfighter: Man or Myth?* (Norman: University of Oklahoma Press, 1974), 119.

44. SELF-DEFENSE AND WAS ACQUITTED: Robert K. De Arment, *Bat Masterson: The Man and the Legend* (Norman: University of Oklahoma Press, 1974), 124–26, 222.

44. SHOOTING WAS SELF-DEFENSE: Ibid. at 235–37.

45. BRAZEL WAS ACQUITTED: Leon C. Metz, *Pat Garrett: The Story of a Western Lawman* (Norman: University of Oklahoma Press, 1974), 289–95.

45. SHE FELL TO HER DEATH: There are many accounts of the story of the lynching of Juanita of Downieville. Among the primary ones are: Hubert H. Bancroft, *Popular Tribunals*, vol. I, ch. 31 (San Francisco: The History Company, 1887); John W. Caughey, *Their Majesties The Mob* (Chicago: University of Chicago Press, 1960); Leonard Pitt, *The Decline of the Californios* (Berkeley: University of California Press, 1966); Josiah Royce, *California* (Boston: Houghton Mifflin, 1914); George R. Stewart, *Committee of Vigilance* (Boston: Houghton Mifflin, 1964).

46. SELF-DEFENSE OR MURDER: Bancroft, *Popular Tribunals*, vol. I, ch. 31, 47; Royce, *California*, 294–95.

46. "INVALUABLE TO THE NATION": Theodore Roosevelt, *Ranch Life and the Hunting Trail*, in *The Works of Theodore Roosevelt*, vol. IV (New York: Scribners, 1924), 428.

47. "FELLOW BEING ON HIS HANDS": Joseph H. Beale, "Retreat from a Murderous Assault," 16 *Harvard Law Review* 577 (1903).

48. BY THE APPELLATE COURTS: Self-defense cases decided by the American courts between 1658 and 1896 are collected at 26 *American Digest* secs. 614–32 (St. Paul: West, 1901).

49. ALL FROM THE 1890S: Emma Cotten was convicted of first-degree murder for killing Henry Harris in Alabama in 1891. They had quarreled during the day and he had threatened to kill her. Later she went to the room where he was, and they argued again. He hit her over the head, and she hit him back. He said he was going to kill her and reached inside his shirt as though to draw a pistol, and she stabbed him. *Cotten v. State*, 9 So. 287 (Ala. 1891).

    Caroline Bowman killed a man named George Ayers in Green County, Texas, in 1892. As the appellate court stated, "there is evidence tending to prove that appellant Bowman struck the deceased but one blow, and when she struck him he was making a violent and dangerous attack on her, threatening to then and there take her life." The jury convicted her of manslaughter. *Bowman v. State*, 20 S.W 558 (Tex. Cr. App. 1892).

    In another Texas case, Lizzie Williams was convicted of manslaughter for killing another woman. The two were walking along arguing; Lizzie was carrying a bucket a water. The other woman said to her, "Just hit the dirt and I will whip you," and picked up a piece of plank three feet long and three fingers wide. Saying she was going to tell her husband, Lizzie went into the house, put down her bucket, and came back outside. The woman hit Lizzie with the plank; and it broke so she dropped it and got Lizzie by the throat, pushing her backwards. Lizzie stabbed her, and she died. The trial judge refused to charge the jury on self-defense and the appellate court upheld him, saying that Lizzie was the aggressor and had voluntarily engaged in combat with the deceased. *Williams v. State*, 22 S.W. 683 (Tex. Cr. App. 1893).

49. SELF-DEFENSE WAS DECIDED IN 1902: *Williams v. State*, 70 S.W. 756 (Tex. Cr. App. 1902). Sadie Williams—whose husband had beaten her bloody on numerous occasions, had stomped on her stomach when she was pregnant, causing her to miscarry, and had repeatedly threatened to kill her—was convicted of second-degree murder when she shot him as he was coming at her with a hoe. She was sentenced to five years in prison. The trial court refused to allow the jury to hear any evidence about her husband's past abuse of her. The Texas Court of Criminal Appeals held this to be error and granted her a new trial.

Chapter 3. THE LAW IN ACTION

51. GRIEVOUS BODILY INJURY: The interchangeable terms "serious bodily harm," "great bodily harm," "grievous bodily injury" and the like have no special,

technical meaning in the self-defense context. They are used in their ordinary sense, and it is generally up to the jury to decide whether the harm threatened on a given occasion was serious enough to justify using deadly force in response.

52. HANDS, FISTS, AND FEET: Lenore Walker, *The Battered Woman* (New York: Harper and Row, 1979), 79 and *passim*.

52. AN OBJECT OR WEAPON: Maria Roy, "A Current Survey of 150 Cases," in *Battered Women: A Psychosociological Study of Domestic Violence*, Maria Roy, ed. (New York: Van Nostrand Reinhold, 1977), 18.

52. MINIMUM, SUFFERED BRUISES: J.J. Gayford, "Wife Battering: A Preliminary Survey of 100 Cases," *British Medical Journal*, 25 January 1975, 194–97.

52. SUCH AS STRAUS: Murray Straus, Richard Gelles, and Suzanne K. Steinmetz, *Behind Closed Doors: Violence in the American Family* (New York: Anchor/ Doubleday, 1980), 31–50.

52. DOBASH AND DOBASH: R. Emerson Dobash and Russell Dobash, *Violence Against Wives* (New York, The Free Press, 1979), 106–8.

52. STACEY AND SHUPE: William A. Stacey and Anson Shupe, *The Family Secret: Domestic Violence in America* (Boston: Beacon Press, 1983), 29.

52. INJURIES TO REPRODUCTIVE ORGANS: Walker, *The Battered Woman*, 105–6; Sue E. Eisenberg and Patricia L. Micklow, "The Assaulted Wife: 'Catch 22' Revisited," 3 *Women's Rights Law Reporter*, 138 (1977) at 144; Del Martin, *Battered Wives* (New York: Pocket Books, 1976), 61.

52. BEATEN WHILE PREGNANT: *The Family Secret*, 31.

52. PAINFUL AND HORRIBLE WAYS: Walker, *The Battered Woman*, 126.

52. KILLED BY BOYFRIENDS: Marvin E. Wolfgang, *Patterns in Criminal Homicide* (Philadelphia: University of Pennsylvania Press, 1958), 207, 213. Although it is quite old, Wolfgang's work is still the most thorough study available of homicide in the United States and one of the few that carefully and consistently analyze data by sex and relationship of perpetrators and victims. A number of subsequent studies of individual cities have replicated parts of Wolfgang's work and have generally supported his results. A study, which compared homicides in Houston with those in Wolfgang's Philadelphia, suggests that there may be regional differences in homicide methods. In Houston, women victims were far more apt to be shot than beaten to death. Alex D. Pokorney, "A Comparison of Homicides in Two Cities," 56 *Journal of Criminal Law, Criminology and Police Sciences* 479 (1965). See, also, Wilbanks, "Murdered Women and Women Who Murder," 170–71.

52. MAN IN THE BEDROOM: Wolfgang, *Patterns in Criminal Homicide*, 162.

53. "RETALIATION WITH DEADLY FORCE": *People v. Jones*, 12 Cal. Rptr. 777 (Cal. App. 1961) at 780.

54. SIX YEARS IN PRISON: *Easterling v. State*, 267 P.2d 185 (Okl. Cr. 1954).

55. LIFE IN PRISON: *State v. Painter*, 620 P.2d 1001 (Wash. App. 1980). Janice Painter's conviction was overturned on appeal; she pleaded guilty to manslaughter to avoid facing another trial.

57. USING A DEADLY WEAPON: *People v. Bush*, 148 Cal. Rptr. 430 (Cal. App. 1978); California Penal Code, section 1699.

58. "ANYTHING HANDY": Stacey and Shupe, *The Family Secret*, 30.

58. MAIMED OR KILLED HER: *Jackson v. State*, 240 S.E.2d 180 (Ga. App. 1977).

59. WASHINGTON SUPREME COURT: *State v. Thompson*, 558 P.2d 202 (Wash. 1977).

59. GUILTY OF INVOLUNTARY MANSLAUGHTER: *State v. Brooks*, 266 S.E.2d 3 (N.C. App. 1980).

60. PROGRESSIVELY MORE VIOLENT: See below, 129ff.

60. "MORE SERIOUS THAN THE OTHERS": *People v. Chapman*, 364 N.E.2d 577 (Ill. App. 1977), at 580.

61. AT THE TIME THERESA JONES': 1961; see above, 53–54.

61. "VIOLENCE IN THE HOUSEHOLD": 12 Cal. Rptr. 777, at 780; see also *State v. Copley*, 418 P.2d 579 (Ariz. 1966) for a very similar ruling.

62. MUTILATE OR KILL HER: See Don B. Kates, Jr. and Nancy Jean Engberg, "Deadly Force Self-Defense Against Rape," 15 *University of California, Davis, Law Journal* 873 (1982); Judith Fabricant, "Homicide in Response to a Threat of Rape: A Theoretical Examination of the Rule of Justification," 11 *Golden Gate University Law Review* 945 (1981).

63. BY THE JUDGE AS WELL: *State v. Martinez*, 230 P. 379 (N. Mex. 1924).

63. RULING AND HER CONVICTION: *People v. Taylor*, 9 Cal. Rptr. 391 (Cal. App. 1960). See also *State v. Harris*, 222 N.W.2d 462 (Iowa 1979), in which an appellate court upheld a trial judge's refusal to instruct the jury that, in addition to death and great bodily harm, a person has a right to use deadly force in defense against a felony about to be committed against him or her. The defendant, Rosetta Harris, testified that the man she killed had begun bothering her in a bar. She rebuffed him and went home, but he followed her to her apartment and demanded sex. She refused, and they struggled. She grabbed a shotgun from a corner of the room and told him to leave. When he refused, she loaded the gun and told him again to get out. He went to the door. Fearing that he was going to lock it and then rape her, she fired the shotgun. Her forty-year prison sentence for second-degree murder was upheld on appeal.

64. ORDINARY RAPE TRIAL: Susan Estrich, *Real Rape* (Cambridge: Harvard University Press, 1987). Professor Estrich's study is the first to systematically analyze the way that rape cases are being decided by the courts in the wake of the rape law reforms of the 1970s. Her conclusion is that although reform has changed the way issues are framed on appeal, it has not substantially changed the way the criminal justice system operates in practice. Suspicion of women's motives and credibility still underlie the courts' approach to rape cases. Ibid. at 57–79 and *passim*.

64. EIGHTY YEARS IN PRISON: *Thomas v. State*, 578 S.W.2d 691 (Tex. Cr. App. 1979), Rosetta Harris (p. 63n, "Ruling and her conviction," above) was also portrayed by the prosecution as a prostitute who murdered a customer. Another case involving a prostitute and self-defense against rape is *State v. Goodseal*, 183 N.W.2d 258 (Neb. 1971) (conviction affirmed).

65. BURGLARY, ROBBERY, OR RAPE: Formerly California Penal Code secs. 461, 213 and 264; now codified at California Penal Code sec. 12022.7.

65. "SIGNIFICANT OR SUBSTANTIAL": *People v. Wells*, 92 Cal. Rptr. 191 (Cal. App. 1971); *People v. Richardson*, 100 Cal. Rptr. 251 (Cal. App. 1972).

65. THESE SENTENCING STATUTES: *People v. Cardenas*, 121 Cal. Rptr. 126 (Cal. App. 1975); *People v. Superior Court (Lozano)*, 137 Ca. Rptr. 767 (Cal. App.

1977); *People v. Superior Court (Vasquez)*, 137 Cal. Rptr. 762 (Cal. App. 1977).

66. TO COVER SUCH INJURIES: *People v. Caudillo*, 146 Cal. Rptr. 859 (Cal. 1978).

66. NEVER WENT ANYWHERE: Kathleen Queneville, "Will Rape Ever Be A Crime of the Past? A Feminist View of Societal Factors and Rape Law Reforms," 9 *Golden Gate University Law Forum*, 581 (1978–79), at 589ff. The California sentence-enhancement statutes have now been consolidated at sections 12022.7 and 12022.8 of the California Penal Code. California's sentencing statutes have been extensively amended since the *Caudillo* case but not in ways that alter *Caudillo*'s view of the type of harm involved in rape. Indeed, that view has been codified in section 12022.8, which adds a five-year enhancement to the sentence of anyone who inflicts great bodily injury during the commission of a sexual crime.

66. DEFENDANT ALLOWED _____: I have omitted the victim's name from this account.

67. WIPING AWAY HIS VICTIM'S VOMIT: 146 Cal. Rptr. 859, at 862. Mr. Caudillo was not only convicted of burglary; he was also convicted of forcible rape, sodomy, oral copulation, and robbery. However, the judge ordered that he serve all of the other sentences concurrently with the burglary sentence. Therefore, the terms of the burglary sentence were all that mattered. From the point of view of punishment, the sex crimes were "for free."

67. ESCALATE INTO DEADLY CONFRONTATIONS: Self-defense cases decided between 1658 and 1896 are collected in 26 *American Digest* secs. 614–32. Cases decided between 1897 and 1916 are collected in West's *First* and *Second Decentennial Digests*, St. Paul: West, 1912 and 1920.

68. PRECEDED BY "MERE" THREATS: See, e.g., Darrel W. Stephen, "Domestic Assault: The Police Response," in Roy, ed., *Battered Women: A Psychosociological Study of Domestic Violence*, 164ff.

70. SHOT COONER IN THE HEAD: *Kontos v. State*, 363 S.2d 1025 (Ala. App. 1978).

71. CONVICTED OF MANSLAUGHTER: *State v. Crigler*, 598 P.2d 739 (Wash. App. 1979). Reversed on appeal and remanded for a new trial. Ms. Crigler chose to plead guilty to a reduced charge to avoid the ordeal of a second trial.

72. TWO YEARS IN PRISON: *Valentine v. State*, 587 S.W.2d 399 (Tex. Cr. App. 1979). Ms. Valentine's conviction was upheld on appeal.

72. BRICK IN HIS HAND: *King v. State*, 355 So.2d 1148 (Ala. App. 1978). Ms. King's first degree manslaughter conviction was upheld on appeal. She was given a seven-year sentence.

72. HANDS OF THE DECEASED: *Commonwealth v. Shaffer*, 326 N.E.2d 880 (Mass. 1975).

73. (A FEW MINUTES) TOO SOON: Mary Yost, "Probation Granted Improperly: Judge," *Columbus Dispatch*, 22 August 1981.

73. BEFORE IT IS TOO LATE: See below, 128–35.

74. TWO-TO-FIVE YEARS IN PRISON: *State v. Hundley*, 693 P.2d 475 (Kan. 1985). Betty Hundley's conviction was overturned on appeal, and she was granted a new trial. The appellate court ruled that the trial judge had erred in using the word "immediate" rather than "imminent" in the self-defense instruction.

75. RATIONAL AND UNDERSTANDABLE: Nan Blitman and Robin Green, "Inez Garcia On Trial," *Ms.*, May 1975, 49ff.

76. SHE WAS ACQUITTED: Elizabeth Schneider and Susan Jordan, "Representation of Women Who Defend Themselves in Response to Physical or Sexual Assault," 4 *Women's Rights Law Reporter*, 149 (Spring 1978). This excellent article is reprinted in slightly different form in Elizabeth Bochnak, ed., *Women's Self-Defense Cases* (Charlottesville, VA: Michie, 1981).

76. THAN A PRISON TERM: Faith McNulty, *The Burning Bed* (New York: Harcourt Brace Jovanovich, 1980).

77. FOR THE REST OF HER LIFE: Marilyn LeVine, "Beaten Wife Free in Husband's Death," *Charlotte (N.C.) News*, 7 October 1977; Marilyn Mather, "No Jail For Wife Who Killed Her Husband," *Charlotte Observer*, 7 October 1977.

78. "ENORMOUS BODILY HARM": *Erwin v. State*, 29 Ohio 186 (1876), at 199.

78. HOW SORELY PROVOKED HE MAY BE: 16 *Harvard Law Review* 567, at 581; see above, at 46–47.

80. OFTEN AT NIGHT: Gelles, *The Violent Home* (Beverly Hills: Sage, 1977), 99–104.

80. OF HER OWN, NO TRANSPORTATION: Walker, *The Battered Woman*, 165ff; Angela Browne, *When Battered Women Kill* (New York: Free Press, 1987), 43–44.

80. BRUNT OF HER HUSBAND'S ANGER: In Stacey and Shupe's survey, for example, of the 542 battered women studied, 452 had children. Forty-five percent of these children had themselves been victims of abuse; their average age was 5½. The authors found that the more severely a man injured his wife, the more likely he was to injure his children as well. *The Family Secret*, 63ff.

80. WITH WHICH THEY LIVE: See below, 131ff.

82. TO LIFE IN PRISON: *People v. Lenkevich*, 229 N.W.2d 298 (Mich. 1975). Ms. Lenkevich's conviction was upheld by the Michigan Court of Appeals but subsequently was reversed and remanded for a new trial by that state's Supreme Court on the grounds that the trial judge had misstated the law; she had no obligation to retreat in this instance because she was in her own home. See below, 82ff.

82. OUTRUN A RIFLE BULLET: *People v. McGrandy*, 156 N.W.2d 48 (Mich App. 1967); reversed on appeal and remanded for a new trial.

82. "GETTING AWAY WITH MURDER": See Annotation: "Duty to Retreat Where Assailant and Assailed Share the Same Living Quarters," 26 *American Law Reports 3rd* 1296. Annotation to *People v. McGrandy*, 156 N.W.2d 48 (Mich. App. 1967).

See, also, Annotation: "Duty to Retreat Where Assailant is Social Guest on Premises," 100 *American Law Reports 3rd* 532. Annotation to *Gainer v. State*, 391 N.E.2d 856 (Md. App. 1978).

The most often-quoted statement of the original rule is Justice Cardozo's opinion in *People v. Tomlins*, 107 N.E. 496 (N.Y. 1914):

> It is not now and never has been the law that a man assailed in his own dwelling is bound to retreat. If assailed there, he may stand his ground and resist the attack. He is under no duty to take to the fields and the highways, a fugitive from his own home.... The rule is the same whether the attack proceeds from some other occupant or from an intruder. It was so adjudged in *Jones v. State* [1884] 76 Ala. 8, 14. "Why," it was there inquired, "should

one retreat from his own house, when assailed by a partner or cotenant, any more than when assailed by a stranger who is lawfully upon the premises? Whither shall he flee, and when may he be permitted to return?''

Although a few very early state cases held that this rule did not apply to co-tenants, this appears to have been the general rule in the United States in this century until the Supreme Court of New Hampshire, in 1949, created an exception to it out of thin air. The case involved a battered woman, Florence Grierson, whose story is told below at pp. 84–85. Following the Grierson case the New Jersey Supreme Court, in *State v. Pontery*, 117 A.2d 473 (N.J. 1955), citing *Grierson* and an old case from 1910, invoked the same rule. Ida Pontery had shot her estranged husband with a pistol.

After that, the exception to the castle doctrine, either as to co-tenants or social invitees, took on a life of its own and over the past thirty years has been applied in a number of cases involving woman defendants (most of which are referred to in the text or notes). Since its establishment in *Grierson* and *Pontery*, it has occasionally been invoked by trial courts in cases involving male defendants as well. However, I have been able to find only a single modern case in which the exception has been upheld by an appellate court to the detriment of a man who killed either a co-tenant or a guest in his own "castle." *Commonwealth v. Walker*, 288 A.2d 741 (Pa. 1972).

83. AGAINST A HOMICIDAL STRANGER: *People v. Stallworth*, 111 N.W.2d 742 (Mich. 1961); *People v. McGrandy*, 156 N.W.2d 48 (Mich. App. 1967); *People v. Paxton*, 209 N.W.2d 251 (Mich. App. 1973); *People v. Lenkevich*, 229 N.W.2d 298 (Mich. 1975).

83. BEFORE SHE CAN DEFEND HERSELF:: *State v. Bobbit*, 415 So.2d 724 (Fla. 1982); see also *State v. Bobbit*, 389 So.2d 1094 (Fla. App. 1980).

83. WHO DOES NOT LIVE WITH HER: *Hedges v. State*, 172 So.2d 824 (Fla. 1965); see also *Hedges v. State*, 165 So.2d 213 (Fla. App. 1964).

83. ARE OTHERWISE IDENTICAL: See also *Watkins v. State*, 197 So.2d 312 (Fla. 1967); *Connor v. State*, 361 So.2d 774 (Fla. 1978); *Cannon v. State*, 464 So.2d 149 (Fla. App. 1985); *Carter v. State* 469 So.2d 194 (Fla. App. 1985).

84. DEFENDANTS WHO ARE BATTERED WOMEN: I have not found any cases in which an appellate court has upheld the social invitee exception to the castle doctrine against a male defendant. See above, p. 82n, ''getting away with murder.''

85. LIKE A TEMPORARY CO-TENANT: *State v. Grierson*, 69 A.2d 851 (N.H. 1949).

85. AND SET HER FREE: *Commonwealth v. Eberle*, 379 A.2d 90 (Pa. 1977).

87. WAS GRANTED A NEW TRIAL: *State v. Lamb*, 366 A.2d 981 (N.J. 1976).

90. IN RETALIATION FOR PAST ABUSE: *State v. Branchal*, 684 P.2d 1163 (N.M. App. 1984).

90. WHICH CAN BE MURDER: The prosecutor in *State v. Griffiths*, above, 17ff, for example, ''portrayed the defendant as having deliberately planned and carried out the murder of her husband in a cold and calculated manner, continuing to fire shots into the body of her husband while he was in a helpless position and pleading for mercy.'' *State v. Griffiths*, 610 P.2d 522 (Idaho 1980), at 525.

92. JURY WHICH CONVICTED HER: *People v. Shipp*, 367 N.E.2d 966 (Ill. App. 1977).

Chapter 4. THE QUESTION OF REASONABLENESS

94. ACTION WAS NOT REASONABLE: See Bochnak, *Women's Self-Defense Cases,* 72–85 for an interesting discussion of defense attorney strategies for selecting unbiased juries in these cases.

94. INTENTION TO KILL HER: See above 55–57.

95. FIRED AGAIN, KILLING HIM: *People v. White,* 414 N.E.2d 196 (Ill. App. 1980).

95. "BEYOND ANY REASONABLE DOUBT": Ibid at 199.

96. AND SET HER FREE: *State v. Lynch,* 436 So.2d 567 (La. 1983). The law in Louisiana requires the prosecutor to prove beyond a reasonable doubt that a homicide defendant did *not* act in self-defense. Since the appellate court found that the prosecutor did not meet that burden of proof, Sheral should have been acquitted at her trial. She was thus entitled to a complete discharge rather than just a retrial.

98. DEFEND HERSELF AGAINST IT: *Commonwealth v. Watson,* 431 A.2d 949 (Pa. 1981). Fortunately, the Pennsylvania Supreme Court, in an extremely sensitive opinion, overruled the trial judge and found that, on the evidence, her fear was reasonable. It ordered her discharged. See, above, p.96, "and set her free."

98. "ONE SUFFICIENT REASON": Oliver W. Holmes, *The Common Law* (New York: Little, Brown, 1881), 108.

99. "BATTERED WOMAN DEFENDANT": Comment, "Battered Wives Who Kill: Double Standard Out of Court, Single Standard In?" 2 *Law and Human Behavior,* 133 (1978) at 158.

100. BIG BRAWNY BOYS: Jeffrey Z. Rubin, Frank Provenzano, and Zella Luria, "The Eye of the Beholder: Parents' Views on Sex of Newborns," *American Journal of Orthopsychiatry* 44 (1974): 512–19.

101. PLAY MORE ROUGHLY WITH THEM: Nancy Romer, *The Sex Role Cycle* (Old Westbury, N.Y.: The Feminist Press, 1981), 7–10; Lenore J. Weitzman, *Sex Role Socialization* (Palo Alto: Mayfield, 1979), 1–4.

101. 15 PERCENT OF THE BOYS: Janet Lever, "Sex Differences in the Games Children Play," *Social Problems* 23 (1976): 478–87.

102. GIRLS DID MAKE: Roger Hart, "Sex Differences in the Use of Outdoor Space," *Perspectives on Non-Sexist Early Childhood Education,* Barbara Sprung, ed. (New York: Teachers College Press, 1978), 101–9.

102. WHICH BOYS TYPICALLY DO: Seppo E. Iso-Ahola, "Sex-Role Stereotypes and Causal Attributions of Success or Failure in Motor Performance," *Research Quarterly* 50 (1979): 630–40; Anne Marie Bird and Jean M. Williams, "A Developmental-Attributional Analysis of Sex-Role Stereotypes for Sport Performance," *Developmental Psychology* 16 (1980): 319–22.

102. EVIDENCE TO THE CONTRARY: N.P. Pollis and D.C. Doyle, "Sex-Role Status and Perceived Competence Among First Graders," *Perceptual and Motor Skills* 34 (1972): 235–38; see also, Judith Bridges and Joseph del Ciampo, "Children's Perceptions of the Competence of Boys and Girls," *Perceptual and Motor Skills* 52 (1981): 503–6.

102. TENNIS, SWIMMING, AND GYMNASTICS: Elmer Spreitzer, Eldon Snyder, and Joseph Kivlin, "A Summary of Some Recent Studies Concerning the Female Athlete," *Frontiers,* vol. 3, no. 1 (1978): 14–19.

103. COVERAGE OF THE LAW: 20 USCA 1681; 34 CFR 106.34 (c); 34 CFR 106.41 (b).

104. SETTLE THE QUESTION: D.R. Omark and M. Edelman, "Peer Group Social Interactions from an Evolutionary Perspective," paper presented at the Society for Research in Child Development Conference, Philadelphia, 1973; D.R. Omark, M. Omark, and M. Edelman, "Dominance Hierarchies in Young Children," paper presented at the International Congress of Anthropological and Ethnological Sciences, Chicago, 1973. Both cited in Eleanor E. Maccoby and Carol N. Jacklin, *The Psychology of Sex Differences* (Stanford: Stanford University Press, 1974), 256–60.

104. A FEW FIST FIGHTS: Straus, Gelles, and Steinmetz, *Behind Closed Doors,* 68.

106. NEED FOR SECURITY: Inge Broverman, Susan Vogel, Donald Broverman, Frank Clarkson, and Paul Rosenkranz, "Sex-Role Stereotypes: A Current Appraisal," *Journal of Social Issues* 28 (1972): 63. See also, Paul Rosenkrantz, Susan Vogel, H. Bee, Inge Broverman, and Donald Broverman, "Sex-Role Stereotypes and Self-Concepts in College Students," *Journal of Consulting and Clinical Psychology* 32 (1968): 287–95; Inge Broverman, Donald Broverman, Frank Clarkson, Paul Rosenkrantz, and Susan Vogel, "Sex-Role Stereotypes and Clinical Judgements of Mental Health," *Journal of Consulting and Clinical Psychology* 34 (1970): 1.

107. "BOTH MEN AND WOMEN": Broverman et al., "Sex Role Stereotypes: A Current Appraisal," 61.

107. STEREOTYPICALLY FEMININE ONES: Ibid. at 65.

107. DOMINANT, AGGRESSIVE, AND COMPETITIVE: Sandra L. Bem, "The Measurement of Psychological Androgyny," *Journal of Consulting and Clinical Psychology* 42 (1974): 155–62. Such lists of gender stereotypes are, of course, extensively prevalidated. They do not merely reflect the biases or assumptions of those who devise them.

108. "TO PIECES UNDER PRESSURE": Janet T. Spence and Robert L. Helmreich, *Masculinity and Feminity: Their Psychological Dimensions, Correlate and Antecedents* (Austin: University of Texas Press, 1978), 231–33.

108. "SUBMISSIVE," "TIMID" AND "WORRYING": Alfred B. Heilbrun, Jr., *Human Sex-Role Behavior* (New York: Pergamon, 1981), 7.

108. FAR FROM CONCLUSIVE: Maccoby and Jacklin, *The Psychology of Sex Differences,* Chapter 10 and *passim.*

109. EYE OF THE BEHOLDER: John Condry and Sandra Condry, "Sex Differences: A Study in the Eye of the Beholder," *Child Development* 47 (1976): 817.

109. FOOTBALL TO THE "BOY": Laura S. Sidorowicz and G. Sparks Lunney, "Baby X Revisited," *Sex Roles* 6 (1980): 67–73.

109. IN VERY YOUNG CHILDREN: Maccoby and Jacklin, *The Psychology of Sex Differences,* 362ff., and Chapter 9 *passim;* cf. Jeanne H. Block, "Assessing Sex Differences: Issues, Problems and Pitfalls," *Merrill-Palmer Quarterly* 22 (1976): 283–308.

110. DOLLS LIKE G.I. JOE: Harriet L. Rheinhold and Kay V. Cook, "The Content of Boys' and Girls' Rooms as an Index of Parents' Behavior," *Child Development* 46 (1975): 459–63.

110. FOCUS OF THEIR ACTIVITIES: Evelyn G. Pitcher and Lynn H. Schultz, *Boys and Girls at Play: The Development of Sex Roles* (South Hadley, MA: Bergin and Garvey, 1983), 27–35.

110. "SEX-APPROPRIATE BEHAVIOR...": Ibid. at 114–15.

111. REPRESENTING SUBMISSIVE BEHAVIORS: Ibid. at 26.

111. STRONGER, ABLER, BRAVER MALE: A particularly good analysis of traditional folk tales can be found in Maria R. Lieberman, "Some Day My Prince Will Come," *Sexism and Youth*, Diane Gersoni-Stavn, ed. (New York: Bowker, 1974), 228–43.

111. DESIGNED FOR PRESCHOOL CHILDREN: Lenore J. Weitzman, Deborah Eifler, Elizabeth Hodaka, and Catherine Ross, "Sex-Role Socialization in Picture Books for Preschool Children," *American Journal of Sociology* 77 (1972): 1125–50.

112. LESSONS FOR LITTLE GIRLS: Shirley St. Peter, "Jack Went Up the Hill...But Where Was Jill?" *Psychology of Women Quarterly* 4 (1979): 256.

113. SUBSEQUENTLY ADMINISTERED TEST: Emily Davidson, Amy Yasuna, and Alan Tower, "The Effects of Television Cartoons on Sex-Role Stereotyping in Young Girls," *Child Development* 50 (1979): 597–600.

113. ABSORBED BY YOUNG VIEWERS: Above, p. 111 "representing submissive behaviors"; see also, Ann Beuf, "Doctor, Lawyer, Household Drudge," *Journal of Communications* 24 (1974): 142–45; M. Frueh, "Traditional Sex-Role Development and Amount of Time Spent Watching Television," *Developmental Psychology* 11 (1975): 109; Paul E. McGee and Terry Frueh, "Television Viewing and the Learning of Sex-Role Stereotypes," *Sex Roles* 6 (1980): 179–88; Laurie Ross, Daniel Anderson, and Patricia A. Wisocki, "Television Viewing and Adult Sex-Role Attitudes," *Sex Roles* 8 (1982): 589; Alexis S. Tan, "T.V. Beauty Ads and Role Expectations of Adolescent Female Viewers," *Journalism Quarterly* 56 (1979): 283–88.

113. REINFORCE THE BEHAVIOR: Romer, *The Sex-Role Cycle*, 37–40; Lisa A. Serbin, "Teachers, Peers and Play Preferences: An Environmental Approach to Sex Typing in Preschool," in *Perspectives on Non-Sexist Early Childhood Education*, 37–40.

114. READERS AND OTHER TEXTBOOKS: See, for example, the many articles on this collected in Judith Stacey, Susan Bereaud, and Joan Daniels, eds., *And Jill Came Tumbling After: Sexism In American Education* (New York: Dell, 1974). See also, Comment: "Sex Discrimination: The Textbook Case," 62 *California Law Review* 1312 (1974).

117. AND KILLED HIM: *State v. Wanrow*, 559 P.2d. 548 (Wash. 1977).

117. DANGER THAT SHE FACED: Respondent's Supplemental Brief, *State v. Wanrow*, Supreme Court of the State of Washington, Case No. 43949, February 10, 1976.

117. "TO BE OBJECTIVELY REASONABLE": *State v. Wanrow*, 559 P.2d 548 at 5.

117. APPLICABLE TO MALE DEFENDANTS: Ibid.

118. ILLICITLY OBTAINED KEY: *State v. Crigler*, 598 P.2d 739 (Wash. App. 1979); above, 71–72.

118. GRABBED THE GUN AND SHOT HIM: *State v. Savage,* 618 P.2d 82 (Wash. 1980).
118. ALL OF THE CHILDEN: *State v. Thacker,* 616 P.2d 655 (Wash. 1980).
118. PARALYZED ON THE FLOOR: *State v. Painter,* 620 P.2d 1001 (Wash. App. 1980); above, vii–viii and 54–55.
119. SHE STABBED HIM: *State v. Bailey,* 591 P.2d 1212 (Wash. App. 1979).
119. TEN YEARS FOR MANSLAUGHTER: *Northwest Passage,* June 1, 1981, p. 10; above, 26-27.
119. WHEN SHE SHOT HIM: *State v. Kelly,* 655 P.2d 1202 (Wash. App. 1982); 685 P.2d 564 (Wash. 1984).
119. THIRTY YEARS IN PRISON: Maggie Brown, "Second thoughts from the judge who sent her to jail," *Seattle Post-Intelligencer,* 14 November 1982, p. B1; *Equal Defense Alliance Newsletter,* January–March 1983; above, 25–26.
119. PURSUANT TO A GUILTY PLEA: Maggie Brown, "In the last 10 years these women have pled self-defense in the state's courts," *Seattle Post-Intelligencer,* 14 November 1982, p. B1.
120. TWENTY YEARS IN PRISON: *State v. Allery,* 682 P.2d 312 (Wash. 1984); *Northwest Passage,* 1 June 1981, p. 12.
120. WAS GOING TO KILL HER: Maggie Brown, "In the past 10 years these women have pled self-defense in the state's courts," *Seattle Post-Intelligencer,* 14 November 1982, p. B1; *Equal Defense Alliance Newsletter,* January–March 1983.
120. BATTERED WIFE FOR TWENTY YEARS: Ibid.
120. ABOUT TO ASSAULT HER: Maggie Brown, "In the past 10 years these women have pled self-defense in the state's courts," *Seattle Post-Intelligencer,* 14 November 1982, p. B1.
120. TEN YEARS IN PRISON: "No proof woman was battered, says judge," *Seattle Post-Intelligencer,* 19 April 1984, p. A3. Happily, the judge was subsequently convinced that Ms. Three Stars had been a battered woman and was defending herself. He vacated the sentence and placed her on probation. Marsha Leslie, "Judge suspends prison term for Paula Three Stars," *Seattle Times,* 14 June 1984.
120. AND HAVE A TRIAL: There have been no appellate cases in Washington involving women and self-defense since these were decided. I do not know whether there have been other convictions in the trial courts because the organization that was monitoring this issue in Washington state, the Equal Rights Alliance, has ceased to operate. In 1984 the Washington Supreme Court ruled that expert testimony about the battered-woman syndrome is admissible in these cases, a development that may well have contributed to a reducton in the number of convictions since then. See Chapter Six, below.
121. "ON WOMEN'S DEFENSE ISSUES": Maggie Brown, "A double standard at work in self-defense cases, too," *Seattle Post-Intelligencer,* 14 November 1982, p. B2.
121. REASONABLENESS REQUIREMENT ALTOGETHER:: States which have done this by statute are Delaware, Hawaii, Kentucky, and Pennsylvania. Colorado, Ohio and Indiana have adopted the same position by court decision. *Model Penal Code,* Article 3, Section 3.04 and Comments, and Section 3.09 and Comments, American Law Institute, 1961. This code was drafted by a group of legal experts to provide a model criminal code for states that are revising and

updating their criminal law. It was intended to represent a systematic analysis and rethinking of the basic premises of criminal responsibility and criminal justice.

121. USING DEADLY FORCE: The existence of two sorts of subjective standard applicable to self-defense—the subjective standard of *reasonableness* and the subjective standard of *belief*—has caused no end of confusion. Court opinions tend to talk about subjective standards without specifying which they mean and often apparently without realizing that there are two different concepts involved. This is confused even further because, in every state that employs an objective "reasonable man" standard, the jury must find that the defendant's belief in the need for using deadly force was genuine as well as reasonable. This means that even the objective standard has a subjective component.

121. TWO LINES OF REASONING: See, generally, Dolores A. Donovan and Stephanie M. Wildman, "Is the Reasonable Man Obsolete? A Critical Perspective on Self-Defense and Provocation," 14 *Loyola of Los Angeles Law Review* 435 (1981); Paul H. Robinson, "A Theory of Justification: Societal Harm as a Prerequisite for Criminal Liability," 23 *University of California at Los Angeles Law Review* 266 (1975); Note: "Manslaughter and the Adequacy of Provocation: The Reasonableness of the Reasonable Man," 106 *University of Pennsylvania Law Review* 1021 (1958); Glanville Williams, "Provocation and the Reasonable Man," 1954 *Criminal Law Review* 740.

122. OF THE PERSON ACCUSED: See, for example, Glanville Williams, *Criminal Law: The General Part*, 2d. ed. (London: Stevens and Sons Ltd., 1961); Jerome Hall, *General Principles of Criminal Law*, 2d. ed. (New York: Bobbs Merrill, 1960); H.L.A. Hart, *Punishment and Responsibility: Essays In The Philosophy of Law* (Oxford: Oxford University Press, 1968) George Fletcher, *Rethinking Criminal Law* (Boston: Little, Brown, 1978).

122. PEOPLE ACCUSED OF CRIMES: See Donovan and Wildman, "Is the Reasonable Man Obsolete?" 462ff., and the sources there cited.

122. INEQUITIES THAT THEY IGNORE: For a telling example of the problems that the reasonable man standard can present for racial and ethnic minorities see Colin Howard, "What Colour is the Reasonable Man?" 1961 *Criminal Law Review* 41, discussing the application of British law to Australian aborigines.

Chapter 5. REASONABLENESS AND THE BATTERED WOMAN

124. MIDDLE OF THE NIGHT: Walker, *The Battered Woman*, p. 61; Elaine Hilberman and Kit Munson, "Sixty Battered Women," *Victimology* 2 (1977–78): 460; Dobash and Dobash, *Violence Against Wives*, 111, 139.

124. "IN MY BED": Hilberman and Munson, "Sixty Battered Women," 464.

125. "THREATENING TO 'TORCH' HER": William A. Stacey and Anson Shupe, *The Family Secret* (Boston: Beacon Press, 1983), 29.

125. VAGINAL AND ANAL RAPE: Lenore E. Walker, *The Battered Woman* (New York: Harper and Row, 1979), 78–126.

125. "OR HELD UNDERWATER": Angela Browne, "Self-Defense Homicides by Battered Women: Relationships at Risk." Paper presented to the American Psychology and Law Conference, Chicago, October, 1983, 9.

126. REPORTED SUCH FREQUENT ASSAULTS: Angela Browne, *When Battered Women Kill* (New York: Free Press, 1987), 68.
126. INJURY TO THE WOMAN: Ibid. at 97–100.
126. "VARIETY OF ASSAULTIVE BEHAVIORS...": Ibid. at 96. Citation in original omitted. The "number of abusive acts" refers to those that occured during the four specific incidents each participant was asked to describe in detail, not to the overall frequency of abusive incidents (each comprised of a variety of acts, such as slaps, kicks, punches) that the women in the two groups experienced.
127. WOMEN IN THE COMPARISON GROUP: Ibid. at 69. Citation in original omitted.
127. COWED AND TERRIFIED: Walker, *The Battered Woman*, 148, 166, 172; Dobash and Dobash, *Violence Against Wives*, 24.
127. A LARGE PART OF IT: Walker, *The Battered Woman*, 172–73.
128. PSYCHOLOGICAL ABUSE OFTEN TAKES: Walker, *The Battered Woman*, 163ff; Walker, *The Battered Woman Syndrome*, 50; Stacey and Shupe, *The Family Secret*, 49–50; Hilberman and Munson, "Sixty Battered Women," 1339–40.
128. KILLS A PET ANIMAL: Angela Browne, *When Battered Women Kill*, 14.
128. DEVASTATION AS PHYSICAL PAIN: Ibid. at 97–100.
128. WILL CAUSE HER TO DIE: Ibid. at 66; Walker, *The Battered Woman*, 10.
129. WILL EVER VOLUNTARILY STOP: Mildred G. Pagelow, *Woman Battering: Women and Their Experience* (Beverly Hills: Sage, 1981); Jean Giles-Simms, *Wife-Battering: A Systems Theory Approach* (New York: Guilford, 1983), 52, 55, 129ff.; Browne, *When Battered Women Kill*, 105–7; Stacey and Shupe, *The Family Secret*, 47; Davidson, *Conjugal Crime*, 35.
129. "DURING A SINGLE BEATING": *The Family Secret*, 47.
129. AND ATTEMPTED RECONCILIATION: *The Battered Woman*, 55–70; Lenore E. Walker, *The Battered Woman Syndrome* (New York: Springer, 1984), 95–104.
131. PATTERN ON THE WALLPAPER: Del Martin, *Battered Wives* (New York: Pocket Books, 1976), 50.
131. CHILD'S BIRTHDAY PARTY: Richard J. Gelles, *The Violent Home* (Beverly Hills: Sage, 1977), 139.
131. "ONE NIGHT FOR DINNER": *The Family Secret*, 87.
131. HAD SAID SHE WOULD: *The Battered Woman*, 90ff.
131. "CONSTANT ANTICIPATORY TERROR": Elaine Hilberman, "Overview: the 'Wife-Beater's Wife' Reconsidered," *American Journal of Psychiatry* 137 (1980): 1340.
132. WORK FOR BATTERED WOMEN: R. Emerson Dobash and Russell Dobash, *Violence Against Wives* (New York: The Free Press, 1979), 103.
132. "GUARANTEE A VIOLENT PUNISHMENT": Ibid. at 103–4.
132. EVEN MORE VICIOUS BEATING: *The Violent Home*, 77.
132. SEVERELY THEY WERE BEATEN: Sue E. Eisenberg and Patricia L. Micklow, "The Assaulted Wife: Catch 22 Revisited," 3 *Women's Rights Law Reporter* 138 (1977): at 144–45.
133. TWISTED OR BROKEN: *The Battered Woman*, 61–62.
133. "END THE SECOND PHASE": Ibid. at 61.
133. GIFTS AND LOVING BEHAVIOR: Ibid. at 65ff.

133. INTO FORGIVING HIM: Walker, *The Battered Woman Syndrome*, 97; Dobash and Dobash, *Violence Against Wives*, 139–40.
133. NORMAL MARRIED LIFE: Walker, *The Battered Woman Syndrome*, 96.
133. A LONG TIME AFTERWARDS: Dobash and Dobash, *Violence Against Wives*, 123.
133. OF KILLING THEM: Walker, *The Battered Woman*, 75; Bruce J. Rounsaville, "Theories in Marital Violence: Evidence from a Study of Battered Women," *Victimology* 3 (1978): 16; Browne, *When Battered Women Kill*, 68–69.
134. DO TO HER AND HOW: Walker, *The Battered Woman*, 10; Browne, *When Battered Women Kill*, 66.
134. WITH A KNIFE OR GUN: Jean Giles-Sims, *Wife-Battering: A Systems Theory Approach* (New York: Guilford, 1983), 49ff; Straus et al., *Behind Closed Doors*, 34.
134. FOR THEIR INTENDED VICTIMS: Gelles, *The Violent Home*, 73–74; Martin, *Battered Wives*, 51; *Glamour*, October 1980, 56. (The story of Deborah Davis, whose husband, after years of horrible sexual abuse, threatened to build a wooden coffin to imprison her in. She was acquitted by a jury of murdering him.)
135. FIRING A BULLET THROUGH IT: See p. 2 above.
135. "WITH EXPLOSIVE SUDDENESS": "Sixty Battered Women," 466.
135. "OR 'DRUNKEN' RAVINGS' ": Peter D. Chimbos, *Marital Violence: A Study of Interspousal Homicide* (San Francisco, R. and E. Research Associates, 1978), 75
136. TO FILE A COMPLAINT: *Under the Rule of Thumb: Battered Women and the Administration of Justice*, United States Commission on Civil Rights, 1982, 14.
136. ONE CASE OUT OF THREE: *The Family Secret*, 107.
136. ARMED EVEN IS HE ISN'T: Ibid. at 109.
137. PROBLEM OF DOMESTIC VIOLENCE: *Final Report, Attorney General's Task Force on Family Violence*, United States Department of Justice, 1984, 11–12, 22–24.
138. ARREST OF HER ASSAILANT: Dobash and Dobash, *Violence Against Wives*, 215.
138. WHERE THEY ARE MARRIED: Ibid. at 207–8.
138. AND ITS ESCALATING NATURE: Ibid at 214.
138. DISPUTES AND DISTURBANCES: *Domestic Violence and the Police: Studies in Detroit and Kansas City* (Washington, D.C.: The Police Foundation, 1977), 9.
138. IN THE SAME TWO-YEAR PERIOD: Ibid.
139. DEPARTMENT'S PART TO PROTECT HER: *Hartzler v. City of San Jose*, 46 Cal. App. 3d 6 (1975). On a happier note, a federal court jury recently awarded 3.6 million dollars in damages to a battered woman in a negligence suit against the Torrington, Connecticut police department, a sum that was subsequently reduced to 1.9 million following an appeal. She claimed that they had failed to protect her from her violent husband, despite her frequent calls to them for help. Ultimately, he attacked her and stabbed her thirteen times, leaving her disfigured and partly paralyzed. *New York Times*, 15 June 1986, p. E8. See Note, "Battered Women and the Equal Protection Clause: Will The Constitution Help Them When The Police Won't?" 95 *Yale Law Journal* 788 (1986).

139. IF SHE EVER TRIED: Browne, *When Battered Women Kill*, 66; Terry Davidson, *Conjugal Crime* (New York: Ballentine Books, 1980), 38; Walker, *The Battered Woman*, 42–43; Roy, "A Current Survey of 150 Cases," 35.

140. BATTERED WOMAN AT EVERY TURN: *Under The Rule Of Thumb*, 12–59; *Final Report, Attorney General's Task Force on Family Violence*, 27–43.

140. THAN TO PROSECUTE THEM: *Under the Rule of Thumb*, 23–34; Eisenberg and Micklow, "The Assaulted Wife: Catch 22 Revisited," 158–59; Lynne A. Sacco, "Wife Abuse: The Failure of Legal Remedies," 11 *John Marshall Journal of Practice and Procedure* 549 (1978) at 563–65; Stacey and Shupe, *The Family Secret*, 161–64; Elizabeth Truninger, "Marital Violence: The Legal Solutions," 23 *Hastings Law Journal* 259 (1971) at 273.

140. MANIPULATE THEIR HUSBANDS: *Under the Rule of Thumb*, 23–34.

140. IN CRIMINAL TRIAL CIRCLES: "The Assaulted Wife: Catch 22 Revisited," 158.

140. PAST ROMANTIC RELATIONSHIP: *Under the Rule of Thumb*, 24.

140. VICTIMS DECLINES DRAMATICALLY: Ibid. at 32–33.

141. DID NOT OCCUR, DO NOT: *The Federal Response to Domestic Violence*, United States Commission on Civil Rights, Washington, D.C., 1982, 26–27.

141. TO PROSECUTE HIM AT ALL: *Under the Rule of Thumb*, 23–34; Eisenberg and Micklow, "The Assaulted Wife: Catch 22 Revisited," 158–59; Lynne A. Sacco, "Wife Abuse: The Failure of Legal Remedies," 11 *John Marshall Journal of Practice and Procedure* 549 (1978) at 563–65; Stacey and Shupe, *The Family Secret*, 161–64; Elizabeth Truninger, "Marital Violence: The Legal Solutions," 23 *Hastings Law Journal* 259 (1971) at 273.

142. JUDGES WHO TRY THEM: *Under the Rule of Thumb*, 55–59; Martin, *Battered Wives*, 115–19; Stacey and Shupe, *The Family Secret*, 167ff; Dobash and Dobash, *Violence Against Wives*, 219–20.

142. EVER REACHES A COURTROOM: *Under the Rule of Thumb*, 36, 55.

142. TRIAL, SENTENCING, AND JAIL: Mildred D. Pagelow, *Woman Battering: Victims and Their Experiences* (Beverly Hills, Sage, 1981), 81.

142. SERIOUS CRIMINAL OFFENSE: *Under the Rule of Thumb*, 55–59.

142. WHO FILES FOR A DIVORCE: *Under the Rule of Thumb*, 48.

143. AGAINST THE BATTERER ANYWAY: Martin, *Battered Wives*, 105–9.

143. INTO WHICH IT HAS LAPSED: Nadine Taub, "Equitable Relief in Cases of Adult Domestic Abuse," 6 *Women's Rights Law Reporter* 241 (Summer 1980) at 267–68; Truninger, "Marital Violence: The Legal Solutions," 265–67.

143. CAN HAVE IMMEDIATE PROTECTION: Lisa Lerman, "Protection of Battered Women: A Survey," 6 *Women's Rights Law Reporter* 271 (Summer 1980).

144. FREQUENTLY BEEN VITIATED: *Under the Rule of Thumb*, 47ff.

145. HAS A LEGAL RIGHT TO BE: 40 *American Jurisprudence Second*, "Homicide," sec. 161:

> No generally recognized rule of law deprives one who expects an attack to be made upon him of going to places where he otherwise has a legal right to go. On the contrary, he may proceed with his legitimate business, and if, without fault on his part, the anticipated attack is made, he may kill his assailant with an assurance that the law will excuse his act. Very

obviously, the law does not require one to secrete himself to avoid one who has threatened his life.

145. EVEN A LETHAL CONFRONTATION: Ibid.

145. CONFRONTATIONS ARE LIKELY TO ARISE: Phyllis Crocker, "The Meaning of Equality for Battered Women Who Kill Men in Self-Defense," 8 *Harvard Women's Law Journal* 121 (1985) at 148, note 127.

145. SUCH A WOMAN'S ACTIONS REASONABLE: Bochnak, *Women's Self-Defense Cases*, 55ff; Schneider, "Describing and Changing: Women's Self-Defense Work and The Problem of Expert Testimony on Battering," 201; Lenore E. Walker, Roberta K. Thyfault, and Angela Browne, "Beyond the Juror's Ken: Battered Women," 7 *Vermont Law Review* 1 (1982) at 5; Stacey and Shupe, *The Family Secret*, 118-19.

Juries are by their nature ephemeral bodies and difficult to study. Experienced trial attorneys, however, develop a very acute sense of what issues juries are troubled by. Jurors' preoccupation with the issue of not leaving is reflected in the arguments to appellate courts made by defense attorneys about why expert testimony is necessary in women's self-defense cases; it is also reflected in appellate court opinions about what jurors are and are not likely to understand about battered women's behavior. See below, Chapter Six, and the articles listed at p. 160n, "the battered woman syndrome," and the cases listed at p. 166n, "state courts of appeals."

147. STILL EXPECT OF THEMSELVES: Philip Blumstein and Pepper Schwartz, *American Couples* (New York: William Morrow, 1983), 28.

147. FOLLOWED BY RATIONALIZATION: Dobash and Dobash, *Violence Against Wives*, 95-96; Davidson, *Conjugal Violence*, 50ff; Browne, *When Battered Women Kill*, 52.

147. SUFFERED FROM THEIR PARTNERS: *Wife-Battering: A Systems Theory Approach*, 59.

147. DENIAL USUALLY TAKES: "Sixty Battered Women," 467; see also, Kathleen J. Ferraro and John M. Johnson, "How Women Experience Battering: The Process of Victimization," *Social Problems* 30, no. 3 (1983): 325; Rounsaville, "Theories in Marital Violence: Evidence from a Study of Battered Women," 22.

148. TO BE A NORMAL MARRIAGE: *The Battered Woman*, 65-70.

149. NUMBER OF SPECIFIC DEVELOPMENTS: Dobash and Dobash, *Violence Against Wives*, 146-48; J. J. Gayford, "Wife Battering: A Preliminary Survey of 100 Cases," *British Medical Journal*, 25 January 1975, 194-97; Rounsaville, "Theories in Marital Violence: Evidence from a Study of Battered Women," 17.

149. BETWEEN LEAVING AND STAYING: *Wife-Battering: A Systems Theory Approach*, 48, 135.

149. DESPITE THE BEATINGS: *The Battered Woman Syndrome*, 95-97.

150. ON THE WOMAN'S PART: *Violence Against Wives*, 159.

150. "NOW YOU LIE IN IT": Stacey and Shupe, *The Family Secret*, 39; Pagelow, *Woman Battering*, 48.

150. LISTS OF THEIR OWN: Pagelow, *Woman Battering*, 212-13.

150. VIOLENT HUSBANDS IS FEAR: Browne, *When Battered Women Kill*, 113ff; Martin, *Battered Wives*, 76-80; Stacey and Shupe, *The Family Secret*, 55-56; Dobash

and Dobash, *Violence Against Wives*, 146ff; Bochnak, *Women's Self-Defense Cases*, 57; Hilberman and Munson, "Sixty Battered Women," 466.

150. BATTERED WOMAN CAN DO: Browne, *When Battered Women Kill*, 115–16;.

151. WOMEN IN THEIR LIVES: Browne, *When Battered Women Kill*, 115–16; Hilberman and Munson, "Sixty Battered Women," 466; Pagelow, *Woman-Battering: Victims and their Experiences,* 106; Rounsaville, "Theories in Marital Violence: Evidence from a Study of Battered Women," 20–21; Stacey and Shupe, *The Family Secret*, 99.

151. KILL HIMSELF AS WELL: Walker, *The Battered Woman Syndrome*, 34, 42; Browne, *When Battered Women Kill*, 65–68.

151. PERCENT OF THE MALE VICTIMS: Wolfgang, *Patterns in Criminal Homicide*, 207, 214.

151. "THREATS ARE INTERTWINED": George W. Bernard, Hernan Vera, Maria I. Vera, and Gustave Newman, "Till Death Do Us Part: A Study of Spouse Murder," *Bulletin of the American Academy of Psychiatry and Law*, vol. 10, no. 4 (1982): 279.

151. "VIOLENCE IN THESE CASES": Ibid. at 278.

152. ASSAULT BUT THE LEAVING: C. Robert Showalter, Richard J. Bonnie, and Virginia Roddy, "The Spousal Homicide Syndrome," *International Journal of Law and Psychiatry* 3 (1980): 117.

152. TRIGGER FOR VIOLENCE: Robert I. Simon, "Type A, AB, B Murderers: Their Relationship to the Victims and to the Criminal Justice System," *Bulletin of the American Academy of Psychiatry and the Law* 5 (1978): 344 at 345. See also, Leroy G. Schultz, "The Wife Assaulter," *Journal of Social Therapy*, vol. 6, no. 2 (1960): 103; E. Tanay, *The Murderers* (N.Y.: Bobbs-Merril, 1976).

153. ESCALATION OF VIOLENCE: Dobash and Dobash, *Violence Against Wives*, 140–41.

153. FREEING THEMSELVES AS FUTILE: Martin, *Battered Wives*, 84.

153. WOMEN'S SELF-DEFENSE CASES: Schneider, "Describing and Changing: Women's Self-Defense Work and the Problems of Expert Testimony on Battering," 201. See also the interviews with jurors in Chapters Four, Five, and Six of Bochnak, *Women's Self-Defense Cases*, 107ff.

154. WILL TO LIVE IN HUMANS: Martin E.P. Seligman, *Helplessness* (San Francisco: W.H. Freeman, 1975); L.Y. Abramson, Martin E.P. Seligman, and J.D. Teasdale, "Learned Helplessness in Humans: Critique and Reformulation," *Journal of Abnormal Psychology* 87 (1978): 49–74. See also Christopher Peterson and Martin E.P. Seligman, "Learned Helplessness and Victimization," *Journal of Social Issues* 39(2) (1983): 103, for the authors' rather cautious approach to the application of learned helplessness theory to victim behavior in humans.

154. ALLEVIATE HER SITUATION: Walker, *The Battered Woman*, 42–54; Walker, *The Battered Woman Syndrome*, 86–94; Lenore E. Walker, "Battered Women and Learned Helplessness," *Victimology* 2 (1977–78): 525.

154. DOGS, RATS AND PEOPLE: Walker, *The Battered Woman*, 47–48.

155. PRECIPITATED THEM IS OVER: Browne, *When Battered Women Kill*, 122–27. See also, Don Dutton and Susan Lee Painter, "Traumatic Bonding: The Development of Emotional Attachments in Battered Women and Other Relationships of Intermittent Abuse," *Victimology* 6 (1981): 139, and Ronnie Janoff-Bulman

and Irene H. Frieze, "A Theoretical Perspective for Understanding Reactions to Victimization," *Journal of Social Issues* 39(2) (1983): 1.

155. PSYCHOLOGICALLY TRAUMATIC EVENT: American Psychiatric Association, *Diagnostic and Statistical Manual*, 3rd ed. (Washington, D.C., 1980), 236ff.

156. POWERLESS TO MAKE CHANGES: Elaine Hilberman, "The 'Wifebeater's Wife' Reconsidered," *American Journal of Psychiatry* 137 (1980): 1341.

156. EXPLANATION IN CLINICAL TERMS: See, for example, Elizabeth M. Schneider, "Describing and Changing: Women's Self-Defense Work and the Problem of Expert Testimony on Battering," 9 *Women's Rights Law Reporter* 195 (1986) and the discussion at 179ff, below. See, also, Susan Schecter, *Women and Male Violence* (Boston: South End Press, 1982) for a penetrating analysis of the effect that the growing involvement of mental health and other professionals has had on the battered women's movement.

Chapter 6. EXPERT TESTIMONY ON BATTERED WOMAN SYNDROME

160. REASONABLE UNDER THE CIRCUMSTANCES: This is not to say, however, that an insanity defense is never appropriate in a homicide case involving a battered woman. As noted in Chapter Three, sometimes a case's facts will be so at odds with male-oriented self-defense law, particularly the imminence requirement, that a plea of insanity or diminished capacity will be the defendant's only reasonable option. See *State v. Felton*, 329 N.W.2d 161 (Wis. 1983) for a case in which a woman's murder conviction was overturned on appeal because her attorney relied entirely on self-defense at her trial when insanity and other defenses could have been raised as well. The appellate court held this amounted to inadequate representation of counsel. This was a "sleeping husband" case that presented very difficult facts under a self-defense theory.

160. THE BATTERED WOMAN SYNDROME: See, for example, James R. Acker and Hans Toch, "Battered Women, Straw Men, and Expert Testimony: A Comment on *State v. Kelly*," 21 *Criminal Law Bulletin* 125 (1985); Julie Blackman and Ellen Brickman, "The Impact of Expert Testimony on Trials of Battered Women Who Kill Their Husbands," 2 *Behavioral Science and Law* 413 (1984); Phyllis L. Crocker, "The Meaning of Equality for Battered Women Who Kill Men in Self-Defense," 8 *Harvard Women's Law Journal* 121 (1985); Elizabeth M. Schneider, "Equal Rights to Trial for Women: Sex Bias in the Law of Self-Defense," 15 *Harvard Civil Rights-Civil Liberties Law Review* 623 (1980); Elizabeth M. Schneider, "Describing and Changing: Women's Self-Defense Work and the Problem of Expert Testimony on Battering," 9 *Women's Rights Law Reporter* 195 (1986); Lenore Walker, Roberta K. Thyfault, and Angela Browne, "Beyond the Juror's Ken: Battered Women," 7 *Vermont Law Review* 1 (1982); Comment, "Expert Testimony on the Battered Wife Syndrome: A Question of Admissibility In the Prosecution of the Battered Wife for the Killing of Her Husband," 27 *St. Louis University Law Journal* 407 (1983); Comment, "The Admissibility of Expert Testimony on Battered Wife Syndrome: An Evidentiary Analysis," 77 *Northwestern University Law Review* 348 (1982); Comment, "Admissibility of Expert Testimony on the Battered Woman Syndrome In Support of a Claim of Self-Defense," 15 *Connecticut Law Review*

121 (1982); Comment, "Battered Wives Who Kill: Double Standard Out of Court, Single Standard In?" 2 *Law and Human Behavior* 133 (1978); Comment, "The Expert As Educator: A Proposed Approach to the Use of Battered Woman Syndrome Expert Testimony," 35 *Vanderbilt Law Review* 741 (1982); Comment, "Self-Defense: Battered Woman Syndrome on Trial," 20 *California-Western Law Review* 485 (1984); Comment, "*State v. Thomas*: The Final Blow to Battered Women?" 43 *Ohio State Law Journal* 491 (1982); Commentary, "Expert Testimony and Battered Women: Conflict Among the Courts and a Proposal," 3 *Journal of Legal Medicine* 267 (1982); Note, "A Woman, A Horse and a Hickory Tree: The Development of Expert Testimony on the Battered Woman Syndrome in Homicide Cases," 53 *UMKC Law Review* 386 (1985); Note, "The Admissibility of Expert Testimony on Battered Wife Syndrome: An Evidentiary Analysis, 77 *Northwestern University Law Review* 348 (1982); Note, "The Battered Wife Syndrome: A Potential Defense to a Homicide Charge," 6 *Pepperdine Law Review* 213 (1978); Note, "Battered Woman Syndrome: Admissibility of Expert Testimony for the Defense: *Smith v. State*," 47 *Missouri Law Review* 835 (1982); Note, "The Battered Woman Syndrome and Self-Defense: A Legal and Empirical Dissent," 72 *Virginia Law Review* 619 (1986); Note, "Criminal Law—Evidence—Expert Testimony Relating to Subject Matter of Battered Women Admissible on Issue of Self-Defense—*Ibn-Tamas v. United States*," 11 *Seton Hall Law Review* 255 (1980); Note: "Evidence: Admitting Expert Testimony on the Battered Woman Syndrome," 21 *Washburn Law Journal* 689 (1982); Note, "Expert Testimony on Battered Woman Syndrome: Its Admissibility in Spousal Homicide Cases," 19 *Suffolk Law Journal* 877 (1985); Note, "Legal and Psychiatric Concepts and the Use of Psychiatric Evidence in Criminal Trials," 73 *California Law Review* 411 (1985); Note, "Limits on the Use of Defensive Force to Prevent Intramarital Assaults," 10 *Rutgers-Camden Law Journal* 643 (1979); Note, "The Use of Expert Testimony in the Defense of Battered Women," 52 *University of Colorado Law Review* 587 (1981).

160. WIDELY HELD IN OUR SOCIETY: *The Battered Woman*, 18–31.
161. EXPERT WITNESS CAN MAKE: Tom DeVries, "Chano & Blanche: A Ballad of Love, Death and the Law in Tulare County," *New West*, 12 March 1979, pp. 48–67. All of the details of Idalia Mejia's story are drawn from this excellent account.
162. "AND THEN I GOT HIT": Ibid. at 50.
162. "BOSS OF THE FAMILY": Ibid.
164. "JUST WOUND HIM?": Ibid. at 61.
166. STATE COURTS OF APPEALS: Opinions that address some aspect of expert testimony on battered woman syndrome include: *Borders v. State*, 433 So.2d 1325 (Fla. App. 1983); *Buhrle v. State*, 627 P.2d 1374 (Wyo. 1981); *Clenney v. State*, 344 S.E.2d 216 (Ga. 1986); *Commonwealth v. Rose*, 725 S.W.2d 588 (Ky. 1987); *Commonwealth v. Stonehouse*, 517 A.2d 540 (Pa. Super. 1982); *Fennel v. Goolsby*, 630 F. Supp. 451 (E.D. Pa. 1985); *Fielder v. State*, 683 S.W.2d 565 (Tex. App. 1985); *Fultz v. State*, 439 N.E.2d 659 (Ind. App. 1982); *Hawthorne v. State*, 408 So.2d 801 (Fla. App. 1982), rev. den. 415 So.2d 1361 (Fla. 1982), 470 So.2d 770 (Fla. App. 1985); *Ibn-Tamas v. U.S.*, 407

A.2d 626 (D.C. 1979), 455 A.2d 893 (D.C. 1983); *Ledford v. State*, 333 S.E.2d 576 (Ga. 1985); *Meeks v. Bergen*, 749 F.2d 322 (6th Cir. 1984); *Mullis v. State*, 282 S.E.2d 334 (Ga. 1981); *People v. Adams*, 430 N.E.2d 267 (Ill. App. 1981); *People v. Emick*, 481 N.Y.S.2d 552 (N.Y. A.D. 1984); *People v. Minnis*, 455 N.E.2d 209 (Ill. App. 1983); *People v. Powell*, 424 N.Y.S.2d 626 (1980), aff'd 442 N.Y.S.2d 645 (N.Y. A.D. 1981); *People v. Torres*, 488 N.Y.S.2d 358 (N.Y. Sup. 1985); *People v. White*, 414 N.E.2d 196 (Ill. App. 1980); *Smith v. State*, 274 S.E.2d 703 (Ga. App. 1980), 277 S.E.2d 678 (Ga. 1981); *State v. Allery*, 682 P.2d 312 (Wash. 1984); *State v. Anaya*, 438 A.2d 892 (Maine 1981), 456 A.2d 1255 (Maine 1983); *State v. Branchal*, 684 P.2d 1163 (N.M. App. 1984); *State v. Burton*, 464 So.2d 421 (La. App. 1985); *State v. Edwards*, 420 So.2d 663 (La. 1982); *State v. Felton*, 329 N.W.2d 161 (Wis. 1983); *State v. Gallegos*, 719 P.2d 1268 (N.M. 1986); *State v. Griffiths*, 610 P.2d 522 (Idaho 1980); *State v. Hodges*, 716 P.2d 563 (Kan. 1986); *State v. Kelly*, 478 A.2d 364 (N.J. 1984); *State v. Kelly*, 655 P.2d 1202 (Wash. App. 1982), 685 P.2d 564 (Wash. 1984); *State v. Leidholm*, 334 N.W.2d 811 (N.D. 1983); *State v. Martin*, 666 S.W.2d 895 (Mo. App. 1984); *State v. Moore*, 695 P.2d 985 (Or. App. 1985); *State v. Necaise*, 466 So.2d 660 (La. App. 1985); *State v. Thomas*, 423 N.E.2d 137 (Ohio 1981), *habeas* petition denied *sub nom. Thomas v. Arn*, 728 F.2d 813 (6th Cir. 1984), aff'd 106 S.Ct 466 (1985); *Terry v. State*, 467 So.2d 761 (Fla. App. 1985).

166. HELP FROM AN EXPERT: *Mullis v. State*, 282 S.E.2d 334 (Ga. 1981); *State v. Thomas*, 423 N.E.2d 137 (Ohio 1981), *habeas* petition denied *sub. nom. Thomas v. Arn*, 728 F.2d 813 (6th Cir. 1984), aff'd 106 S. Ct. 466 (1985).

167. IN JANUARY 1978: *State v. Thomas*, 423 N.E.2d 137 (Ohio 1981), *habeas* petition denied *sub nom. Thomas v. Arn*, 728 F.2d 813 (6th Cir. 1984), aff'd 106 S.Ct. 466 (1985); Ann Jones, *Women Who Kill* (New York: Holt, Rinehart and Winston, 1980), 298.

167. REASONABLENESS OF HER ACT: Leslie Kay, "Murder Verdict Reversed in 'Battered Woman' Case," *Cleveland Plain Dealer*, 24 July 1980, p. A1.

168. "KEN OF THE AVERAGE PERSON": *State v. Thomas*, 423 N.E.2d 137 (Ohio 1981) at 139.

168. ASLEEP IN HIS BED: W. James Van Vliet, "Battered Woman Testimony Helps Wife in Killing Case, *Cleveland Plain Dealer*, n.d. 1981, p.1.

169. EFFECTS OF BATTERING: *Smith v. State*, 277 S.E.2d 678 (Ga. 1981).

170. CALLED THE POLICE: Ibid. at 679.

170. COURT OF APPEALS, WHICH UPHELD IT: *Smith v. State*, 274 S.E.2d 703 (Ga. App. 1980).

170. KEN OF THE AVERAGE JUROR: *Smith v. State*, 277 S.E.2d 678 (Ga. 1981) at 683.

171. INVOLVING A BATTERED WOMAN: *Ibn-Thomas v. U.S.*, 407 A.2d 626 (D.C. 1979); *State v. Anaya*, 438 A.2d 892 (Me. 1981); *Hawthorne v. State*, 408 So.2d 801 (Fla. App. 1982); *Borders v. State*, 433 So.2d 1325 (Fla. App. 1983); *State v. Kelly*, 478 A.2d 364 (N.J. 1984); *People v. Torres*, 488 N.Y.S.2d 358 (Sup. 1985); *People v. Minnis*, 455 N.E.2d 209 (Ill. App. 1983); *State v. Hodges*, 716 P.2d 593 (Kan. 1986); *Commonwealth v. Rose*, 725 S.W.2d 588 (Ky. 1987); *State v. Allery*, 682 P.2d 312 (Wash. 1984).

171. IN FEBRUARY OF 1976: *Ibn-Tamas v. U.S.*, 407 A.2d 626 (D.C. 1979).

172. "ONE WAY OR THE OTHER": Ibid. at 630.

173. GOING TO KILL ME: Ibid. at 633.

173. I HAD SHOT HIM: Ibid.

174. BEVERLY'S MURDER CONVICTION: *Ibn-Tamas v. U.S.*, 455 A.2d 893 (D.C. 1983).

174. IS NOT SUFFICIENTLY ADVANCED: *Buhrle v. State*, 627 P.2d 1374 (Wyo. 1981); *State v. Thomas*, 423 N.E.2d 137 (Ohio 1981).

174. SETTLED IN A NEW TRIAL: *Hawthorne v. State*, 408 So.2d 801 (Fla. App. 1982), 470 So.2d 770 (Fla. App. 1985); *State v. Kelly*, 478 A.2d 364 (N.J. 1984); *Borders v. State*, 433 So.2d 1325 (Fla. App. 1983); *Terry v. State*, 467 So.2d 761 (Fla. App. 1985).

174. IDENTITY AS A BATTERED WOMAN: *State V. Allery*, 682 P.2d 312 (Wash. 1984); see below, p. 119–20.

175. IN NEW YORK STATE: *State v. Hodges*, 716 P.2d 563 (Kan. 1986); *People v. Torres*, 488 N.Y.S.2d 358 (N.Y. Sup. 1985).

175. WITHOUT THE EVIDENCE: McCormick, *Handbook on the Law of Evidence*, 2d. ed., Edward W. Cleary, ed. (St. Paul: West, 1972), 474–77.

175. TELL ANYONE OR SEEK HELP: *Borders v. State*, 433 So.2d 1325 (Fla. App. 1983); *People v. Minnis*, 455 N.E.2d 209 (Ill. App. 1981); *People v. Torres*, 488 N.Y.S.2d 359 (N.Y. Sup. 1985); *Smith v. State*, 277 S.E.2d 678 (Ga. 1981); *State v. Allery*, 682 P.2d 312 (Wash. 1984); *State v. Anaya*, 438 A.2d 892 (Maine 1981); *State v. Branchal*, 684 P.2d 1163 (N.M. 1984); *State v. Hodges*, 716 P.2d 563 (Kan. 1986); *State v. Kelly*, 478 A.2d 364 (N.J. 1984); *Terry v. State*, 467 So.2d 761 (Fla. App. 1985).

175. PROSECUTION WAS ASKING FOR: Lenore E. Walker, "A Response to Elizabeth M. Schneider's 'Describing and Changing: Women's Self-Defense Work and the Problem of Expert Testimony on Battering,' " 9 *Women's Rights Law Reporter* 223 (1986), at 224.

175. AGAINST BATTERED WOMEN DISMISSED: See Julie Blackman, "Potential Uses for Expert Testimony: Ideas Toward the Representation of Battered Women Who Kill," 9 *Women's Right Law Reporter* 227 (1986), and Betty Levinson, "Using Expert Testimony in the Grand Jury to Avoid a Homicide Indictment for a Battered Woman: Practical Considerations for Defense Counsel," 9 *Women's Rights Law Reporter* 239 (1986).

176. CITY OF DECATUR, ILLINOIS: *People v. Minnis*, 455 N.E.2d 209 (Ill. App. 1983). A similar case was that of Diane Barson, a Houston, Texas, woman who shot her husband, dismembered his body, packed it in bags and drove it in the trunk of her car to California. She had been a battered wife for two years and during the three days leading to his death, her husband had threatened and tormented her with loaded guns and an ice pick. She was acquitted by a jury on the grounds of temporary insanity (episodic dysfunction). Wayne King, "Right of Women to Self-Defense Gaining in 'Battered Wife' Cases: Powerful Strategy for Battered Wives," *New York Times*, 7 May 1979, pp. A1, A18.

176. "WOULDN'T HAVE TO DO THIS": Ibid. at 214.

177. SLEEP IN THAT CORNER: Ibid. at 215.

178. ACTIONS BY EXPERT TESTIMONY: Compare, for example, *Mullis v. State*, 282 S.E.2d 334 (Ga. 1981) with *Smith v. State*, 277 S.E.2d 678 (Ga. 1981); see

also the attorney's testimony about his similar belief in *Meeks v. Bergen* 749 F.2d 322 (6th Cir. 1984), a case in which the woman brought a *habeas corpus* proceeding arguing she had been denied effective assistance of counsel at her trial because her attorney had failed to present expert testimony on battering.

179. EVIDENCE THAT IT *WAS* REASONABLE: *Fultz v. State*, 439 N.E.2d 659 (Ind. App. 1982). See also Phyllis R. Crocker, "The Meaning of Equality for Battered Women Who Kill in Self-Defense," 8 *Harvard Women's Law Journal* 121 (1985), at 137ff., and the cases cited there.

179. DIRECTION THAT IT IS TAKING: See, in particular, Elizabeth M. Schneider, "Describing and Changing: Women's Self-Defense Work and the Problem of Expert Testimony on Battering," 9 *Women's Rights Law Reporter* 195 (1986), and Phyllis L. Crocker, "The Meaning of Equality for Battered Women Who Kill Men in Self-Defense," 8 *Harvard Women's Law Journal* 121 (1985).

179. AS AGGRESSIVE AS KILLING: Schneider, "Describing and Changing: Women's Self-Defense Work and the Problem of Expert Testimony on Battering," 197–200.

180. CRAZY OR HELPLESS OR BOTH: Ibid. at 214–15.

180. *BONA FIDE* BATTERED WOMAN: Crocker, "The Meaning of Equality for Battered Women Who Kill Men in Self-Defense," 144–50.

180. FOUGHT BACK IN THE PAST: *State v. Kelly*, 655 P.2d 1202 (Wash. App. 1982); *State v. Anaya*, 438 A.2d 892 (Maine 1981), 456 A.2d 1255 (Maine 1983); *Mullis v. State*, 282 S.E.2d 334 (Ga. 1981).

180. HELD A GOOD JOB: *State v. Anaya*, 438 A.2d 892 (Maine 1981), 456 A.2d 1255 (Maine 1983).

180. KNEW HOW TO USE A PISTOL: *Commonwealth v. Shaffer*, 326 N.E.2d 343 (Mass. 1975); *People v. Powell*, 442 N.Y.S.2d 645 (N.Y. 1981).

180. UNABLE TO LEAVE HER HUSBAND: *Buhrle v. State*, 627 P.2d 1374 (Wyo. 1981).

180. BEFORE THE FINAL ASSAULT: *State v. Griffiths*, 610 P.2d 522 (Idaho 1980).

180. REALLY A BATTERED WOMAN: Crocker, "The Meaning of Equality for Battered Women Who Kill Men in Self-Defense," 144–50.

181. ECONOMIC OR ETHNIC BACKGROUNDS: Schneider, "Describing and Changing: Women's Self-Defense Work and the Problem of Expert Testimony on Battering," 211, note 146.

181. NECESSARY SELF-DEFENSE: Ibid. at 149–50.

181. WOMAN'S RIGHT TO SELF-DEFENSE: Ibid. at 151. For Yvonne Wanrow's story, see above, 9, 116–18; for Inez Garcia's, see above, 9, 74–75.

Chapter 7. SUMMING UP

183. "REGARD FOR REASON": *Brown v. U.S.*, 256 U.S. 335, 41 S. Ct. 501, 65 L. Ed. 961 (1921).

184. TECHNIQUES OF LEGAL REFORM: The highest appellate court in New York state, for example, recently changed the standard of reasonableness in self-defense cases in New York from a subjective to an objective one. It was a decision that will have a serious impact on women who defend themselves there, but it was a case involving a male defendant, Bernhard Goetz, the so-called "subway vigilante," and women's concerns were simply absent from the court's

deliberations. *People v. Goetz,* 506 N.Y.S.2d 18 (N.Y. 1986). See "A Hard Case For Feminists—*People v. Goetz,*" 10 *Harvard Women's Law Journal* 253 (1987).

185. WANROW DECISION IS ANOTHER: *State v. Wanrow,* 559 P.2d 548 (Wash. 1977). See above, 116ff. For a particularly sensitive appellate opinion on the appropriateness of expert testimony in self-defense cases involving battered women see *State v. Kelly,* 478 A.2d 364 (N.J. 1984).

185. APPLICABLE THERE AFTER ALL: *Commonwealth v. Shaffer,* 326 N.E.2d 880 (Mass. 1975). See above, 72.

185. TO BE LAID TO REST: See, for example, the cases cited at 40 *American Jurisprudence Second,* "Homicide," sec. 155.

186. OF HIS OWN ACCORD: Maria L. Marcus, "Conjugal Violence: The Law of Force and the Force of Law," 69 *California Law Review* 1657 (1981) at 1710.

186. "ON THE PRESENT OCCASION": *Model Penal Code,* 3.04 (1). The official comments to the code explain: "The actor must believe that his defensive action is immediately necessary and the unlawful force against which he defends must be force that he apprehends will be used on the present occasion, but he need not apprehend that it will be immediately used. There would, for example, be a privilege to use defensive force to prevent an assailant from going to summon reinforcements, given belief and reason to believe that it is necessary to disable him to prevent an attack by overwhelming numbers—as long as the attack is apprehended on the "present occasion." The latter words are used in preference to "imminent" or "immediate" to introduce the necessary latitude for the attainment of just results in cases of this kind." *Model Penal Code* 3.04, Comment (Tent. Draft No. 8, 1958).

186. PROVISION OF THE CODE: These states include Hawaii, New Jersey, and Pennsylvania.

187. LOOKS BEYOND IMMEDIACY: See, for example, *State v. Matthews,* 49 S.W. 1095 (Mo. 1899); *Orta v. State,* 71 S.W. 755 (Tex Cr. App. 1903); *Furlow v. State,* 73 So. 362 (Fla. 1916).

187. SHOULD BE PURSUED ELSEWHERE: *State v. Hundley,* 693 P.2d 475 (Kan. 1985); *State v. Osbey,* 710 P.2d 676 (Kan. 1985); *State v. Hodges,* 716 P.2d 563 (Kan. 1986).

187. NOT BEEN THREATENED BEFORE: The full instruction read: "One who has received threats against her life or person made by another is justified in acting more quickly and taking harsher measures for her own protection in the event of assault either actual or threatened, than would be a person who had not received such threats; and if in this case you believe from the evidence that the deceased made threats against the defendant and that the defendant because of such threats made previously to the transaction complained of had reasonable cause to fear greater peril in the event of an altercation with the deceased than she would have otherwise, you are to take such facts into consideration in determining whether the defendant acted in a manner in which a reasonable person would act in protecting her own life or bodily safety." *People v. Bush,* 148 Cal. Rptr. 430 (Cal App. 1978) at 435–36. A male defendant would, of course, be entitled to a similar instruction in appropriate circumstances.

188. REFUSED TO ADOPT IT: See, for example, *State v. Ison,* 39 So.2d 247 (Ala. App. 1949); *People v. McGrandy,* 156 N.W.2d 48 (Mich. App. 1967); *People v. Lenkevich,* 229 N.W.2d 298 (Mich. 1975); *People v. Mroue,* 315 N.W.2d 192 (Mich. App. 1981); *Gainer v. State,* 391 N.E.2d 856 (Md. App. 1978).

188. RIGHT OF MEN AS WELL: Some courts have recognized the right of men to resist homosexual rape. See, for example, *State v. Robinson,* 328 S.W.2d 667 (Mo. 1959); *People v. Collins,* 11 Cal. Rptr. 504 (Cal. App. 1961); *Commonwealth v. Lawrence,* 236 A.2d 768 (Pa. 1968); *Commonwealth v. Robson,* 337 A.2d 573 (Pa. 1975); *State v. Philbrick,* 402 A.2d 59 (Maine 1979); *State v. Molko,* 274 S.E.2d 271 (N.C. 1981). Indeed, some feminist commentators have argued that modern courts are more willing to recognize the right in men than in women. Schneider, "Representation of Women Who Defend Themselves in Response to Physical or Sexual Assault," 153–54.

189. ACTED AS SHE DID: Some courts have begun to find a way around this problem by identifying both a subjective and an objective element in the objective standard and admitting the evidence as relevant to the former. See, for example, *State v. Kelly,* 478 A.2d 364 (N.J. 1984).

189. FAIR TO WOMEN DEFENDANTS: See above, 120ff.

190. INAPPROPRIATE MASCULINE STANDARD: See *State v. Wanrow,* 559 P.2d 548 (Wash. 1977).

190. KILLING OF HIS PARTNER: Julie Emery, "Battered-woman defense gets gay man acquitted of murder," *Seattle Times,* 21 November 1986.

190. RESULTED IN ACQUITTALS: Charles P. Ewing, *Battered Women Who Kill: Psychological Self-Defense as Legal Justification* (Lexington, MA: D.C. Heath, 1987), 55. Similarly, Dr. Lenore Walker reports that one quarter of the cases in which she has participated as an expert witness have resulted in acquittals. Walker, "A Response to Elizabeth M. Schneider's 'Describing and Changing: Women's Self-Defense Work and the Problem of Expert Testimony on Battering.'"

190. MUST DEFEND THEMSELVES: For a much more radical proposal see Charles Patrick Ewing's recent book, *Battered Women Who Kill: Psychological Self-Defense as Legal Justification.* Drawing on the insights of existential psychiatric theorists that "self" encompasses more than the mere physical aspects of existence but includes those psychological aspects of the self that give meaning and value to physical existence, Professor Ewing suggests an expansion of self-defense law that would permit one to defend oneself against serious threatened harm to one's "psychological self." Specifically, he proposes that use of deadly force should be justified where such force appears "reasonably necessary to prevent the infliction of serious psychological injury," defined as "gross and enduring impairment of one's psychological functioning which significantly limits the meaning and value of one's physical existence." (Ibid. 79.)

As Professor Ewing acknowledges, recognition of psychological self-defense would represent a major change in substantive criminal law (Ibid. 97), and he discusses a number of potential problems the doctrine might raise. From a feminist perspective, the most troubling aspect of Ewing's proposal is that it would seem to move the legal analysis of battered women's defensive acts towards—rather than away from—an insanity defense, with acquittal hinging on psychiatric testimony about a woman's actual mental state at the time of the killing and courtroom debate focusing on what constitutes gross impairment of one's psychological functioning. One certainly must question whether it would serve to reinforce the very stereotypes about battered women that feminist lawyers have worked so hard to counter in these cases.

191. DISCRIMINATED AGAINST IN THE COURTS: "Report of New York Task Force on Women in the Courts," 15 *Fordham Urban Law Journal* 1 (1986–87); "The First Year Report of the New Jersey Supreme Court Task Force on Women in the Courts—June 1984," 9 *Women's Rights Law Reporter* 129 (1986). A number of other states are currently undertaking similar studies.

191. "IN THE MARITAL RELATIONSHIP": "Report of New York Task Force on Women in the Courts," 27.

192. QUESTION TO THE JURY: *People v. Scott,* 424 N.E.2d 70 (Ill. App. 1981). See above, 1ff.

193. DO IT WAS REASONABLE?: Theresa Carpenter, ". . . And Then She Shot Him," *Redbook,* April 1984, 126ff.

193. PAROLED, RESENTENCED, OR PARDONED: See Ginny Cook, "Twice Imprisoned," *Maryland in Baltimore,* Fall 1987, 21ff, for a description of an innovative program being run by New Directions for Women and the House of Ruth, with the assistance of students from the University of Maryland Law School.

193. DIFFERENCE IN THESE CASES: An example is the recent public support of Karen Straw by feminists in New York City and extensive, sympathetic coverage of the case by the *New York Times.* Ms. Straw was acquitted on October 1, 1987. A public outcry can sometimes convince a prosecutor to drop charges or not to file them at all. When a Tacoma, Washington, woman named Cherri Lauderdale shot her former husband as he hurled a pot of boiling soup at her, local women's and church groups rose to her defense, generated a lot of press coverage, and met with representatives of the prosecutor's office. They succeeded in getting the charges dropped. Carrie Webster, "Charge is dropped in slaying of ex-husband," *Seattle Post-Intelligencer,* 5 March 1983, p. A5.

Sources

BOOKS

Atkins, Burton, and Mark Pogrebin, eds. *The Invisible Justice System: Discretion and the Law.* Cincinnati: Anderson, 1978.

Bancroft, Hubert H. *Popular Tribunals,* vol. 1 ch. 31. San Francisco: The History Company, 1887.

Blackstone, Sir William. *Commentaries on the Laws of England* (London, 1765–1769).

Blumstein, Philip, and Pepper Schwartz. *American Couples.* New York: William Morrow, 1983.

Bochnak, Elizabeth, ed. *Women's Self-Defense Cases.* Charlottesville, VA: Michie, 1981.

Browne, Angela. *When Battered Women Kill.* New York: Free Press, 1987.

Brownmiller, Susan. *Against Our Will: Men, Women and Rape.* New York: Simon and Schuster, 1975.

Caughey, John W. *Their Majesties The Mob.* Chicago: University of Chicago Press, 1960.

Chimbos, Peter D. *Marital Violence: A Study of Interspousal Homicide.* San Francisco: R. and E. Research Associates, 1978.

Critchley, T.A. *The Conquest of Violence: Order and Liberty in Britain.* New York: Schocken, 1970.

Davidson, Terry. *Conjugal Crime.* New York: Ballantine Books, 1980.

De Arment, Robert K. *Bat Masterson: The Man and the Legend.* Norman: University of Oklahoma Press, 1974.

Dobash, R. Emerson, and Russell Dobash. *Violence Against Wives.* New York: The Free Press, 1979.

Domestic Violence and the Police: Studies in Detroit and Kansas City. Washington, D.C.: The Police Foundation, 1977.

Drago, Harry S. *Outlaws on Horseback.* New York: Dodd, Mead, 1964.

Estrich, Susan. *Real Rape.* Cambridge: Harvard University Press, 1987.

Ewing, Charles P. *Battered Women Who Kill: Psychological Self-Defense as Legal Justification.* Lexington, MA: D.C. Heath, 1987.

233

Feild, Herbert S., and Leigh B. Beinen. *Jurors and Rape: A Study In Psychology and Law.* Lexington, MA: Lexington Books, 1980.

Fell, Christine. *Women in Anglo-Saxon England and the Impact of 1066.* Bloomington: Indiana University Press, 1984.

Fletcher, George. *Rethinking Criminal Law.* Boston: Little, Brown, 1978.

Friedman, Lawrence M. *A History of American Law.* New York: Simon and Schuster, 1973.

Geis, Frances, and Joseph Geis. *Women in the Middle Ages.* New York: Barnes and Noble, 1980.

Gelles, Richard J. *The Violent Home.* Beverly Hills: Sage, 1977.

Gersoni-Stavn, Diana, ed. *Sexism and Youth.* New York: Bowker, 1974.

Giles-Sims, Jean. *Wife-Battering: A Systems Theory Approach.* New York: Guilford, 1983.

Givens, James B. *Society and Homicide in Thirteenth-Century England.* Stanford: Stanford University Press, 1977.

Hall, Jerome. *General Principles of Criminal Law.* 2d ed. New York: Bobbs-Merrill, 1960.

Hanawalt, Barbara. *Crime and Conflict in English Communities, 1300-1348.* Cambridge: Harvard University Press, 1979.

Hart, H.L.A. *Punishment and Responsibility: Essays in the Philosophy of Law.* Oxford: Oxford University Press, 1968.

Heilbrun, Alfred B., Jr. *Human Sex-Role Behavior.* New York: Pergamon, 1981.

Holmes, Oliver W. *The Common Law.* New York: Little, Brown, 1881.

Horan, James D. *The Authentic Wild West: The Gunfighter.* New York: Crown, 1976.

Jones, Ann. *Women Who Kill.* New York: Holt, Rinehart and Winston, 1980.

Labarge, Margaret W. *A Small Sound of the Trumpet: Women in Medieval Life.* Boston: Beacon Press, 1986.

Langley, Roger, and Richard C. Leavy. *Wife Beating: The Silent Crisis.* New York: Simon & Schuster, 1977.

Maccoby, Eleanor E., ed. *The Development of Sex Differences.* Stanford: Stanford University Press, 1966.

————, and Carol N. Jacklin. *The Psychology of Sex Differences.* Stanford: Stanford University Press, 1974.

Martin, Del. *Battered Wives.* New York: Pocket Books, 1976.

McCormick's Handbook on the Law of Evidence. 2d. ed. Edited by Edward W. Cleary. St. Paul: West, 1972.

McNulty, Faith. *The Burning Bed.* New York: Harcourt Brace Jovanovich, 1980.

Metz, Leon C. *Pat Garret: The Story of a Western Lawman.* Norman: University of Oklahoma Press, 1974.

Miller, Frank. *Prosecution: The Decision To Charge A Suspect With A Crime.* Boston: Little, Brown, 1970.

Page. *Northumberland Assize Rolls.* The Surtees Society, vol. 88, 1891.

Pagelow, Mildred G.. *Woman Battering: Women and Their Experiences.* Beverly Hills: Sage, 1981.

Pitcher, Evelyn G., and Lynn H. Schultz. *Boys and Girls at Play: The Development of Sex Roles.* South Hadley, MA: Bergin and Garvey, 1983.

Pitt, Leonard. *The Decline of the Californios.* Berkeley: University of California Press, 1966.

Pollock, Sir Frederick, and Frederick W. Maitland. *The History of English Law* (2d ed., 1895). Cambridge: Cambridge University Press, 1968.

Radcliffe and Cross. *The English Legal System,* 6th ed. Edited by G.J. Hand and D.J. Bently. London: Butterworths, 1977.

Rafter, N.H., and E.A. Stanko, eds. *Judge, Lawyer, Victim, Thief: Women, Gender Roles and Criminal Justice.* Boston: Northeastern University Press, 1982.

Rayner, J.L., and G.T. Cook, eds. *The Complete Newgate Calendar,* vol. 4. London: The Navarre Society, 1926.

Roosevelt, Theodore. *Ranch Life and the Hunting Trail,* in *The Works of Theodore Roosevelt,* vol. IV. New York: Scribners, 1924.

Rosa, Joseph G. *The Gunfighter: Man or Myth?* Norman: University of Oklahoma Press, 1974.

Roy, Maria, ed. *Battered Women: A Psychosociological Study of Domestic Violence.* New York: Van Nostrand Reinhold, 1977.

Romer, Nancy. *The Sex Role Cycle.* Old Westbury, N.Y.: The Feminist Press, 1981.

Royce, Josiah. *California.* Boston: Houghton Mifflin, 1914.

Rush, Florence. *The Best Kept Secret: Sexual Abuse of Children.* New York: McGraw-Hill, 1980.

Russell, Diana E. *Rape in Marriage.* New York: MacMillan, 1982.

Schecter, Susan. *Women and Male Violence.* Boston: South End Press, 1982.

Seligman, Martin E.P.. *Helplessness.* San Francisco: W.H. Freeman, 1975.

Spence, Janet T., and Robert L. Helmreich. *Masculinity and Femininity: Their Psychological Dimensions, Correlates and Antecedents.* Austin: University of Texas Press, 1978.

Sprung, Barbara, ed. *Perspectives on Non-Sexist Early Childhood Education.* New York: Teachers College Press, 1978.

Stacey, Judith, Susan Bereaud, and Joan Daniels, eds. *And Jill Came Tumbling After: Sexism In American Education.* New York: Dell, 1974.

Stacey, William A., and Anson Shupe. *The Family Secret: Domestic Violence in America.* Boston: Beacon Press, 1983.

Stanko, Elizabeth A. *Intimate Intrusions: Women's Experience of Male Violence.* London: Routledge & Kegan Paul, 1985.

Steinmetz, Suzanne K., and Murray K. Straus. *Violence in the Family.* New York: Dodd, Mead, 1974.

Stewart, George R. *Committee of Vigilance.* Boston: Houghton Mifflin, 1964.

Straus, Murray A., Richard J. Gelles, and Suzanne K. Steinmetz. *Behind Closed Doors: Violence in the American Family.* New York: Anchor/Doubleday, 1980.

Tanay, E. *The Murderers.* New York: Bobbs-Merrill, 1976.

Totman, Jane. *The Murderess: A Psychosocial Study of Interspousal Homicide.* San Francisco: R.& E. Research Associates, 1978.

Trevelyan, George M. *Illustrated English Social History.* London: Longmans, Green, 1949.

Walker, Lenore E. *The Battered Woman.* New York: Harper and Row, 1979.

———. *The Battered Woman Syndrome.* New York: Springer, 1984.

Weitzman, Lenore J. *Sex Role Socialization.* Palo Alto: Mayfield, 1979.

Williams, Glanville. *Criminal Law: The General Part,* 2d ed. London: Stevens and Sons Ltd., 1961.

Wolfgang, Marvin E. *Patterns in Criminal Homicide.* Philadelphia: University of Pennsylvania Press, 1958.

ARTICLES

Abramson, L.Y., Martin E.P. Seligman, and J.D. Teasdale. "Learned Helplessness in Humans: Critique and Reformulation." *Journal of Abnormal Psychology* 87 (1978): 49.

Acker, James R., and Hans Toch. "Battered Women, Straw Men, and Expert Testimony: A Comment on *State v. Kelly.*" 21 *Criminal Law Bulletin* 125 (1985).

Annotation: "Duty to Retreat Where Assailant and Assailed Share the Same Living Quarters." 26 *American Law Reports 3rd.* 1296.

Annotation: "Duty to Retreat Where Assailant is Social Guest on Premises." 100 *American Law Reports 3rd.* 532.

Beale, Joseph H. "Retreat from a Murderous Assault." 16 *Harvard Law Review* 577 (1903).

Bem, Sandra L. "The Measurement of Psychological Androgeny." *Journal of Consulting and Clinical Psychology* 42 (1974): 155.

Bernard, George W., Hernan Vera, Maria I. Vera, and Gustave Newman. "Till Death Do Us Part: A Study of Spouse Murder." *Bulletin of the American Association of Psychiatry and Law* 10 (1982): 271.

Beuf, Ann. "Doctor, Lawyer, Household Drudge." *Journal of Communications* 24 (1974): 142.

Bird, Anne Marie, and Jean M. Williams. "A Developmental-Attributional Analysis of Sex-Role Stereotypes for Sport Performance." *Developmental Psychology* 16 (1980): 319.

Blackman, Julie. "Potential Uses for Expert Testimony: Ideas Toward the Representation of Battered Women Who Kill." 9 *Women's Rights Law Reporter* 227
(1986).

————, and Ellen Brickman. "The Impact of Expert Testimony on Trials of Battered
Women Who Kill their Husbands." 2 *Behavioral Science and Law* 413 (1984).

Blitman, Nan, and Robin Green. "Inez Garcia on Trial." *Ms.*, (May 1975): 49.

Block, Jeanne H. "Assessing Sex Differences: Issues, Problems and Pitfalls." *Merrill-
Palmer Quarterly* 22 (1976): 283.

Bridges, Judith, and Joseph del Campo. "Children's Perceptions of the Competence
of Boys and Girls." *Perceptual and Motor Skills* 52 (1981): 503.

Broverman, Inge, Donald Broverman, Frank Clarkson, Paul Rosenkrantz, and Susan
Vogel. "Sex-Role Stereotypes and Clinical Judgements on Mental Health." *Journal
of Consulting and Clinical Psychology* 34 (1970): 1.

————, Susan Vogel, Donald Broverman, Frank Clarkson, and Paul Rosenkrantz.
"Sex-Role Stereotypes: A Current Appraisal." *Journal of Social Issues* 28 (1972):
63.

Brown, Bernard. "Self-Defense in Homicide from Strict Liability to Complete
Exculpation." 1958 *Criminal Law Journal* 583.

Browne, Angela. "Self-Defense Homicides by Battered Women: Relationships at
Risk." Paper presented to the American Psychology and Law Conference, Chicago,
October 1983.

Carpenter, Theresa. "...And Then She Shot Him." *Redbook,* (April 1984): 126.

Collins, Ronald K.L. "Language, History and the Legal Process: A Profile of the
Reasonable Man." 8 *Rutgers-Camden Law Journal* 311 (1976–7).

Comment, "Admissibility of Expert Testimony on the Battered Woman Syndrome
in Support of a Claim of Self-Defense." 15 *Connecticut Law Review* 121 (1982).

Comment, "Battered Wives Who Kill: Double Standard Out of Court, Single
Standard In?" 2 *Law and Human Behavior* 133 (1978).

Comment, "Expert Testimony on the Battered Wife Syndrome: A Question of
Admissibility in the Prosecution of the Battered Wife for the Killing of Her
Husband." 27 *St. Louis University Law Journal* 407 (1983).

Comment, "Self-Defense: Battered Woman Syndrome on Trial." 20 *California-
Western Law Review* 485 (1984).

Comment, "*State v. Thomas*: The Final Blow to Battered Women?" 43 *Ohio State
Law Journal* 491 (1982).

Comment, "The Admissibility of Expert Testimony on Battered Wife Syndrome:
An Evidentiary Analysis." 77 *Northwestern University Law Review* 348 (1982).

Comment, "The Expert as Educator: A Proposed Approach to the Use of Battered
Woman Syndrome Expert Testimony." 35 *Vanderbilt Law Review* 741 (1982).

Commentary, "Expert Testimony and Battered Women: Conflict Among the Courts
and a Proposal." 3 *Journal of Legal Medicine* 267 (1982).

Condry, John, and Sandra Condry. "Sex Differences: A Study in the Eye of the Beholder." *Child Development* 47 (1976): 817.

Crocker, Phyllis L. "The Meaning of Equality for Battered Women Who Kill Men in Self-Defense." 8 *Harvard Women's Law Journal* 121 (1985).

Davidson, Emily, Amy Yasuna, and Arnold Tower. "The Effects of Television Cartoons on Sex-Role Stereotyping in Young Girls." *Child Development* 50 (1979): 597.

DeVries, Tom. "Chano & Blanche: A Ballad of Love, Death and the Law in Tulare County." *New West* (12 March 1979): 50.

Donovan, Dolores A., and Stephanie M. Wildman. "Is the Reasonable Man Obsolete? A Critical Perspective on Self-Defense and Provocation." 14 *Loyola of Los Angeles Law Review* 435 (1981).

Dutton, Don, and Susan Lee Painter. "Traumatic Bonding: The Development of Emotional Attachments in Battered Women and Other Relationships of Intermittent Abuse." *Victimology* 6 (1981): 139.

Eber, Loraine P. "The Battered Wife's Dilemma: To Kill or Be Killed." 32 *Hastings Law Journal* 895 (1981).

Eisenberg, Alan D., and Earl J. Seymour. "The Self-Defense Plea and Battered Women." *Trial* (July 1978): 75.

Eisenberg, Sue E., and Patricia Micklow. "The Assaulted Wife: 'Catch 22' Revisited." 3 *Women's Rights Law Reporter* 138 (1977).

Fabricant, Judith. "Homicide in Response to Rape: A Theoretical Examination of the Rule of Justification." 11 *Golden Gate University Law Review* 945 (1981).

Ferraro, Kathleen J., and John M. Johnson. "How Women Experience Battering: The Process of Victimization." *Social Problems* 30, No. 3 (1983): 325.

"First Year Report of the New Jersey Supreme Court Task Force on Women in the Courts, The." 9 *Women's Rights Law Reporter* 129 (1986).

Frueh, M. "Traditional Sex-Role Development and Amount of Time Spent Watching Television." *Development Psychology* 11 (1975): 109.

Gayford, J.J. "Wife Battering: A Preliminary Survey of 100 Cases." *British Medical Journal* (25 January 1975).

Green, Thomas A. "The Jury and the English Law of Homicide, 1200–1600." 74 *Michigan Law Review* 413 (1976).

Hart, Roger. "Sex Differences in the Use of Outdoor Space." In *Perspectives on Non-Sexist Early Childhood Education,* ed. Barbara Sprung. New York: Teachers College Press, 1978.

Hilberman, Elaine. "Overview: The 'Wife-Beater's Wife' Reconsidered." *American Journal of Psychiatry* 137 (1980): 1336.

————, and Kit Munson. "Sixty Battered Women." *Victimology* 2 (1977–8): 460.

Howard, Colin. "What Colour is the Reasonable Man?" 1961 *Criminal Law Review* 41.

Iso-Ahola, Seppo E. "Sex-Role Stereotypes and Causal Attributions of Success or Failure in Motor Performance." *Research Quarterly* 50 (1979): 630.

Janoff-Bulman, Ronnie, and Irene H. Frieze. "A Theoretical Perspective for Understanding Reactions to Victimization." *Journal of Social Issues* 39 (2) (1983): 1.

Jones, Ann. "When Battered Women Fight Back." 9 *Barrister* 12, (Fall 1983).

Kates, Don B., Jr., and Nancy Engberg. "Deadly Force Self-Defense Against Rape." 15 *University of California, Davis, Law Journal* 873 (1982).

Kilpatrick, Dean G., Patricia Resnick, and Lois J. Vernon. "Effects of Rape Experience: A Longitudinal Study." *Journal of Social Issues* 37, No. 4 (1981): 105.

Lerman, Lisa. "Protection of Battered Women: A Survey." 6 *Women's Rights Law Reporter* 271 (Summer 1980).

Lever, Janet. "Sex Differences in the Games Children Play." *Social Problems* 23 (1976): 478.

Levinson, Betty. "Using Expert Testimony in the Grand Jury to Avoid a Homicide Indictment for a Battered Woman: Practical Considerations for Defense Counsel." 9 *Women's Rights Law Reporter* 239 (1986).

Lieberman, Maria R. "Some Day My Prince Will Come." In *Sexism and Youth,* ed. Diana Gersoni-Stavn. New York: Bowker, 1974.

Marcus, Maria L. "Conjugal Violence: The Law of Force and The Force of Law." 69 *California Law Review* 1657 (1981).

McGhee, Paul E., and Terry Frueh. "Television Viewing and Adult Sex-Role Attitudes." *Sex Roles* 6 (1980): 179.

Note. "A Hard Case For Feminists—*People v. Goetz.*" 10 *Harvard Women's Law Journal* 253 (1987).

Note. "A Woman, A Horse and a Hickory Tree: The Development of Expert Testimony on the Battered Woman Syndrome in Homicide Cases." 53 *U.M.K.C. Law Review* 386 (1985).

Note. "The Admissibility of Expert Testimony on Battered Wife Syndrome: An Evidentiary Analysis." 77 *Northwestern University Law Review* 348 (1982).

Note. "The Battered Wife Syndrome: A Potential Defense to a Homicide Charge." 6 *Pepperdine Law Review* 213 (1978).

Note. "Battered Woman Syndrome: Admissibility of Expert Testimony for the Defense: *Smith v. State.*" 47 *Missouri Law Review* 835 (1982).

Note. "The Battered Woman Syndrome and Self-Defense: A Legal and Empirical Dissent." 72 *Virginia Law Review* 619 (1986).

Note. "Battered Women and the Equal Protection Clause: Will The Constitution Help Them When the Police Won't?" 95 *Yale Law Journal* 788 (1986).

Note. "Criminal Law—Evidence—Expert Testimony Relating to Subject Matter of Battered Women Admissible on Issue of Self-Defense—*Ibn-Tamas v. United States.*" 11 *Seton Hall Law Review* 255 (1980).

Note. "Does Wife Abuse Justify Homicide?" 24 *Wayne Law Review* 1705 (1978).

Note. "Evidence: Admitting Expert Testimony on the Battered Woman Syndrome." 21 *Washburn Law Journal* 689 (1982).

Note. "Expert Testimony on Battered Woman Syndrome: Its Admissability in Spousal Homicide Cases." 19 *Suffolk Law Review* 877 (1985).

Note. "Legal and Psychiatric Concepts and the Use of Psychiatric Evidence in Criminal Trials." 73 *California Law Review* 411 (1985).

Note. "Limits on the Use of Defensive Force to Prevent Intramarital Assaults." 10 *Rutgers-Camden Law Journal* 643 (1979).

Note. "The Use of Expert Testimony in the Defense of Battered Women." 52 *University of Colorado Law Review* 587 (1981).

Omark, D.R., and M. Edelman. "Peer Group Social Interactions from an Evolutionary Perspective." Paper presented at the Society for Research in Child Development Conference, Philadelphia, 1973. Cited in Eleanor E. Maccoby and Carol N. Jacklin, *The Psychology of Sex Differences.* Stanford: Stanford University Press, 1974.

————, M. Omark, and M. Edelman. "Dominance Hierarchies in Young Children." Paper presented at the International Congress of Anthropological and Ethnological Sciences, Chicago, 1973. Cited in Eleanor E. Maccoby and Carol Jacklin. *The Psychology of Sex Differences.* Stanford: Stanford University Press, 1974.

Perkins, Rollin M. "Self-Defense Reexamined." 1 *U.C.L.A. Law Review* 133 (1953).

Peterson, Christopher, and Martin E.P. Seligman. "Learned Helplessness and Victimization." *Journal of Social Issues* 39 (2) (1983): 103.

Pokorney, Alex D. "A Comparison of Homicides in Two Cities." 56 *Journal of Criminal Law, Criminology and Police Sciences* 479 (1965).

Pollis, N.P., and D.C. Doyle. "Sex-Role Status and Perceived Competence Among First Graders." *Perceptual and Motor Skills* 34 (1972): 235.

Queneville, Kathleen. "Will Rape Ever Be A Crime of the Past? A Feminist View of Societal Factors and Rape Law Reforms." 9 *Golden Gate University Law Forum* 581 (1978–9).

"Report of New York Task Force on Women in the Courts." 15 *Fordham Urban Law Journal* 1 (1986–7).

Rheinhold, Harriet L., and Kay V. Cook. "The Content of Boys' and Girls' Rooms as an Index of Parents' Behavior." *Child Development* 46 (1975): 459.

Robinson, Paul H. "A Theory of Justification: Societal Harm as A Prerequisite for Criminal Liability." 23 *U.C.L.A. Law Review* 266 (1975).

Rosen, Cathryn Jo. "The Excuse of Self-Defense: Correcting a Historical Accident on Behalf of Battered Women Who Kill." 36 *American University Law Review* 11 (1986).

Rosenkrantz, Paul, Susan Vogel, H. Bee, Inge Broverman, and Donald Broverman. "Sex-Role Stereotypes and Self Concepts in College Students." *Journal of Consulting and Clincial Psychology* 32 (1986): 287.

Ross, Laurie, Daniel Anderson, and Patricia A. Wisocki. "Television Viewing and Adult Sex-Role Attitudes." *Sex Roles* 8 (1982): 589.

Rounsaville, Bruce J. "Theories in Marital Violence: Evidence from a Study of Battered Women." *Victimology* 3 (1978): 11.

Rubin, Jeffrey Z., Frank Provenzano, and Zella Luria. "The Eye of the Beholder: Parents' Views on Sex of Newborns." *American Journal of Orthopsychiatry* 44 (1974): 512.

Sacco, Lynne A. "Wife Abuse: The Failure of Legal Remedies." 11 *John Marshall Journal of Practice and Procedure* 549 (1978).

Schneider, Elizabeth M. "Describing and Changing: Women's Self-Defense Work and the Problem of Expert Testimony on Battering." 9 *Women's Rights Law Reporter* 195 (1986).

————. "Equal Rights to Trial for Women: Sex Bias and the Law of Self-Defense." 15 *Harvard Civil Rights Law Review* 623 (1980).

————, and Susan B. Jordan. "Representation of Women Who Defend Themselves in Response to Physical or Sexual Assault." 4 *Women's Rights Law Reporter* 149 (Spring 1978).

————, Susan B. Jordan, and Christina C. Arguedas. "Representation of Women Who Defend Themselves in Response to Physical or Sexual Assault." In *Women's Self-Defense Cases,* ed. Elizabeth Bochnak. Charlottesville, VA: Michie, 1981.

Schultz, Leroy G. "The Wife Assaulter." *Journal of Social Therapy* Vol. 6, No. 2 (1960): 103.

Showalter, C. Robert, Richard J. Bonnie, and Virginia Roddy. "The Spousal Homicide Syndrome." *International Journal of Law and Psychiatry* 3 (1980): 117.

Sidorowicz, Laura S., and G. Sparks Lunney. "Baby X Revisited." *Sex Roles* 6 (1980): 67.

Simon, Robert I. "Type A, AB, B Murderers: Their Relationship to the Victims and to the Criminal Justice System." *Bulletin of the American Academy of Psychiatry and the Law* 5 (1978): 344.

Spreitzer, Elmer, Eldon Snyder, and Joseph Kivlin. "A Summary of Some Recent Studies Concerning the Female Athlete." *Frontiers* Vol. 3, No. 1 (1978): 14.

St. Peter, Shirley. "Jack Went Up the Hill...But Where Was Jill?" *Psychology of Women Quarterly* 4 (1979): 256.

Stanko, Elizabeth A. "Would You Believe This Woman? Prosecutorial Screening for 'Credible' Witnesses and A Problem of Justice." In *Judge, Lawyer, Victim, Thief: Women, Gender Roles and Criminal Justice,* eds. N.H. Rafter and Elizabeth A. Stanko. Boston: Northeastern University Press, 1982.

Stephen, Darrel W. "Domestic Assault: The Police Response." In *Battered Women: A Psychosociological Study,* ed. Maria Roy. New York: Van Nostrand Rheinhold, 1977.

Tan, Alexis S. "T.V. Beauty Ads and Role Expectations of Adolescent Female Viewers." *Journalism Quarterly* 56 (1979): 283.

Taub, Nadine. "Equitable Relief in Cases of Adult Domestic Abuse." 6 *Women's Rights Law Reporter* 241 (Summer 1980).

Truninger, Elizabeth. "Marital Violence: The Legal Solutions." 23 *Hastings Law Journal* 259 (1978).

Walker, Lenore E. "A Response to Elizabeth M. Schneider's 'Describing and Changing: Women's Self-Defense Work and the Problem of Expert Testimony on Battering.'" 9 *Women's Rights Law Reporter* 223 (1986).

————. "Battered Women and Learned Helplessness." *Victimology* 2 (1977–8): 525.

————, Roberta K. Thyfault, and Angela Browne. "Beyond the Jurors' Ken: Battered Women." 7 *Vermont Law Review* 1 (1982).

Weitzman, Lenore J., Deborah Eifler, Elizabeth Hokada, and Catherine Ross. "Sex-Role Socialization in Picture Books for Preschool Children." *American Journal of Sociology* 77 (1972): 1125.

Wilbanks, William. "Murdered Women and Women Who Murder." In *Judge, Lawyer, Victim, Thief: Women, Gender Roles and Criminal Justice*, eds. N.H. Rafter and Elizabeth A. Stanko. Boston: Northeastern University Press, 1982.

MISCELLANEOUS

American Digest, vol. 26, secs. 614–632, St. Paul: West, 1901.

American Jurisprudence Second, vol. 40, "Homicide," 1968.

American Psychiatric Association, *Diagnostic and Statistical Manual*, 3rd ed., Washington, D.C.: 1980.

Appellant's Supplemental Brief Appealing Conviction and Opening Brief Appealing Denial of New Trial Motion, *State v. Painter*, Case #5678-6-I, Court of Appeals, Division I, State of Washington, 1979.

Brown v. U.S., 256 U.S. 335, 41 S. Ct. 501, 65 L. Ed. 961 (1921).

Commonwealth v. Lawrence, 236 A.2d 768 (Pa. 1968).

Commonwealth v. Robson, 337 A.2d 573 (Pa. 1975).

Commonwealth v. Walker, 288 A.2d 741 (Pa. 1972).

Crime in the United States–1986 (Uniform Crime Reports), Washington, D.C.: U.S. Government Printing Office, 1987.

Crimes of Violence, Staff Report to the National Commission on the Causes and Prevention of Violence, Washington, D.C.: U.S. Government Printing Office, 1969.

Erwin v. State, 29 Ohio 186 (1876).

Federal Response to Domestic Violence, The, Washington, D.C.: United States Commission on Civil Rights, 1982.

Final Report, Attorney General's Task Force on Family Violence, Washington, D.C.: United States Department of Justice, 1984.

First Decentennial Digest, St. Paul: West, 1912.

Furlow v. State, 73 S. 362 (Fla. 1916).

Gainer v. State, 391 N.E.2d 856 (Md. App. 1978).

Hartzler v. City of San Jose, 46 Cal. App.3d 6 (1975).

Model Penal Code 3.04, Comments, Tentative Draft No 8, American Law Institute, 1958.

Model Penal Code 3.04, Final Draft, American Law Institute, 1961.

National Prosecutor Standards, Chicago: National District Attorneys Association, 1977.

Orta v. State, 71 S.W. 755 (Tex. Cr. App. 1903).

People v. Cardenas, 121 Cal. Rptr. 426 (Cal. App. 1975).

People v. Caudillo, 121 Cal. Rptr. 859 (Cal. 1978).

People v. Goetz, 506 N.Y.S.2d 18 (N.Y. 1986).

People v. Mroue, 315 N.W.2d 192 (Mich. App. 1981).

People v. Richardson, 100 Cal. Rptr. 251 (Cal App. 1972).

People v. Superior Court (Lozano), 137 Cal. Rptr. 767 (Cal. App. 1977).

People v. Superior Court (Vasquez), 137 Cal. Rptr. 762 (Cal. App. 1977).

People v. Tomlins, 107 N.E. 496 (N.Y. 1914).

People v. Wells, 92 Cal. Rptr. 191 (Cal. App. 1971).

Report of Proceedings, *State v. Kelly,* Case No. 10452-7-I, Court of Appeals, Division I, State of Washington, 1982.

Respondent's Supplemental Brief, *State v. Wanrow,* Supreme Court of the State of Washington, Case No. 43949, 10 February 1976.

Second Decentennial Digest, St. Paul: West, 1920.

State v. Ison, 39 So.2d 247 (Ala. App. 1949).

State v. Matthews, 49 S.W. 1085 (Mo. 1899).

State v. Molko, 274 S.E.2d 271 (N.C. 1981).

State v. Philbrick, 402 A.2d 59 (Maine 1979).

State v. Robinson, 328 S.W.2d 667 (Mo. 1959).

Under the Rule of Thumb: Battered Women and the Administration of Justice, Washington, D.C.: United States Commission on Civil Rights, 1982.

Index